"Some books are to be tasted, others to be swallowed, and some few to be chewed and digested."
— *Sir Francis Bacon*

"Page 47 makes a great napkin." — *Wilbur*

"One of the most profound and important works of our times. Two snouts up."
— *Sizzle and Eggbearer*

"Seven days without barbecue makes one weak."
— *Harris Hollans*

"This smells like trouble to me."
— *overheard at a hog lot*

"This thing really does fit in my glove box!"
— *Chuck Perry*

"Mmmm. I wonder if they will choose me for the centerfold when they print the second edition?"
— *Ms. Piggy*

"People should eat more pork."
— *the National Pork Council*

"This guide is the best thing since sliced bread!"
— *the National Sliced Bread Council*

THE PEACH STATE
GLOVE BOX GUIDE
TO BAR-B-QUE

STEVE STOREY

PHOTOGRAPHS BY JAMES R. LOCKHART

IN CONJUNCTION WITH

DIGEST

THE COMPLETE STATEWIDE GUIDE
TO BAR-B-QUE IN GEORGIA

LONGSTREET PRESS
Atlanta, Georgia

Published by
LONGSTREET PRESS, INC.
A subsidiary of Cox Newspapers,
A subsidiary of Cox Enterprises, Inc.
2140 Newmarket Parkway
Suite 122
Marietta, GA 30067

Printed in the United States of America

1st printing 1997
Library of Congress Card Catalog Number: 96-79807
ISBN: 1-56352-375-2

Jacket and book design by BBQ Digest

To Adam —
the first man
to share his ribs

CONTENTS

ACKNOWLEDGMENTS

A very special thanks to Leigh Anne Zalants for serving as a research assistant on this project. I also appreciate the assistance of the following: Mason Adams, John Bassett, Arden Brey, Bob Callaway, Renita Davis, Jill Dible, Karen Easter, Anne Floyd, Chris Goswick, Mary Lee Lockhart, Shannon Maggio Mason, Teresa Noles, Steve Nordmeyer, Chuck Perry, Lucy Puckett, Martha Reimann, Sara Reimann, Leamon Scott, Todd Steadman, Leslie Storey, Bill Towson, Fred Van Dyck, Patrick Vickers, Brian Williamson, Adriane Wood, and Andy Yarn. (I hope to treat each of you to a double-meat pork plate and beverage of your choice at a barbecue place to be named later.)

S. S.

DIGEST

THE
PEACH STATE
GLOVE BOX GUIDE
TO BAR-B-QUE

Pro-Hog Prologue:
The Guide to the Guide

We'd like to get something straight right up front—this is not a rating of barbecue restaurants in Georgia. That's a task best left to higher powers—such as your own palate. Instead, what you hold in your hands is the most complete directory of Georgia barbecue restaurants available at any cost or any place. For each listing you'll find information about where a place is, how to get there, the telephone number, the days and hours of operation, what they serve, and any specialties of the house you should be sure not to miss—whether it's a special sauce, a collection of memorabilia, or the owner him (or her) self.

As you'll notice, about the same amount of space is given to each listing. This avoids showing favoritism. Now, rest assured we have our favorites. But we can't even agree among ourselves about what's best, much less with the thousands of other barbecue lovers—such as yourself. We decided to keep our opinion to ourselves and let you be the judge.

Our job was to provide the essential information you need for each restaurant. The hard part was deciding what to include. We figured the name, address, phone number, directions, and hours of operation were essential. We also wanted to offer a description of the place and let you know what they served.

"Trying to come up with a standard for barbecue is like nailing jello to a tree."

— Todd Steadman

BBQ DIGEST

1

Naturally, we couldn't include everything on the menu, so we chose the following ten things to list for each restaurant: pork, beef, chicken, ribs, fries, onion rings, desserts, alcoholic beverages, Brunswick stew, and food other than barbecue.

For quick and easy reference there are symbols for each of these items. Beside each listing, you'll find the appropriate symbols. A guide to these symbols is found conveniently on page 224. They should be pretty self-explanatory, but, until you're familiar with the symbols, you can flip back to find out if a symbol is for dessert or french fries.

"You just can't cook barbecue in an oven!"

— B. Duke

Now, it's important to keep in mind that a lot of restaurants have other specific items that didn't make it on our list of symbols. Part of that is because almost every restaurant serves slaw, beans, and potato salad. All of them have sauce. And you can dine in at most of them. Because these features were so common, we figured they didn't need special attention. On the other hand, a lot of the places serve steaks. A lot have green beans. Some even have salads and shrimp. That's hardly barbecue if you ask us, but that's another story for another time.

We also wanted to let you know that some places said they served barbecue when, in fact, what they did was parboil their ribs, slather 'em with sauce, and serve them. To be included in *The Glove Box Guide*, a restaurant had to slow-cook its meat over flame. We hope you agree with us on that one.

In regard to the directions, well, you know how that goes. As hard as we tried to get everything right, you can count on a new road being added or one being closed, or there being another (and better) way to get there. However, these are the best directions we can offer, and they come from a combination of personal experience and the words of the proprietor.

To further help you find your way to good barbecue, we carved the state into twenty-two sections. There are maps for each section that show most of the various towns and counties. For each county you'll find numbers that correspond to all the listings in that county. The maps may not get down to street level. Their purpose is simply to put you in the general area. From there, with the written directions, you shouldn't have any problems. If all else fails, ask a friendly local. We've never had a bad experience when talking barbecue.

Please, give a place a call before venturing out. Getting an accurate set of listings was definitely aiming at a moving target. Over the course of the year it took to develop this book, about one out of ten places went out of business, changed ownership, or moved locations. We'd hate to have you take your sweetheart, brother, or potential client down a dead-end trail.

On the flip side of that coin, we apologize up front to any new places that opened that we're not aware of. Like the phone book, this directory will be out of date before it's even published.

Information was gathered in a variety of ways—we used phone books, local chambers of commerce, listings of business licenses, restaurant data bases, the Internet, word of mouth, and plain ol' driving around. But, despite our efforts, at least one place probably

"Wait a minute— I think you can get there from here!"

— Anon.

BBQ
DIGEST

3

escaped us. Please drop us a line or give us a call if you know of a place we left out or if you find that a place listed in the book is no longer in business. That way, when the next version comes out, we'll be closer to being 100 percent accurate. You'll find our phone number, mailing address and e-mail address on page 223.

The listings are in alphabetical order—from A&J to Zeb's. Each listing has an ID number that can help you locate information. For example, knowing that you may be in southeast Georgia, unfamiliar with the territory but looking for some good barbecue, check the indexes which start on page 196. These are broken down county by county and include a simplified list with the name, city, and ID number of each listing. You can also refer to the actual maps to get a list of ID numbers of barbecue restaurants within a given county.

"I get by with a little help from my friends."

— J. Lennon

Please call or write us with ideas for making *The Glove Box Guides* better. We value your input. Plus, we love to talk about anything that has to do with barbecue. In fact, that general interest and fascination for barbecue is how our company and this book came about.

We've always considered the barbecue restaurant a special place. A place where amidst the variety—the range of people, busy waitresses, sounds of traffic, clanking plates and trays, thick hickory air, the sweet smell of smoked meat, a mouthful of pork—we were coated by a peacefulness as real as the smoky air. In short? We're happy there. And much like those pieces of pig on the pit, the concept for *The Glove Box Guides* started with a basic, raw product. And just like good barbecue, hours of passion, work, and sweat wielded a suitable product. In our case, this guide to one of Georgia's purest art forms: barbecue.

The idea that eventually led to *The Glove Box Guide* was a concept for a barbecue newsletter (for more on that, see page 223). One day, as we waited for our ribs, mindlessly staring at some football newsletter (like we'd do the back of a box of cereal), we started talking about how much fun it would add to the barbecue experience if there were a witty barbecue newsletter. Soon, from that simple beginning, the idea for a statewide guide to barbecue emerged.

Our dreams are the same as yours. Like you, we want to know how to find barbecue. Regardless of where it is.

Like you, we want to be able to find that golden egg in the barbecue restaurant hunt of life—to find that place hidden in the woods that a friend keeps telling us we "have to try." Or to find a new place to meet with a client in Macon or a different one to eat at after appraising real estate in LaGrange or when driving to the coast or the mountains. So, we set out to locate every barbecue restaurant in the state.

"Dream the impossible dream."

— *Not sure*

We hit the hickory-smoked trail and we hit it hard. We ate high on the hog (see Glossary). And often. We drove from barbecue restaurant to barbecue restaurant gathering the information we thought would be most useful to you. There are six of us. Chris Pomar, Harris Hollans, Scott Walton, and Todd Steadman wrote the guides to Alabama and South Carolina. Steve Storey and Jim Lockhart did

BBQ

DIGEST

5

this volume. We're all Southern and we all love barbecue—the culture and the people. We hope *The Glove Box Guide* drifts like the sweet smell of smoked meat from the printing press to your glove box. We think it's entertaining enough for a vegetarian to buy and enticing enough for someone in New York City to get in the car and drive down South for some fantastic barbecue.

Happy trails.

"How much for just one rib?"

— Chris Rock in "I'm Gonna Get You Sucka"

Barbecue: A Slow, Savory Science

Humanity's devotion to and craving for barbecue is a phenomenon as old as the history of man. From the nomadic tribes of Mesopotamia who hunted and ate wild game to those network television college football broadcasters who rave on the air about their annual pilgrimages to certain barbecue places and rib shacks, barbecue has an unchallenged romance with our souls as well as our palates.

So, how did barbecue come to achieve such an important status in our culture? Where exactly did barbecue come from and why? Or, as an inquisitive Southern matron might ask of a sliced pork sandwich the same she'd ask of her daughter's date, "Who are your people?"

Well, that depends on whom you ask.

"For I was hungered and ye gave me meat."

— The Bible

To start with, it's important to note that everywhere we use the word *barbecue* (or *BBQ*, or *Bar-B-Que*, or any other variation) we are referring to the term as it is known in the South: some type of meat, most often pork, slow-cooked or smoked in such a way as to produce a supple tenderness, then flavored liberally or conservatively with some type of sweet, spicy, or spicy-sweet sauce. That, my friends, is barbecue as Southerners know it. Not as the word is used in other parts of the country, which usually refers to

BBQ DIGEST

anything cooked outdoors or slapped on a grill. From shrimp to arugula.

There are several different versions of the origin of the term *barbecue*. The French term *barbe-a-queue*—which means grilling from beard to tail—receives some credit for bringing us the current name for barbecue. French explorers referred to the hunters and smokers of Hispaniola and the Tortugas as *boucaniers*, a word which can be cut, sliced, and chopped to *buccaneer* and even *barbecuer*. But it is the Spanish history of the word which is usually associated with the current use of *barbecue*. Spanish explorers in the Caribbean discovered natives who prepared meat on long, green wooden sticks, or *barbacoa*, involving slow-cooking over hot embers. This is the most accepted origin of the word we know today as barbecue.

"There are at least a dozen ways to spell what we all know as barbecue."

— The Pork Boys

Other rumors persist that the word involves some combination of the words *bar* (as in the place you go for a drink), *beer* (what you drink when you get there), and *cue* (as in the stick you use in the game of pool). But, these don't allow for as much history or romance.

The history and evolution of barbecue in the five hundred years since European explorers first discovered the *barbacoa* is as rich and complicated as the history of the American South itself. In fact, the two are permanently wed in a rich marinade. The history of barbecue includes flavorful influences from both Spanish and French settlers. Caribbean and African spices and cooking methods imported via the slave trade and the unique touch of Native Americans also added flavor to the table.

The popularity of barbecue at church gatherings and political rallies is as old as at least several hymns. It was at these community assemblies—where the pork was slow-cooked and served at its peak of flavor—that barbecue was first recognized for its undeniable appeal to rich and poor of all races and creeds.

According to John Egerton, an excellent author on all things Southern, Virginia had laws on the books in the late 1600s prohibiting the shooting of firearms at barbecues, and Carolinians incorporated the word into their common language before the colonial period was over. Soon after 1800, when Kentucky was a young state, barbecues there were a primary form of summer social entertainment and, by the end of that century, the same could be said for every state in the region. In an excerpt from his book *Southern Food*, Egerton recalls the heritage of the first true pit men, the grandfathers and architects of barbecue as we know it today: "The South's great barbecue tradition is in large measure a cultural gift from black men. . . . In the early decades of the nineteenth century, when accounts of huge barbecue feasts in the region first appeared in print, it was almost always black men who were described as tenders of the fires and cookers of the meat and makers of the sauce. Over the years, black cooks have mastered the ancient art, adapted it to their time and place in Southern history, then passed the wisdom on to others, black and white. Today the region's proud reputation for pit cooking is shared by men and women of both races."

"I have a dream!"
— *MLK*

BBQ
DIGEST

Spell it how you like. Make your own guess as to how it got here. But have no doubt that barbecue is gaining in popularity. For example, last year's Memphis in May World Championship Barbecue Cookoff had no less than 350 teams competing for the title of Grand Champion. Teams that traveled from as far away as New Zealand, Germany, and Canada came to slow-cook their pork. And over 10,000 people came to witness the event.

Now, before we talk about the specifics of barbecue in Georgia, we'd like to leave you with a thought expressed by Stephen A. Smith from a 1985 article he wrote for the journal *Studies in Popular Culture*. For us, it does a pretty good job of summing up the hold barbecue has on this part of the country:

> "Barbecue is serious business in the South. . . . The Barbecue Eucharist serves as the perfect metaphor for understanding contemporary Southern society. The catechism contains a reverence for tradition and the heritage of the past, the vestiges of rural camp meetings, a chorus of regional chauvinism, a pulpit for oratory, an opportunity for community participation, appreciation for the vernacular, equality of opportunity, and subtle interracial respect. . . . The community values represented by the high priest cooks and the dedication of their congregations suggests that the rhetorical ritual of barbeque . . . may also serve to further human understanding and humanitarian values among the faithful."

It's a deep thought. But it smells good to us.

"United we stand, divided we fall."

— Not sure

Barbecue in Georgia

Mention "barbecue" in Georgia and the image most likely to come to mind is a pile of chopped pork covered with a sweet tomato-based sauce, with Brunswick stew on the side. In eastern North Carolina the word brings forth visions of "pulled" pork with a thin vinegar-and-pepper sauce and hushpuppies on the side. In South Carolina, it probably will be pork with a mustard-based sauce and a side of hash. In Texas, it might not be pork at all, but beef instead.

Actually, you can have any of those varieties of barbecue and never leave the Peach State.

For example, in north metro Atlanta (the Olym-pig city), you can have it Memphis-style (Corky's in Duluth), Chicago–style (Leon's in downtown Atlanta), North Carolina-style (Dusty's in north DeKalb County), and Texas-style (The Rib Ranch in Marietta). And it's not only in the Atlanta area either. In our travels around the state, we've dined on Cajun barbecue, St. Louis–style ribs, Lexington, N.C.–style pulled pork, and barbecued goat (we're not sure where that came from). In Macon, we even found barbecued ostrich.

"Welcome to the South. Confusing, ain't it?"

—John Shelton Reed

While we enjoy expanding our horizons when it comes to smoked meat, we also appreciate plain ol' Georgia barbecue as it's been done here for generations. Time and technology have taken a toll on these traditions, unfortunately, but there's still plenty of old-fashioned wood-cooked true 'cue out there. That's why this book was written—to help you find it. But first, a little background and some notes on how it's done in the Peach State:

The Pit

Traditionally, a hole was dug in the ground, wood was thrown in and burned down to coals, and meat was placed on a grill or rack over the coals. Later, as barbecue became a commercial venture, the wood would be burned to coals on a hearth. The coals were then shoveled into the "pit," now likely to be above ground and built of brick, concrete block, rock, or steel.

Pits are sometimes classified as "open" or "closed." The former are similar to backyard grills, but much larger. The meat might lie anywhere from one to four feet above the coals. Sheets of metal or cardboard are placed over the meat to keep the smoke concentrated around it. Closed pits have permanent covers and often use indirect heat to cook the meat.

Most barbecue nowadays is cooked not in pits but in homemade or manufactured steel "cookers" or "smokers" that can be moved from one location to another. Configurations vary, but it is typical to have a firebox at one end, a smokestack at the other end, and a cooking chamber in the middle.

Wood

In a perfect world, all barbecue would be cooked over hardwood coals. Pitmasters would use various mixtures of oak, hickory, pecan, walnut, cherry, apple, and other nut-bearing and fruit-bearing trees. These impart desirable flavors into the meat and lend themselves to slow cooking.

While hickory is ubiquitous, many a ham or butt is cooked with oak. Red oak is popular in much of the state. Some pitmasters on the Georgia coast use live oak because hickory can be hard to get.

Cooking pork the old way with wood requires a lot of time and patience, and it's hard work. Many old-time barbecue places were husband-and-wife operations in which the husband would keep the meat cooking while the wife ran the inside operation. If the husband died, the wife might try to hire someone to maintain the fires in the pit, but often she just chose to cook with electricity or gas. The result, of course, would be roasted pork. It might be drowned in barbecue sauce, but it wouldn't be barbecue.

Cooking Technique

Essentially, "low and slow," that is, low heat and slow cooking is the proper technique. Patience is as important to barbecue as is smoke. Properly cooked meat will have a "smoke ring," a pinkish-to-red color just under the crust caused by the smoking process. Note that the ring is near the outside of the meat. It is not undercooked meat.

"Perfection is attained by slow degrees; it requires the hand of time."

— Voltaire

Think about it. Pit-cooked meat simply can't be cooked well-done inside and be undercooked outside.

Meat

In Georgia, barbecue is pork. While there are hundreds of places with barbecued beef, one shouldn't expect to find it everywhere. The meat is usually chopped (sometimes referred to as "chipped"), occasionally sliced, and often "pulled" (that is, pulled from the bone in big chunks and served that way). Chicken is common enough, but don't expect to find it everywhere either. Smoked turkey is found here and there, and goat and lamb are on a handful of menus. J.L.'s in Macon has ostrich; we haven't seen that anywhere else.

Brunswick Stew and Hash

Brunswick stew is a rich mixture of pork, beef, chicken, potatoes, tomatoes, corn, and spices. We hasten to note, however, that many stew-makers wouldn't think of putting one or more of the just-mentioned ingredients in their stew. Tomatoes in particular seem to generate varying opinions. Some stews are tomato-less; we've found others that are essentially tomato soup with bits of meat and corn. We've also found stews with such nontraditional ingredients as peas, green beans, okra, and noodles. (Actually, we've found only one place in Georgia that puts noodles in its stew, and amazingly it's still in business!)

Georgia is without a doubt a Brunswick stew state, but

over toward the South Carolina border, stew gives way to hash. Think of it as Brunswick stew without corn that you can eat with a fork. Hash developed as a way to use pig organs such as livers and brains and meat from the head and feet. (Poor farmers tried to use everything from the pig except the squeal.) The meat was chopped up and boiled with potatoes and onions. The result was hash.

Today, hardly any barbecue place uses liver or other organs or even head meat or pig's feet. Instead, for their hash they use the same cuts that make up barbecued pork. Even thought it's not the real thing anymore, you can get hash at Sconyers in Augusta, Peanut's Redneck Bar-B-Q in Athens, Chandlers' and Carithers' in Athens, Big Pig in Cordele, and Brinson's in Millen, among other places.

Sauces

Many barbecue connoissooeys contend smoked pork doesn't need sauce because the smoke mixes with the natural juices to provide all the flavor needed. Other e-pig-ures believe that barbecue sauce is to meat as clothes are to the man, and they just don't hold with nakedness. (We agree with the first group. On the other hand, we've tasted some marvelous sauces. We'll just agree with both.)

There are three great sauce cultures: the vinegar-and-pepper, the tomato-base, and the mustard-base. Georgia stands firmly in the tomato camp.

"Everyone lays claim to the one true sauce."
— Jim Auchmutey

BBQ DIGEST

It's extremely rare to find a sauce here without at least a little tomato. We've found only two or three places offering eastern North Carolina–style sauces, mixtures of vinegar and pepper with no tomato whatsoever.

Mustard-based sauces such as those from central South Carolina are rare, too. In parts of central Georgia, sauces with mustard in varying degrees are common. Most have as much or more tomato (or ketsup) than mustard, but enough of the latter is present to give it a distinct mustard taste.

"The real secret to sauce is the mystique."

— Jim Auchmutey

As a rule, it's not a good idea to ask a barbecue man for his sauce recipe, especially if the menu or ads for the place mention SECRET SAUCE, HOME RECIPE SAUCE, OLD FAMILY RECIPE SAUCE, OR MILLION-DOLLAR RECIPE SAUCE. Many won't tell you anything about the ingredients or even confirm correct guesses. "Just because it's yellow doesn't mean it has mustard in it; it could be food coloring," one owner told us. Another was a bit more forthcoming: "I could tell you what's in the sauce, but then I'd have to kill you."

Dessert

Don't expect it. Many of the places that serve the best barbecue have little or nothing in the way of desserts. Banana pudding, however, is a tradition in some places. Pies are a bit more common. Fried pies are exciting finds for many Southerners, but they're likely to be mass-produced rather than homemade as in the past.

The Places

We found barbecue in million-dollar buildings and in the humblest of shacks. We found places with no phone, no seats, no street address, no side orders, no beverages, and no employees other than the owner. And places with multiple locations and staffs numbering in the hundreds. Places that once were gas stations or barns or schoolbuses. Places that also sell gas, groceries, fresh produce, and bait.

Such variety is one of the things that attracts us to barbecue. It's the antithesis of standardized, processed fast food served in the cookie-cutter buildings that, if not already in your neighborhood, soon will be. It's one of the reasons we sometimes take 700-mile round trips over a weekend just to eat smoked pork. (Who would drive more than a few miles to eat at McDonald's or Burger King?)

We call them barbecue *places* not only because the word restaurant so often doesn't fit, but also because we feel the strong sense of place that is characteristic of so many Georgia barbecue outlets—Jimbo's in Homerville, Twin Oaks in Brunswick, Wall's in Savannah, Dean's in Jonesboro, Two Brothers in Ball Ground, and Zeb's in Danielsville, to name a few. These are not "restaurant concepts" that can be reproduced and placed in a new shopping mall. It might be possible to prepare the food the same perhaps, but the place itself can never be replicated. Jane and Michael Stern said it as eloquently as we've ever heard in their book *Roadfood and Goodfood*, "There is no seasoning as pungent as authenticity."

"It's the best barbecue I've ever eaten at a place that hasn't been condemned."
— Overheard at Col. Poole's

BBQ
DIGEST

DIGEST

Restaurant Listings

The sample listing below may help you follow how we break down the information for each restaurant.

Restaurant name, address, & phone number.
This is pretty straightforward. If you get a wrong number, always check with directory assistance.

Map ID - This number corresponds to the numbers found within each county and for the numbers found in the regional index.

Hours - Pretty simple.

Directions - We did the best we could, but still suggest a phone call before making a major excursion.

Name/Map ID

Hours/Directions

Really Good Barbecue (387)

718 Ribshack Ave.
Sooee, Ga. 39090
706-555-5555
County: Pigpickins

Mon. - Sat. 8 a.m. - 8 p.m.
From Hickory take Hwy. 9 exit north. Then go west on
U.S. 78 to Sooee. Take a right at the first major intersec-
tion (Ribshack Ave.). It's on the left.

When Joe Pitmaster decided to open a barbecue house, he knew it had to be special — his employees would be like family and the service like Thanksgiving Day. Really Good is located in the oldest building in Sooee. The meat consists of pork butts smoked over hickory. The homemade sauce is red and mild.

Date Visited _____ *Remarks* _____

Icons - These symbols represent some food items and features you can expect to find at a restaurant. A key to these symbols is found on page 224.

Date Visited & Remarks - This is so you can make your own notes about a place.

Comments - A few thoughts on what the place is all about.

A&J Tasty Pig Bar-B-Q (1)

2567 W Main St.
Snellville, Ga. 30278
770/979-1676
County: Gwinnett

Mon - Sat 5:00 a.m. - 8:30 p.m, (til 9 on Friday).
From Atlanta, take U.S. 78 to its junction with Hwy. 124
in Snellville. A&J is on the left.

It's the hickory-smoked barbecued pork that has been attracting folks to A&J for over fourteen years, but the menu also includes fresh vegetables, catfish, and a variety of other non-barbecue items. The vinegar-based sauce is spicy, but not hot. Cafeteria-line service and 150 seats ensure that plenty of folks get fed quickly and get back out on the streets of this busy Atlanta suburb.

Date visited _____*Remarks* _____

A. B. Lee Meat Market (2)

Hwy. 257
Dublin, Ga. 31021
912/272-3084
County: Laurens

Mon - Sat 9 a.m. - 6 p.m.
From Dublin, take Hwy. 257 three miles south.
It's on the right.

Look for a small cinderblock building with a barbecue smoker to one side. A. B. Lee's is primarily a meat market, but it sells plenty of barbecue. The place is known for its super tender meat. The barbecue (hams cooked with oak) is available every day except Sunday. A.B.'s sweet sauce is homemade. The meat, whether cooked or not, is available for take-out only; there's no dining area inside or outside. Sorry, no side orders either.

Date visited _____*Remarks* _____

A. B.'s Bar-B-Que (3)

328 Broad St.
Hawkinsville, Ga. 31036
912/892-3264
County: Pulaski

Mon - Sat 11 a.m. - 9 p.m.
Look for a red building a block or so behind
the courthouse in Hawkinsville.

"Original country recipe bar-b-que" is the slogan at A.B.'s. The hickory-smoked pork is served in big moist chunks. The cole slaw is creamy. The Brunswick stew has plenty of corn and a few green peas. The hot sauce is a tangy brown mixture with a mouth-watering black pepper taste. The sweet tea is cold and plentiful. Dine in, order at the counter, 84 seats. Nonsmokers' area. Drive-thru window. Opened 1976.

Date visited _____*Remarks* _____

Bar-B-Quote

"A wash pot of heavy iron should be used for cooking.
Chicken, rabbit, squirrel, or lamb may be used."

—*From Brunswick stew in* Southern Cooking *by Mrs. S. R. Dull, pub. 1941.*

Abdullah the Butcher, House of Ribs (4)

2387 Fairburn Rd. SW
Atlanta, Ga. 30331
404/629-2332
County: Fulton

Mon - Thu 11 a.m. - 9 p.m., Fri & Sat 11 a.m. - 10 a.m.
From 285, go west on Campbellton Rd. a half mile to
Fairburn Rd. Turn left; it's the third building on the right.

It's rare to find a rib shack that serves Chinese meals too. At Abdullah's, you can
get combo plates with both foods. Barbecue offerings include hickory-smoked
pork shoulders, tasty short end ribs, rib tips, and BBQ wings. The pitmaster,
"Mr. Red," has been barbecueing for thirty years. Dine in, 120 seats.

Date visited _____ *Remarks* _____

Ace Barbecue Barn (5)

30 Bell St. NE
Atlanta, Ga. 30303
404/659-6630
County: Fulton

Mon - Thu 11 a.m. - 9 p.m., Fri & Sat 11 a.m. - 10 p.m.
From Peachtree St. in downtown Atlanta, go east on
Auburn Ave. Turn right at the police station
onto Bell St. It's on the right.

Situated in the heart of the historic Sweet Auburn district in downtown Atlanta,
Ace Barbecue Barn has been serving sweet 'n' smoky pork for nearly three
decades. Owner Mamie Seagraves cooks Boston butts on an open pit and serves
the meat with a sweet, mild sauce. She also offers pigs' feet, ox tails, turkey legs,
pork chops, turnip greens, and string beans. Dine in, 20 or so seats.

Date visited _____ *Remarks* _____

Adams' Bar-B-Q (6)

140 Felton Rd.
Cartersville, Ga. 30120
770/382-8240
County: Bartow

Mon - Thu 10:30 a.m. - 8:30 p.m., Fri - Sat 10:30 a.m. - 9:00 p.m.
From I-75, take exit 124 (Main St.). Go west to J.F.
Harris Parkway and turn right. Go north to 4th light and
turn left onto Felton Rd. It's on the right.

This 85-seat place serves up toothsome hickory-smoked pork, beef, chicken,
and baby back ribs along with the usual sides. Steaks and catfish are available
for those rare occasions on which smoked meats are not desired. Whatever your
choice, finish off your meal with Adams' scrumptious chocolate pecan pie.

Date visited _____ *Remarks* _____

Aleck's Barbecue Heaven (7)

783 Martin L. King, Jr. Dr. NW
Atlanta, Ga. 30314
404/525-2062
County: Fulton

Mon - Wed 11 a.m. - 10 p.m., Thu 11 a.m. - 11 p.m.,
Fri & Sat 11 a.m. - 1 a.m.
From the Georgia Dome, take MLK, Jr. Dr. west past
Morris Brown College. It's on the right, before Ashby St.

Voted Best Barbecue by *Atlanta Magazine* 1992-1996. No wonder. Aleck's barbecue is carefully open-pit cooked with oak and hickory. It's anointed with a thin,
spicy, but not hot, red sauce. On the side are home-cooked vegetables. If you
have room for dessert, there might be some red velvet or German chocolate
cake. Dine in, 20 seats. "Serving Atlanta since 1942."

Date visited _____ *Remarks* _____

Allen's Barbeque (8)

1447 Norman Dr.
College Park, Ga. 30349
770/996-9089
County: Fulton

Mon - Fri 11 a.m. - 9 p.m., Sat 11 a.m. - 11 p.m.
Take I-85 to Riverdale Rd. Go south on Riverdale
to second light. Allen's is behind Checkers.

Memphis-style ribs are the specialty at James Allen's College Park place.
Choose a mild or hot vinegar-based sauce to go with them. If it's no-bones-about-
it pork you're hankering for, Allen cooks Boston butts with oak and hickory on a
closed pit and turns them into heaven on a plate. Dine in, table service, 40 seats.

Date visited _____*Remarks* _____

Anderson's Old Fashion Bar-B-Q (9)

65 Willis Mill Rd. SW
Atlanta, Ga. 30311
404/696-8144
County: Fulton

Tue - Thu 11 a.m. - 11 p.m., Fri & Sat 11 a.m. - 2 a.m.,
Sun 12 p.m. - 6 p.m.
Exit I-20 at Hightower Rd., go south to MLK Jr. Dr., turn left, turn right at Willis
Mill Rd. It's on the right, near Peyton Road, across from West Building Materials.

The barbecue is cooked on an open pit and served with Anderson's own
Original Bar-B-Que & Buffalo Wing sauce (also sold in local grocery stores).
Other old-fashioned items include pork and beef ribs, rib tips, pig ear sandwich-
es, oxtails, potato salad, and collard greens. Dine in, table service, 4 seats.

Date visited _____*Remarks* _____

Applewood Smoke House (10)

4840 Flat Shoals Pkwy.
Decatur, Ga. 30034
770/987-7633
County: DeKalb

Tue - Sat 11 a.m. - 8:30 p.m., Sun 1 p.m. - 8 p.m.
From I-20 East, exit at Wesley Chapel Rd., go south 2
miles to Flat Shoals Pkwy. It's at the corner.

The smoke-anointed meat at Applewood smells so good it makes vegetarians
reconsider. The menu includes hickory-smoked all-ham chopped pork, pork ribs,
barbecued beef brisket, chicken wings and legs, Brunswick stew, beans, cole
slaw, potato salad, greens, mac & cheese, and yams. There's cobbler for dessert,
if you get that far. The sauce is smoky, mild, and tomato-based. Dine in, 60 seats.

Date visited _____*Remarks* _____

Armstrong's Bar-B-Q (11)

216 N Commerce St.
Summerville, Ga. 30747
706/857-9900
County: Chattooga

Mon. - Sat. 8 a.m. - 8 p.m .
From the courthouse in Summerville, take U.S. 27 north.
It's on the right, at the edge of downtown.

"Buying the best to serve the best, since 1965." Summervillians have long
enjoyed the moist and flavorful pork in this popular establishment. The prices
are right too! (around $6.00 for a double-meat pork plate). Desserts are coconut,
chocolate, or lemon ice box pies. Armstrong's "World Famous Bar-B-Q Sauce" is
available to take home by the bottle or the gallon.

Date visited _____*Remarks* _____

Art's Bar-B-Q & Grill (12)

2978 Hwy. 5
Douglasville, Ga. 30135
770/920-1644
County: Douglas

Tue - Thu 11:30 a.m. - 2:30 p.m. and 5:00 p.m. - 9:30 p.m.,
Fri 11:30 a.m. - 2:30 p.m. and 5:00 p.m. - 10:00 p.m.,
Sat 11:30 a.m. - 10:00 p.m., Sun 11:30 a.m. - 9:00 p.m.
From I-20, take exit 8, go south on Hwy. 5. It's on the left.

Art's sizable modern building looks more "Grill" than "Bar-B-Q," but don't let
the slick exterior fool you. Some fine Southern barbecue is served inside.
There's also smoked turkey, Brunswick stew, beans, cole slaw, corn on the cob,
and other items. Fried flounder and fried shrimp are available, too. If iced tea
won't satisfy your thirst, Art can provide both draft and bottled beer, as well as
wine by the glass or carafe.

Date visited_____Remarks_____

Ashby Street Rib Shack (13)

22 Ashby St. NW
Atlanta, Ga. 30314
404/659-4747
County: Fulton

Thu - Sat 12 p.m. - 12 a.m.
From I-20 west of downtown, exit at Ashby St. and go
north. It's just past MLK, Jr. Dr., on the left.

This little rib shack is near a MARTA rapid-rail station, so it's fairly easy to get to
from all over the city. Ribs are the specialty, as the name suggests. Buy 'em by
the rack or in smaller amounts. Rib tips and short ends are available too. The
meats are cooked with oak in a closed pit, and customers can choose a hot or
mild barbecue sauce. Sides include Brunswick stew, beans, cole slaw, fries, and
potato salad. Take-out only.

Date visited_____Remarks_____

Armstrong's

Autry's Bar-B-Que (14)

1809 S Patterson St.
Valdosta, Ga. 31601
912/241-9449
County: Lowndes

Mon - Thu 10 a.m. - 7 p.m.,
Fri 10 a.m. - 8 p.m., Sat 10 a.m. - 7 p.m..
Autry's is on South Patterson St. in downtown Valdosta.

Downtown Valdosta workers know about Autry's terrific barbecue. Thanks to this book, others will find it, too. (We hope you regulars don't mind a longer wait in the lunch lines.) Autry's serves pit-cooked, chopped pork with a tomato-based sauce already mixed in. Beef, chicken, and pork ribs are also available. Sides include Brunswick stew, chili, baked beans, fried okra, cole slaw, fries, chips, and potato salad. Also smoked mullet. Take-out only, with limited seating on porch.

Date visited _____*Remarks* _____

B&B Bar-B-Que (15)

1001 Radium Springs Rd.
Albany, Ga. 31705
912/436-5911
County: Dougherty

Mon 11 a.m. - 3 p.m., Tue - Sat 11 a.m. - 9 p.m.
From downtown Albany, go east on Oglethorpe Ave.
(U.S. 19/82 Bus.); cross the river and turn right on
Radium Springs Rd.

The menu at B&B is basically barbecued pork, beef, chicken, and ribs, along with the usual sides, plus baked potatoes, plus battered-and-fried pickles (yes, pickles, battered and fried). And smoked turkey. B&B's pork barbecue, by the way, is Boston butts barbecued beautifully with white oak or pecan in a smoker. Mild red sauce. Dine in, 100-plus seats.

Date visited _____*Remarks* _____

B&B Barbecue (16)

708 N Church St.
Homerville, Ga. 31634
912/487-3585
County: Clinch

Thu - Sat 10:30 a.m. - 1 p.m. & 3 p.m. - 9 p.m.
From the junction of U.S. 84 and U.S. 441 in downtown
Homerville, go north on 441. You'll be there in a jiffy.

The house specialty is barbecue rice, a treat that combines barbecue sauce, a little smoked meat, and rice. Owner Thomas Brown Sr. says it's an American version of fried rice. As for the pork, it's cooked with oak in a closed pit. A mustard/ketchup–type sauce is served on the meat or on the side. Vegetables and salads complement the meats, and cakes make up the dessert options. A small but adequate dining room permits eating in.

Date visited _____*Remarks* _____

Bar-B-Fact

Harold's Barbecue in Atlanta opened in 1947, a year before the South's first television station, WSB Atlanta, began broadcasting.

B&E Bar-B-Q (17)

2403 Plant Ave.
Waycross, Ga. 31501
912/283-3516
County: Ware

Mon - Sat 10:30 a.m - 9 p.m.
From downtown, go northeast on Plant Ave.
(U.S. 84) towards Blackshear a couple of miles.
It's on the left near KFC.

Owner Emory Cox has been cooking a long time and knows what he's doing. You can sample his tasty open-pit-cooked ham meat at this little take-out shack alongside U.S. 84. Barbecue stuffed potato is the specialty, but the other menu items are very popular, too. The sauce is Cattleman's.

Date visited _____*Remarks* _____

B&E Bar-B-Q (18)

105 S Augusta Ave.
Waycross, Ga. 31501
912/287-0077
County: Ware

Mon - Sat 10 a.m. - 9 p.m.
From downtown Waycross, take U.S. 82 (Corridor Z) west
toward Tifton. B&E is on the right at South Augusta Ave.
across from Waycross College.

B&E's ribs were recently voted Best in Southeast Georgia. This west Waycross location offers the same delicious foods as found at the Plant Avenue original.

Date visited _____*Remarks* _____

B.A.B. Smokehouse (19)

3050 Canton Rd.
Marietta, Ga. 30066
770/422-0604
County: Cobb

Mon. - Sat. 8 a.m. - 8 p.m.
From Marietta, take Canton Rd. north. It's just beyond
Piedmont Rd., on the right.

Built as a burger joint, but now serving "Bar-B-Que At Its Best," B.A.B. is the home of the "best ribs in town." It's also a fine place for Brunswick stew and BBQ beans, brisket of beef, and boneless chicken breast. Add cole slaw, lima beans, or collard greens and you've got some good eatin'. Non-BBQ items include spiral-cut hams, steaks, and seafood. Lunch special plates available from 11 to 4. Seats about 50. Drive-thru.

Date visited _____*Remarks* _____

B.J.'s BBQ (20)

1900 Savannah Hwy.
Jesup, Ga. 31545
912/427-3358
County: Wayne

Mon - Thu 10 a.m. - 8 p.m.,
Fri 10 a.m. - 9 p.m., Sat 10 a.m. - 8 p.m.
From downtown Jesup, take U.S. 25 2 miles north.
It's on the right.

Owner Benny Fowler cooks butts in a smoker using red oak. Ribs are available by the plate or in slabs. The sauce is a mild ketchup-based mixture (not sweet). Other items are stew, beans, slaw, fries, potato salad, chicken fingers, steak sandwiches, and hot dogs. It's take-out only, but there are three tables outside.

Date visited _____*Remarks* _____

Baba's Barbecue and Soul Food (21)

3554 Martin L. King Jr. Dr.
Atlanta, Ga. 30336
404/699-0055
County: Fulton

Mon - Sat 7 a.m. - 11 p.m.
From downtown Atlanta, go west on MLK, Jr. Dr.
Cross over I-285. It's on the left, just past McDonald's,
near Fairburn Rd.

Atlanta's Martin Luther King Jr. Drive begins in downtown and extends to the western edge of the city. A wealth of barbecue places and rib shacks is found along the way, and one of the best is Baba's. The nicely smoked meats are complemented by a medium spicy and not-too-sweet red sauce, and the sides (beans, cole slaw, potato salad, and fries) are flavorful. Home-style vegetables and fish are available, too. Dine in, order at counter, 15 seats, all nonsmoking.

Date visited_____Remarks_____

Bailey's BBQ (22)

11967 Hwy. 41 S
Tunnel Hill, Ga. 30755
706/935-2969
County: Catoosa

Mon - Thu 7 a.m. - 8 p.m., Fri & Sat 7 a.m. - 9 p.m.
Off I-75, south of Ringgold. Take Exit 139, go south on
U.S. 41 towards Tunnel Hill.

Bailey's serves chopped pork with a sweet, vinegar-based sauce (choice of hot or mild). Also on the menu: steaks, fish, baked potatoes, sandwiches, chocolate pie, and coconut pie. (Ribs and BBQ chicken plates served only on Friday nights.) Dine in, table service, seats 100. Opened 1978.

Date visited _____Remarks_____

Baker's BBQ & Country Style Buffet (23)

1046 Holcombe Rd.
Decatur, Ga. 30032
404/292-2592
County: DeKalb

Tue - Sat 11 a.m. - 8 p.m., Sun 12 p.m. - 7 p.m.
From I-285, exit at Memorial Dr. Go a half-mile west,
turn left onto Kensington Rd., go about a mile. It's on the
left just before Redan Rd.

This neighborhood cafeteria offers a nice assortment of vegetables and non-BBQ items like fried chicken, catfish, lasagna, meat loaf, and oxtails over rice. In fact, you could easily fill your plate before you get any barbecue. The sauce is homemade and comes in hot or mild. Desserts vary daily but look for cobblers, banana pudding, sweet potato pie, and punch bowl cake. Dine in, about 50 seats.

Date visited _____Remarks_____

Banks Barbecue (24)

1684 Fortson Dr.
Elberton, Ga. 30635
706/283-8741
County: Elbert

Wed 6 a.m. - 2 p.m., Thu - Sat 6 a.m. - 8 p.m.
From Elberton, take the Hartwell highway (Ga. 77).

Expect barbecued pork, baby back ribs, Brunswick stew, and the customary sides at this dine-in/drive-in place in "the Granite City." A bonus is a country-cooking buffet. They also serve breakfast daily.

Date visited _____Remarks_____

Bar-B-Q Shack (25)

Hwy. 17 Alt. S
Toccoa, Ga. 30598
706/886-7440
County: Stephens

Thu - Sat 10 a.m. - 9 p.m.
From Gainesville, take U.S. 23 30 miles north,
then Hwy. 17 11 miles to its end. Turn left onto 17 Alt.
It's a half mile on the right.

Praising the food at the nearby Traveler's Inn, now a state historical museum, an 1837 visitor wrote, "I got an excellent breakfast of coffee, ham, chicken, good bread and butter, honey and plenty of good new milk for a quarter of a dollar." Travelers can still find good food at reasonable prices in Toccoa. Here at the Shack, they can get perfectly palatable pork, pork ribs, chicken, Brunswick stew, and the appropriate sides. And homemade cakes for dessert. Excellent indeed. Dine in, table service, seats 70.

Date visited_____Remarks _____

Bar-B-Que House (26)

541 Thornton Rd.
Lithia Springs, Ga. 30057
770/941-1155
County: Douglas

Mon - Thu 11 a.m - 9 p.m, Fri & Sat 11 a.m. - 10 p.m.
From I-20 west of Atlanta, take exit 12 (Hwy. 6), go north
about 2 miles. It's on the left.

Some folks say that the Brunswick stew here is the best in town. The barbecued pork, well accented with a tomato/vinegar–based sauce, calls for superlatives as well. A non-BBQ specialty is the "Yellow Jacket Dog," named after a long-gone but still-loved hot dog house that once stood near Georgia Tech. Order at counter, 120 seats, nonsmokers' area. Opened 1983. (Also known as Fred's Bar-B-Que House.)

Date visited_____Remarks _____

Barbecue Billy's (27)

2151 Fort Benning Rd.
Columbus, Ga. 31903
706/687-0097
County: Muscogee

Mon - Sun 11 a.m. - 10 p.m.
From I-185, take exit 1 (U.S. 27), go west on Victory Dr.
toward Phenix City. It's a couple of miles
on the right at Fort Benning Rd.

This family-owned place has walls decorated with cowboy boots, guitars, and Elvis pictures. An extensive buffet, available every day for lunch and dinner, is quite popular. It includes ribs during evenings. Three sauces are offered: the mild one is a thick tomato-based sauce, while the medium and hot sauces are mustard-based. Dine in, table service, 120 seats. Opened 1992.

Date visited_____Remarks _____

Bar-B-Fact

Armstrong's Bar-B-Q in Summerville opened in 1965, the year Augusta's James Brown made the Billboard Top Ten with "I Got You (I Feel Good)."

Barbecue Kitchen (28)

1437 Virginia Ave.
College Park, Ga. 30337
404/766-9906
County: Fulton

Mon - Sun 7:30 a.m. - 10:30 p.m.
From downtown College Park, go toward the airport on
Virginia Ave. It's on the left.

Barbecue Kitchen opened for business about twenty years ago and has been feeding airport-area workers well ever since. Delectable pork and finely smoked chicken are accompanied by veggies such as greens, squash, corn, beans, peas, and fried okra. Corned beef hash, grilled ham, catfish, ribeyes, meat loaf, and other non-BBQ meats round out the menu. Good value for your money. Country music on the jukebox. Dine in, table service, plenty of seats, all nonsmoking.

Date visited _____*Remarks* _____

Bar-B-Fact

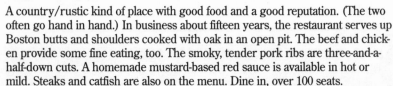

Fincher's was the first barbecue to go into space, traveling on the space shuttle with astronaut Sonny Carter on November 22, 1989.

Barbecue Pit (29)

RR 2, Hwy. 121
Metter, Ga. 30439
912/685-4940
County: Candler

Mon - Sat 11 a.m. - 6:00 p.m.
On Hwy. 121 a couple of miles north of Metter.

The Barbecue Pit has a full menu in the warm seasons, but serves only sandwiches in the winter. This arrangement helps the owner avoid throwing away any food, which he hates to do. It really would be a shame to discard even an ounce of the pit-smoked Boston butts and shoulders found here. The meat is especially good with the homemade vinegar/ketchup/mustard/Worcestershire sauce.

Date visited _____*Remarks* _____

Barbecue Pit (30)

311 First Ave. SE
Moultrie, Ga. 31768
912/985-5314
County: Colquitt

Mon - Thu 11 a.m. - 9 p.m., Fri - Sat 11 a.m. - 10 p.m.
First Avenue is in downtown Moultrie.

A country/rustic kind of place with good food and a good reputation. (The two often go hand in hand.) In business about fifteen years, the restaurant serves up Boston butts and shoulders cooked with oak in an open pit. The beef and chicken provide some fine eating, too. The smoky, tender pork ribs are three-and-a-half-down cuts. A homemade mustard-based red sauce is available in hot or mild. Steaks and catfish are also on the menu. Dine in, over 100 seats.

Date visited _____*Remarks* _____

Barbeque King (31)

701 Lippitt Dr.
Albany, Ga. 31701
912/438-7470
County: Dougherty

Wed - Sat 11 a.m. - 10 p.m.
From downtown Albany, take Slappey Blvd. south. Turn
left at the post office onto Lippitt Dr.
It's just before Newton Rd.

This take-out place specializes in ribs and chopped barbecue. The 'que is hickory, smoked in a closed pit, chopped, and served with the homemade tomato-based sauce. Barbecued turkey is available, too. On the side: Brunswick stew, beans, chili, cole slaw, potato salad, and pork skins. Canned drinks. Opened 1991.

Date visited_____Remarks _____

Barbeque Shack (32)

4320 Lexington Rd.
Athens, Ga. 30605
706/613-6752
County: Clarke

Fri & Sat 10 a.m. - 9 p.m.
From downtown Athens, take Oconee St. (U.S. 78 Bus)
east. It's about a mile beyond the Bypass on the right.

Barbeque Shack sells barbecue sandwiches, platters, Brunswick stew, ribs, chicken, slaw, beans, and other items at this small place, which is open only on weekends. All are available in bulk. Eat it in or take it out.

Date visited_____Remarks _____

Barnes' Barn Bar-B-Que (33)

124 Old LaFayette Rd.
Rocky Face, Ga. 30740
706/278-0434
County: Whitfield

Thu 11 a.m. - 8 p.m., Fri & Sat 11 a.m. - 9 p.m.
Off U.S. 41, 2 miles north of Dalton. Look for the sign.

Here's something you won't find in many restaurants: smoked fillet mignon. The pork and beef are slow-cooked in a closed pit and served chopped or sliced. A spicy tomato-based sauce is served separately. Barnes' Barn has won numerous awards at barbecue contests in Chattanooga, Charleston, Daytona Beach, and Stone Mountain. Dine in, order at counter, 70 seats. Opened 1990.

Date visited _____Remarks _____

Barnes Restaurant (34)

5320 Waters Ave.
Savannah, Ga. 31404
912/354-8745
County: Chatham

Mon - Sun 10:30 a.m. - 10:30 p.m.
On Waters Ave. at 68th St., between Memorial and
Candler Hospitals.

Closed-pit, hickory-smoked pig meat, served chopped or sliced, draws a cross section of people to this long-established eatery. The barbecue is served with the tomato-based sauce already mixed in. Also on the bill of fare are Brunswick stew, barbecued turkey, fried chicken, rotisserie chicken, burgers, seafood, baked potatoes, hush puppies, and onion rings. Dine in, table service, tables and booths, seats 210. Nonsmokers' area. Opened 1975.

Date visited_____Remarks _____

Barnes Restaurant (35)

4685 Hwy. 80 E
Savannah, Ga. 31410
912/898-0220
County: Chatham

Mon - Sun 10:30 a.m. - 10:30 p.m.
From central Savannah, take U.S. 80 (Victory Dr.) east
to Whitemarsh Island. It's on the right
beyond Johnny Mercer Blvd.

Barnes' other location offers the same varied menu, comfortable environment, and fair prices found at the Waters Avenue restaurant described above.

Date visited _____Remarks _____

Bartow's Barbecue (36)

U.S. 441 S
Wiley, Ga. 30581
706/782-4038
County: Rabun

Sun, Mon, Tue, Thu 11 a.m. - 8 p.m.
Fri & Sat 11 a.m. - 8:30 p.m.
From Clayton, take U.S. 441 about 5 miles south of town.
It's on the left.

After a long day of leaf-looking, knick-knack shopping, whitewater rafting, or whatever else you enjoy doing in Georgia's mountains, what could be better than a plate of barbecued pork? Bartow's slow-cooked meat is complemented by a thin, tangy sauce. Either smoked or grilled chicken is available, as are burgers, shrimp, and country fried steak. Vegetables include mashed potatoes, corn, beans, okra, and fried mushrooms. For dessert there are cobblers and cheesecake. Dine in, nonsmokers' area.

Date visited _____Remarks _____

BBQ Express (37)

121 Lower Alabama St. SW
Atlanta, Ga. 30303
404/577-2777
County: Fulton

Mon - Sat 10 a.m. - 10 p.m., Sun 12 p.m. - 6 p.m.
In the food court at Underground Atlanta. Take Peachtree
St. south, look for the Underground Atlanta sign.

Beneath the streets of Atlanta is the twelve-acre shopping and entertainment district known as Underground Atlanta. BBQ Express, in the food court, serves hickory-smoked meats, fourteen fresh vegetables, and pasta salads. Opened 1996.

Date visited _____Remarks _____

Bar-B-Fact

"Today, Americans spend $480 million a year on barbecue
sauce, making it the third-largest-selling condiment
after salsa and ketchup."
—Jim Auchmutey and Susan Puckett,
The Ultimate Barbecue Sauce Cookbook

> *"Classic Southern barbecue is the antithesis of fast food:*
> *it is slow food, requiring hours of patient preparation."*
> — *John Egerton*, Southern Food

Name/Map ID	Hours/Directions

Becky's Bar-B-Q (38)

Hwy. 76/515
Blue Ridge, Ga. 30513
706/632-2197
County: Fannin

Mon - Sat 7 a.m. - 7 p.m.
From Ellijay, take Hwy. 515 (Zell Miller Pkwy.) to
Blue Ridge. It's at the junction of U.S. 76.

Open about three years, this small place on a busy corner sells a variety of barbecued meats and most of the standard barbecue-related side orders. The ribs are baby backs and the mild red sauce is homemade. Dine in or drive-through.

Date visited_____Remarks _____

Bell's Barbecue and Steaks (39)

3815 Cherokee St. NW
Kennesaw, Ga. 30144
770/419-2626
County: Cobb

Tue - Thu 10:30 - 9, Fri & Sat 10:30 - 10.
From I-75, take exit 118 (Wade Green Rd.). Go towards
Kennesaw about a mile; look for the sign.

Closed-pit, hickory-smoked, pulled and chopped barbecue is served with a vinegar and ketchup-based sauce made according to an old recipe used by Austell's Wallace Barbecue in the 1940s and 1950s. Other items include Brunswick stew, beans, creamy cole slaw, fries, onion rings, baked potato, corn on the cob, steaks, and sandwiches. Bell's Super Stew is a large order of Brunswick stew smothered in cheddar and topped with chunks of pork. Dine in, table service, 170 seats, nonsmokers' area. Opened 1992.

Date visited_____Remarks _____

Benny's Barbecue (40)

2150-B Johnson Ferry Rd. NE
Atlanta, Ga. 30319
770/454-7810 Fax: 454-6615
County: DeKalb

Mon. - Sat. 8 a.m. - 8 p.m.
In a small shopping center on Johnson Ferry Rd. at
Ashford-Dunwoody Rd. in northeast Atlanta.

A wonderful aroma greets you at the door of this simply furnished place. Ample portions are the rule; two plates will serve three persons, in many cases. Owner Benny Esslinger cooks Boston butts in an unusual convection smoker using wood only (no gas). Also: BBQ turkey, Brunswick stew, baked beans, potato salad, fries, marinated slaw, chips. For dessert there's peach or apple cobbler. Lunch specials. Two homemade tomato-based sauces: mild and very hot. Dine in, order at counter, about 50 seats. Opened 1991.

Date visited_____Remarks _____

Benny's Barbecue (41)

2271 Atlanta Hwy.
Cumming, Ga. 30130
770/889-7600
County: Forsyth

Mon - Thu 11 a.m. - 3 p.m., Fri & Sat 11 a.m. - 9 p.m.
(Open 'til 8 Mon - Thu in summer).
From Hwy. 400, take exit 13, go one block west to Hwy. 9,
turn right; Benny's is a block north, on the right.

Benny's Cumming place has some items not available at the Atlanta location, including catfish, whiting, hushpuppies, and hot dogs. In addition, there's a buffet. "Best in Georgia" is his claim. Benny's is so good, he says he gets unsolicited letters from travelers praising his 'cue as No. 1 in the Southeast. Dine in, table service, or self-service buffet. Seats about 45 in one medium-sized room. Opened 1995.

Date visited _____*Remarks* _____

Benny's Que Shack (42)

Hwy. 18
Warm Springs, Ga. 31830
706/663-2839
County: Meriwether

Mon - Sat 8 a.m. - 11 p.m.
From Warm Springs, take Hwy. 194 6 miles to Durand.
Turn left onto Hwy. 18. It's on the right.

The sign out front reads "Stew & Que," but the place could also be called "Cue & Que" because inside is a cozy room with pool tables, dining tables, and a fireplace. The barbecue is cooked in a smoker and served with a semi-sweet tomato-based sauce. To go with it, there's Brunswick stew and the usual sides. So grab a quick bite and then rack 'em up. Dine in, order at counter, seats 12. Opened 1993.

Date visited _____*Remarks* _____

Big Al's Bar B-Q Restaurant (43)

301 Johnny Mercer Blvd.
Savannah, Ga. 31410
912/897-0948
County: Chatham

Mon - Sun 11 - 9.
On Wilmington Island. From downtown Savannah, take
U.S. 80 to Johnny Mercer Blvd.

A few years ago, Al Hirsch's place only had two inside seats and one large picnic table outside. Now he has 150 seats with table service, a nonsmokers' area, and he accepts credit cards. His slogan is: "Real Hickory Smoked BBQ. Our BBQ is 100% wood cooked and all our food is prepared on the premises." The ingredients in the mildly flavored Brunswick stew include okra and potatoes. Big Al's tomato-based sauce is served on the finely chopped pork. Sliced Bar-B-Q lamb plate is another option. Also served are freshly made sides including potato salad and corn on the cob. The everyday buffet includes fried chicken, mashed potatoes, corn, and other items. Opened 1989.

Date visited _____*Remarks* _____

Bar-B-Fact

Wallace Barbecue in Austell opened in 1966, the year the Braves
played the first official big-league baseball game in the South.

Big-Chic Barbecue (44)

415 S Mulberry St.
Jackson, Ga. 30233
770/775-4263
County: Butts

Mon - Wed 10 a.m. - 9 p.m.,
Thu - Sat 10 a.m. - 10 p.m., Sun 11 a.m. - 8 p.m.
Big-Chic is three blocks off the square in downtown
Jackson. (Turn right at Western Auto.)

Richard McBride's Big-Chic serves barbecue plates and sandwiches, ribs,
Brunswick stew, and the usual barbecue sides. Catfish, seafood, and vegetables
are other menu items. Hams are cooked over an open pit fired with half hickory
and half oak. The thick brown tomato/vinegar-based–sauce is a little spicy. Take-
out only. Picnic table seating for about 14. Opened 1969.

Date visited _____ *Remarks* _____

Big Daddy's House Bar-B-Que and Southern Style Cooking (45)

5611 Memorial Dr.
Stone Mountain, Ga. 30083
404/508-1800
County: DeKalb

Tue - Thu 11 a.m. - 10 p.m.,
Fri - Sat 11 a.m. - midnight, Sun 12 p.m. - 9 p.m.
From I-285, go east on Memorial Dr. about 3 miles. Look
for it on the hill to the right.

Big Daddy's serves BBQ pork, beef, ribs, rib tips, and chicken, accompanied by
a tomato-based sauce. Also on the menu are ox tails, potato salad, corn on the
cob, Southern-style vegetables, chicken, and fish. Try Big Daddy's Punch. Dine
in, plenty of seats, nonsmokers' area. Meeting room available. Opened 1995.

Date visited _____ *Remarks* _____

Big Ed's Pig 'N Pit Barbecue (46)

1410 Terrell Mill Rd.
Marietta, Ga. 30067
770/952-9841
County: Cobb

Mon - Fri 10:30 a.m. - 9 p.m., Sat 10:30 a.m. - 3 p.m.
From I-75, exit at Windy Hill Rd. Go east to Powers Ferry
Rd. Turn left, go one mile. Turn left on Terrell Mill.
It's on the right.

Picky people have been known to pig out on Pig 'N Pit's stew, a piquant pottage
with plenty of shredded pork (and a few kernels of corn). The pork is pretty
palatable, too. The thick tomato-based sauce is a little hot, a little sweet, and a
little smoky. Sweet cole slaw. Also chicken fingers, chicken wings, and the usual
sides. Country vegetable lunches, but only on weekdays. Dine in. Since 1973.

Date visited _____ *Remarks* _____

Big Greg's Barbecue (47)

1479 Scott Blvd.
Decatur, Ga. 30030
404/378-6041
County: DeKalb

Mon 7 a.m. - 4 p.m., Tue - Sun 7 a.m. - 9 p.m.
On Scott Blvd. (U.S. 78) at North Decatur Rd.,
3 miles inside I-285.

A smokiness permeates most everything here: the food, the sauce, the wood-
paneled walls, the deer and boar heads, the photos of politicians (mostly
Democrats), the bumper stickers, and other interesting clutter. The award-
winning open-pit-cooked pork is excellent. The stew is mostly meat with just the
right accent of tomatoes and corn. Table service, 90 seats, nonsmokers' area.

Date visited _____ *Remarks* _____

Big John's Treat Shoppe (48)

3230 Underwood Rd. NE
Dalton, Ga. 30721
706/259-5511
County: Whitfield

Mon - Fri 10 a.m. - 8 p.m.
From I-75, take Rocky Face/Dalton exit; go east. Turn left
onto Underwood Rd. It's 2 miles on the left.

In business nineteen years, Big John's specializes in "food." John says he doesn't need to advertise much because his food is so good. His meats are cooked in a closed pit using hickory. A mild ketchup-based sauce is the house standard, and a hot relish is available. Homemade pies. Dine in, order at counter, 60 seats.

Date visited _____ *Remarks* _____

Big O Bar-B-Que (49)

Hwy. 100 S
Tallapoosa, Ga. 30176
770/574-2881
County: Haralson

Mon - Sun 10 a.m. - 10 p.m.
From I-20 in west Georgia, take exit 1; turn south. It's in
an old wooden building on the left, at the exit.

Owner Gene Owens also has the place next door which sells lottery tickets, beer, and fuel. Many truckers stop at Big O to get diesel fuel, take a shower, buy a lottery ticket, and eat some barbecue. Pork shoulders, sides of beef, and pork ribs are smoked in a hickory-fired smoker. The meat is coated three or four times with the red-brown sauce, which is then allowed to cook off. The pork is served chopped or sliced. The beef is chopped only. Dine in, order at counter, 25 seats. Drive-thru. Opened 1971.

Date visited _____ *Remarks* _____

Big Pig Bar-B-Q

Bar-B-Fact

Aleck's Barbecue Heaven in Atlanta opened in 1942, the year the Atlanta metro area's population passed the half-million mark.

Name/Map ID   **Hours/Directions**

Big Pig Bar-B-Q (50)

1015 16th Ave.
Cordele, Ga. 31015
912/276-0690
County: Crisp

Tue - Sat 10 a.m. - 9 p.m.
From I-75, take exit 33 and go west on U.S. 280.
It's on the right.

The hickory-smoked, chopped-pork "keeps you squealin' for more," as they say at Big Pig. The barbecue beef, chicken, goat, and turkey might elicit a squeal too. As for the sauces (tomato-based), they note, "We have three sauces: mild, hot, and the Sizzler. We don't put the Sizzler on the table because it burns the table cloths. Just ask for it!" Excellent sweet and tangy Brunswick stew, Georgia-style hash on rice, hobo stew, beans, cole slaw, potato salad, corn on the cob, fries, and fried sweet potatoes. All-you-can-eat specials. Dine in, table service, 50 seats, nonsmokers' area. Also drive-thru.

Date visited _____*Remarks*

Bilbo's Old Hickory Smoke Bar-B-Que (51)

769 Atlantic Ave.
Bremen, Ga. 30110
770/537-4180
County: Haralson

Tue - Sat 11 a.m. - 9 p.m.
From I-20, take exit 3 and go north.
Its's at Hwy. 78 and Hwy. 27.

Earnest and Millie Bilbo serve up ample portions of chipped or sliced pork at this old roadside diner at the edge of Bremen. They also prepare beef and chicken, Brunswick stew, beans, cole slaw, hand-cut fries, baked potato, and hand-sliced onion rings, among other items. Vegetable lunches are served Tuesday through Saturday. The ketchup-based sauce comes hot or mild. The sauce doesn't overpower the hickory-smoke flavor in the meat. There's also a salad bar. Table service (seats 88 at tables and booths). Separate nonsmokers' area. Opened 1985.

Date visited _____*Remarks* _____

Bill Hilliard's Restaurant and Spirits (52)

3005 E Victory Dr.
Thunderbolt, Ga. 31404
912/354-5430
County: Chatham

Sun - Thu 11 a.m. - 10 p.m.,
Fri & Sat 11 a.m. - midnight.
Take Victory Drive (U.S. 80) to the eastern city limits of
Savannah. It's on the right.

"Home for fine barbecue and seafood" is the claim at Bill Hilliard's. It's tough to do both well, but Hilliard's has handled the job for thirty-something years. Bill Hilliard's BBQ sauce is a red, tangy, spicy mixture that is bottled and sold here. Besides open-pit smoked meat there's shrimp, crab, and other fresh seafood, fried chicken, and prime rib. A big daily buffet, a children's menu, and a full bar provide even more options.

Date visited _____*Remarks* _____

Bill's, Kingston

Name/Map ID	**Hours/Directions**

Bill's Bar B Q (53)

38 Turner St. NW
Kingston, Ga. 30145
770/336-5200
County: Bartow

Tue - Thu 11 a.m. - 6 p.m., Fri, Sat & Sun 11 a.m. - 10:30 p.m.
From I-75, take exit 125 and go 2 miles west to
U.S. 41. Go 3 miles north on 41 to
Hwy. 293. Take 293 to Kingston.

In 1862, Andrews' Raiders, having stolen the Confederate locomotive "General" at Big Shanty, raced to Kingston — where they had to sit and wait for a southbound freight to pass. If Bill Sanders' take-out barbecue place had been here then, the wait might not have seemed so long. They could have enjoyed the slow-cooked Boston butts, doused with Bill's vinegar-based sauce, and might have feasted on his tender, smoky ribs. And, since it's a take-out-only place, they could have been back on track in a jiffy.

Date visited _____ *Remarks* _____

Bill's Bar-B-Q (54)

3061 N Dug Gap Rd. SW
Dalton, Ga. 30720
706/277-1884
County: Whitfield

Mon - Fri 6:30 a.m. - 2 p.m.
From I-75 northbound, take exit 135, turn left. Go a half
block and turn right on Dug Gap Rd. It's on the right.

"Bill" is owner Bill Hartman. The barbecue comes from his son's restaurant just up the road in Chattanooga. He serves the smoke-seasoned pork, beef, or chicken with his "self-mixed" red sauce, which is quite spicy, but not hot. Everybody is very friendly at Bill's Bar-B-Q. If they don't know you, they pretend like they do, he says.

Date visited _____ *Remarks* _____

Bill's Bar-B-Q (55)

5410 Matt Hwy.
Cumming, Ga. 30130
770/889-1028
County: Forsyth

Mon - Wed 11 a.m. - 3 p.m., Thu - Sat 11 a.m.- 6 p.m.
From Hwy. 19/400 north of Cumming, take Hwy. 369
5 miles west to the community of Matt.

Bill's is a tiny take-out shack at the BP station/store at the corner of Bannister Rd. and Matt Hwy. near Cumming. This "Little House with the Big Taste" serves real barbecue cooked with hickory wood in a large smoker. Barbecue is available by the plate, sandwich, or pound. Grilled spicy chicken, chick fillet, hot dogs, and burgers too. The tangy red sauce is served warm. "Best iced tea in Georgia." Brownies for dessert. Take-out only. One (sheltered) picnic table.

Date visited_____Remarks _____

Bill's BBQ (56)

RR 3, Box 212
Hull, Ga. 30646
706/549-4949
County: Madison

Mon - Thu 10 a.m. - 8 p.m., Fri & Sat 10 a.m.- 9 p.m.
From Athens, take U.S. 29 north toward Hull to
Hwy. 106, just north of the Clarke County line.
It's at the junction.

This place, just north of Athens, is owned by three brothers. One of them, Bill Lance, is the pitmaster. "Just a country place," is how they describe it. The sauce is vinegar-based and is served on the meat. Like many Athens area establishments, they serve hash, a thick mix of beef and pork, instead of stew. Dine in.

Date visited_____Remarks _____

Black River Bar-B-Q (57)

Hwy. 129 S
Cleveland, Ga. 30528
706/865-6384
County: White

Sun - Thu 11 a.m. - 8 p.m., Fri & Sat 11 a.m. - 9 p.m.
From downtown Cleveland go south on U.S. 129 4 miles.
It's on the right.

"Taste the Legend" is the slogan at Black River. It's a greaseless meat trimmed of fat and then steamed for 45 minutes to dissolve more fat. The rest of the cooking process is more traditional: hams and Boston butts cooked with oak, hickory, or apple in a closed pit all night. Dine inside or outside. Opened 1988.

Date visited_____Remarks _____

Blue's Bar-B-Q (58)

2121 Martin Luther King Jr. Dr.
Augusta, Ga. 30901
706/722-7004
County: Richmond

Thu - Sat 11 a.m. - 10 p.m.
From downtown Augusta, take 15th Street to
Martin Luther King Jr. Drive.

Barbecued goat is served at Rev. Edward E. Blueford's place. He describes pit-cooked goat as tasting like a cross between beef and venison. Old-time hash and three types of barbecue sauce—sweet, mild "Georgia Peach," hot "Louisiana Cajun Queen," and extra hot "Arkansas Razorback Special"—are two more reasons to visit Blue's. Bread pudding for dessert. Dine in, 15 seats. Opened 1988.

Date visited_____Remarks _____

Bo James Bar-B-Que (59)

Route 5, Box 1265
Blakely, Ga. 31723
912/723-5301
County: Early

Mon - Sat 4 p.m. - 10:30 p.m.
From the courthouse in Blakely, take Hwy 62, about 10
miles toward Dothan, Alabama. It's on the right.

Georgia has some nontraditional barbecue places and this one probably fits into that category. It's in a trailer with six tables, a bar, and pool tables, and it has good music on the jukebox. But what about the food? At Bo James, the pork is cooked in a wood-burning smoker and provided with a homemade secret-recipe sauce. It's served on sandwiches or plates. Brunswick stew, beans, cole slaw, and fries are the sides. Fish is available, too.

Date visited _____*Remarks* _____

Bob's Bar-B-Q (60)

1435 Thompson Bridge Rd. NW
Gainesville, Ga. 30501
770/531-7500
County: Hall

Mon - Sat 11 a.m. - 6:30 p.m.
From downtown, take Hwy. 129 Bus. north to Hwy. 60
and go left. Bob's is 8/10 mile on the left near Bi-Lo.

Bob's is a clean, well-lit storefront place with a "country lite" decor. The meats are cooked with hickory in a smoker out back. Baby back ribs are cooked to order on Friday and Saturday nights for regular customers, so call ahead for these. Also Brunswick stew, baked potatoes, corn on the cob, beans, slaw, hot dogs, chicken fingers, chili, grilled cheese. A wider variety of fresh vegetables is available in the summer. Althought it's mostly take-out, there's seating for 25 or so.

Date visited _____*Remarks* _____

Bono's Pit Bar-B-Q and Grill (61)

139 City Smitty Dr.
St. Marys, Ga. 31558
912/882-2666
County: Camden

Mon - Sun 11 a.m. - 9 p.m.
From I-95, take exit 2 (Kingsland/St. Marys). Go east on
Hwy. 40 about 5 miles to 40 Spur. Turn right into Kings
Bay Village shopping center.

"Quality food and great atmosphere at fair prices over four decades." Jacksonville-based Bono's had five restaurants in Georgia in 1997 and has plans for more. Each serves real open-pit barbecue cooked over oak and chopped. A smoky mustard-based sauce comes on the side. Specialties are baby back ribs and Colorado-style spare ribs. Along with the traditional sides, there's barbecue rice, fried okra, fried yellow squash, and corn on the cob. Also BBQ turkey, char-grilled shrimp, pork sausage, steak, salmon, burgers, sandwiches, salads, beer and wine, desserts, and a kids' menu. Dine in, table service, plenty of seats.

Date visited _____*Remarks* _____

Bar-B-Fact

The barbecue at Spruce's in Griffin is so good it has stopped trains.
Railroad men used to halt their locomotives there to grab some 'que.

Bono's Pit Bar-B-Q and Grill (62)

13040 Abercorn St.
Savannah, Ga. 31419
912/927-6344
County: Chatham

Sun - Thu 11 a.m. - 10 p.m., Fri & Sat 11 a.m. - 11 p.m.
Across from Savannah Mall in the Publix shopping center.

Bono's "Bono-fied Best Ribs" are smoked in an open pit and then grilled to perfection. Available in full or short racks.

Date visited _____Remarks _____

Bono's Pit Bar-B-Q and Grill (63)

1531 Baytree Rd.
Valdosta, Ga. 31602
912/244-5006
County: Lowndes

Sun - Thu 11 a.m. - 10 p.m., Fri & Sat 11 a.m. - 11 p.m.
From I-75, take exit 5, go east to McDonald's. Turn left.
Go until the road ends at Baytree Rd. Look for the sign.

Try Lou's Favorite Duo, a short rack of baby back ribs paired with a grilled boneless, skinless barbecued chicken breast.

Date visited _____Remarks _____

Bono's Pit Bar-B-Q and Grill (64)

1636 Veterans Blvd.
Dublin, Ga. 31021
912/275-8809
County: Laurens

Mon - Sun 10 a.m. - 10 p.m.
From U.S. 80 at U.S. 441 in downtown Dublin, take U.S.
80 west about 1.5 miles. It's on the left in the Oaks Plaza.

Weight watchers might want to try Bono's Lite Turkey. It's barbecued turkey served with a house salad.

Date visited _____Remarks _____

Bono's Pit Bar-B-Q and Grill (65)

1303 E Lyons Hwy.
Vidalia, Ga. 30474
912/538-0988
County: Toombs

Sun - Thu 11 a.m. - 10 p.m., Fri & Sat 11 a.m. - 11 p.m.
On the U.S. 280 commercial strip in Vidalia.

Not worrying about your weight? Try the Bar-B-Q Feast, a combo of ribs, beef, pork, turkey, chicken, beans, potato, corn, slaw, applesauce, and bread.

Date visited _____Remarks _____

Boyd's Pit Barbeque (66)

302 Northside Dr.
Statesboro, Ga. 30458
912/764-9995
County: Bulloch

Mon - Wed 6 a.m. - 6 p.m., Thu 6 a.m.- 9 p.m.,
Fri & Sat 6 a.m. - 10 p.m., Sun 7 a.m. - 3 p.m.
On Northside Dr. (U.S. 80 West), near junction with U.S.
301, just north of downtown Statesboro.

Boyd's succulent pork ribs slathered with the mustard-based barbecue sauce will satisfy any cravings for "pig on a stick." The big buffet is rather "fulfilling," too.

Date visited _____Remarks _____

Brennan Road Barbeque (67)

456 Brennan Rd.
Columbus, Ga. 31903
706/689-9334
County: Muscogee

Mon - Sat 10 a.m. - 8 p.m.
From I-185 southbound, take exit 2 (St. Marys Rd.), turn
right, go to third light, turn left on Brennan Rd.

Look for a small block building with an orange door. Inside is a friendly atmosphere and the "Best barbecue in the Columbus area." The pork (Boston butts cooked with oak and hickory in an open pit), chicken, and ribs are first-rate. Try the barbecue slaw (fresh cabbage ground with barbecue sauce). Made-from-scratch, ketchup-based sauce comes in mild or hot. Cakes for dessert. Dine in or carry out. Opened 1987.

Date visited _____*Remarks* _____

Brinson's Bar-B-Que Restaurant (68)

Rt. 4, Box 106
Millen, Ga. 30442
912/982-4570
County: Jenkins

Tue - Thu 9 a.m. - 7 p.m.,
Fri & Sat 9 a.m. - 9 p.m., Sun 9 a.m. - 7 p.m.
Go 3 miles south of Millen on U.S. 25; turn right on Ga.
23; go one mile to crossroads.

Brinson's barbecue is cooked over oak coals in an open pit and served up chopped or sliced. The sauce is a mix of ketchup, mustard, sugar, mayonnaise, salt, pepper, and vinegar, and is served on the side. Recommended sides are Brunswick stew, potato salad, and hash and rice. Dine in, order at counter, 36 seats. Opened 1966.

Date visited _____*Remarks* _____

Bryant's Barbeque Pit (69)

A Street North
Vienna, Ga. 31092
912/268-4179
County: Dooly

Thu - Sat 4 p.m. - 7 p.m.
From I-75, take exit 37. Go west about 3 miles to Vienna.
Turn right on A Street. Go 2 blocks.

J. B. Bryant sells out of a pit in his yard. He just took it up as something to do. He's always cooked at his house; he's never had a restaurant. His wife makes the Brunswick stew. J. B. cooks hams and shoulders with oak in his open pit. His hot-and-spicy homemade BBQ sauce is mostly a blend of vinegar and red pepper. Just pull up in front of his house and follow your nose, he says. Meat and stew are the only items, no sides.

Date visited _____*Remarks* _____

Bar-B-Fact

Sconyers Bar-B-Que in Augusta opened in 1956, the year Little Richard of Macon, Ga., earned a gold record with "Tutti Frutti."

> *D.K.'s Barbeque in Waycross opened in 1960, the year CBS first televised the "The Andy Griffith Show."*

Name/Map ID   **Hours/Directions**

Bubba's B-B-Q (70)

1 Broad St.
Rome, Ga. 30161
706/291-1238 or 706/291-0618
County: Floyd

Tue - Thu 11 a.m. - 7 p.m., Fri & Sat 11 a.m. - 8 p.m.
In downtown Rome on historic Broad Street
at the Etowah River bridge.

In operation since 1991, Bubba's is a take-out shack featuring "Authentic Southern Cuisine." Authentic Southerners know that means barbecued pork, chicken, and ribs (we're not so sure about that beef), Brunswick stew, potato salad, and chips. Outside seating on a nice deck. Or take the old railroad bridge (now a walking bridge) over the river to eat it in the park.

Date visited_____Remarks _____

Bubba's B B Que (71)

902 Langdale Dr.
Nashville, Ga. 31639
912/686-7021
County: Berrien

Mon - Sat 5 a.m. - 8 p.m.
From Nashville, go east on Hwy. 76 to the airport. It's in
a two-story building at the west end of the airport.

Look for a seven-foot pig by the road. It was crafted by a Swedish sculptor, but get Bubba to tell you about that. We're interested in food, not swine art. The meats are cooked out back about 16 hours with oak and hickory the old-time way. Bubba is good at finding low-fat cuts such as pork loin. His unique "Bubba's Southern Blend" sauce is a mix of mustard, vinegar, and spices. His establishment is a store with seating at picnic tables on an open-air porch.

Date visited__ _____Remarks _____

Bubba's Ribs & Q (72)

1629 N Tift Ave.
Tifton, Ga. 31794
912/386-2888
County: Tift

Mon 10:30 a.m. - 2:00 p.m., Tue - Sat 10:30 a.m. - 8:30 p.m.
From I-75, take exit 21, turn onto U.S. 41 South. Go one block, turn
left at light, then right at next light.
Bubba's is one block on the left.

"The best barbecue you ever flopped a lip over!" is how Tifton's Bubba describes his open-pit-cooked meat. If you like, you can douse it with "The Sauce," available in "hot, mild, and wild." It's not one of those sweet sauces, says Bubba with disdain. Beer, you ask? Bubba says Momma don't allow no guitar pickin' or beer drinkin'. No dessert either. Bubba doesn't let sugar ruin the experience of having eaten his barbecue. Dine in, table service, 45 seats.

Date visited_____Remarks _____

Buck's Bar-B-Que (73)

1129 Ethridge Mill Village Rd.
Griffin, Ga. 30223
770/227-8444
County: Spalding

Wed - Sat 11 a.m. - 9 p.m.
From downtown, go south on U.S. 19/41 Bus. Past the
airport, turn left into Ethridge Mill Village.
It's on the right.

Buck's was originally opened in 1975 by the Buchanan family (from whence the name). Although the ownership has changed, the sweet aroma of slow-cooked pig meat still attracts a crowd. Buck's serves hams and pork shoulders cooked with oak and hickory over an open pit. The sauce is a mix of ketchup, mustard, Worcestershire sauce, and vinegar. Among the sides are Brunswick stew, beans, cole slaw, and fries. Desserts are apple and pecan pies. Dine in, table service, seats 50.

Date visited _____ *Remarks* _____

Buck's Express (74)

345 Battlefield Pkwy.
Fort Oglethorpe, Ga. 30742
706/866-2204
County: Catoosa

Sun - Thu 11 a.m.- 10 p.m., Fri & Sat 11 a.m. - 11 p.m.
From I-75, take exit 141. Go west about 7 miles on
Hwy. 2. It's a tiny drive-thru place on the left.

Buck's serves pork shoulders cooked with hickory in a closed pit, then pulled off the bone. The sauce is homemade; it's red and very spicy. The ribs are normally served "wet" (with the sauce). Also available are vegetables, Brunswick stew, other standard barbecue side orders, and hot dogs. Drive-thru only. Opened 1994.

Date visited _____ *Remarks* _____

Bar-B-Fact

Sprayberry's Barbecue in Newnan has been family owned and
operated since 1926, the year Margaret Mitchell began writing
Gone With The Wind.

Bucky's Bar-B-Q (75)

1402 Brown's Bridge Rd.
Gainesville, Ga. 30501
770/503-9113
County: Hall

Sun - Thu 11 a.m.- 9:00 p.m., Fri - Sat 11 a.m.- 10 p.m.
From downtown Gainesville, take Browns Bridge Rd.
(GA 369.) west to West End Ave. It's on the right.

Housed in a former fast-food building on the highway strip, Bucky's looks more like a franchise burger outlet than a real barbecue restaurant, but don't let the contemporary exterior turn you away. Inside, you'll find smoked pork, beef, chicken, turkey, spare ribs, baby back ribs, Brunswick stew, beans, cole slaw, and other delicious items. Bucky's gives you a choice of a hot mustardy sauce or a thick, sweet, smoky tomato-based sauce. Desserts include banana pudding and a variety of cream pies. Eat in, table service. Nonsmokers' area. Drive-thru.

Date visited _____ *Remarks* _____

Name/Map ID	Hours/Directions

Buffalo Bill's Bar-B-Que (76)

3167 Hwy. 411 NE
White, Ga. 30184
770/606-0285
County: Bartow

Mon - Sat 10 a.m.- 9 p.m.
From I-75, take exit 126, and go 2.5 miles north toward
Chatsworth. You'll see it in the little town of White.

Pork and beef barbecue and baby back ribs are the main attractions at this log cabin restaurant north of Cartersville. The pork is Boston butts cooked with hickory in a smoker. A sweet red sauce (Cattleman's) is normally served already mixed in with the meat, but you can get it on the side.

Date visited _____ *Remarks* _____

Buford's Hickory Grill (77)

Hwy. 100
Hogansville, Ga. 30230
706/637-6300
County: Troup

Sun - Thu 11:30 a.m. - 9 p.m.,
Fri & Sat 11:30 a.m.- 10 p.m.
Buford's is between Newnan and LaGrange at the
intersection of I-85 and Hwy. 100.

This is surely the most upscale barbecue house in Georgia. The chief cook is a Danish master chef who does specials every night (for example, lobster and potato Napoleon, salmon stuffed with crabmeat). Instead of fries, there are herb-roasted potatoes. The barbecue is hickory-cooked whole hams. BBQ sauces include a mild red sauce and a hot and spicy watermelon sauce. Also home-made desserts, beer, and an extensive wine list. Table service, 100 seats.

Date visited _____ *Remarks* _____

C&D Bar-B-Que (78)

3815 Flat Shoals Pkwy.
Decatur, Ga. 30034
404/244-0329
County: DeKalb

Tue - Thu 11:30 a.m.- 8:30 p.m.,
Fri & Sat 11:30 a.m. - 11 p.m.
Exit I-285 at Flat Shoals Pkwy. (Hwy. 155). Go one block
south (outside of I-285). It's on the right.

"Love at first bite" is the typical reaction to C&D's closed pit-cooked, oak-and-hickory-smoked meats. Along with the main offerings are rib tips, Polish sausage, smoked wings, beans, potato salad, and cole slaw. For dessert, choose sweet potato pie or red velvet cake. Take-out only.

Date visited _____ *Remarks* _____

C&M Bar-B-Que (79)

Camp Pinckney Dr.
Folkston, Ga. 31537
912/496-3224
County: Charlton

Thu 4 p.m.- 8:30 p.m., Fri & Sat 11 a.m. - 8:30 p.m.
From Folkston, take Hwy. 40 about a mile east toward
Kingsland. Turn right at Exxon; C&M is less
than a mile on the left.

C&M cooks Boston butts in a smoker and over an open pit with oak and pecan. A thick, mild ketchup-based homemade sauce is added to the meat, if you like. Choose your sides: Brunswick stew, beans, cole slaw, fries, or potato salad. Finish up with pecan pie or sour cream pound cake. Then waddle home. Dine in, order at counter, 50 seats. Opened 1981.

Date visited _____ *Remarks* _____

C.H. Mitchell Barbecue

| **Name/Map ID** | **Hours/Directions** |

C. H. Mitchell Barbecue (80)

515 S Ashley St.
Valdosta, Ga. 31601
912/244-2684
County: Lowndes

Mon, Tue, Thu 8 a.m.- 8 p.m., Wed 8 a.m.- 2 p.m.,
Fri & Sat 8 a.m.- 9 p.m.
On South Ashley Street in downtown Valdosta.

A Valdosta favorite for many decades, C. H. Mitchell Barbecue cooks it as traditional as you'll find it: open-pit and hickory-smoked. On the side there's Brunswick stew, potato salad, collard greens, corn, and rice and gravy. Non-BBQ items include fried chicken, chitterlings, and other items varying daily. Dine in, table service, seats 16.

Date visited _____ *Remarks* _____

Canyon Barbecue (81)

4746 Memorial Dr.
Decatur, Ga. 30083
404/299-1877
County: DeKalb

Mon - Thu 11:30 a.m.- 8 p.m.,
Fri & Sat 11:30 a.m.- 9 p.m.
On Memorial Dr. a quarter-mile outside (east of) I-285,
on the left.

Owners Leon and Jeannine Craft opened this place in 1996 expecting to draw crowds hungry for authentic pit-cooked 'que. They say they're doing well after only being in business a short time. Maybe it's the Boston butts cooked with hickory in an open pit near the counter. It could be the pork spare ribs; they're the best-selling item. Or the thin, brown sweet and spicy sauce. Or the beans made according to an old recipe of Leon's mom. Or the pecan pie, sweet potato pie, or pound cake. Dine in, table service. Seats 40. All nonsmoking. Kids' menu. Opened 1996.

Date visited _____ *Remarks* _____

Carey Hilliard's (82)

514 U.S. Hwy. 80
Savannah, Ga. 31304
912/964-5671
County: Chatham

Mon - Sun 11 a.m. - 1 a.m.
From downtown Savannah, take Bay St. west (upriver) to
U.S. 80. Go left. It will be on the left.

Carey Hilliard's restaurants offer casual, relaxed family dining and a menu that should satisfy just about everyone (barbecue, seafood, chicken, steak, sandwiches, side orders, and beer). All five Savannah-area Carey Hilliard's restaurants have dine in, take-out, and curb service (but no drive-thru.) Banquet rooms are available, too.

Date visited _____ *Remarks* _____

Carey Hilliard's (83)

11111 Abercorn St.
Savannah, Ga. 31419
912/925-3225
County: Chatham

Mon - Sun 11 a.m. - 1 a.m.
From downtown Savannah, take Abercorn St. to
the south side of town. It's about two miles
past Oglethorpe Mall near the Toyota place.

Carey Hilliard's Abercorn Street location offers barbecue, seafood, chicken, steak, sandwiches, side orders, and beer.

Date visited _____ *Remarks* _____

Carey Hilliard's (84)

3316 Skidaway Rd.
Savannah, Ga. 31404
912/354-7240
County: Chatham

Mon - Sun 11 a.m. - 1 a.m.
From downtown Savannah, take U.S. 80 (Victory Dr.)
east. Turn right on Skidaway Rd. It's two or three blocks
on the left, just past the Enmark station.

Carey Hilliard's Skidaway Road location offers barbecue, seafood, chicken, steak, sandwiches, side orders, and beer.

Date visited _____ *Remarks* _____

Carey Hilliard's (85)

5350 Hwy. 21
Garden City, Ga. 31304
912/963-0060
County: Chatham

Mon - Sun 11 a.m. - 1 a.m.
From downtown Savannah, follow Bay Street west to
Augusta Road (Hwy. 21). Go about 3 miles;
it's on the right.

Carey Hilliard's Garden City location offers barbecue, seafood, chicken, steak, sandwiches, side orders, and beer.

Date visited _____ *Remarks* _____

Carey Hilliard's (86)

8410 Waters Rd.
Savannah, Ga. 31306
912/355-2468
County: Chatham

Mon - Sun 11 a.m. - 1 a.m.
From downtown Savannah, take Waters Ave. south to
Montgomery Cross Rd. It's on the corner.

Carey Hilliard's Waters Road location offers barbecue, seafood, chicken, steak, sandwiches, side orders, and beer.

Date visited _____ *Remarks* _____

Carithers' Bar-B-Que (87)

2025 S Milledge Ave.
Athens, Ga. 30605
706/354-0284
County: Clarke

Tue - Wed 11 a.m. - 2 p.m., Thu - Sat 11 a.m.- 9 p.m.
On South Milledge Ave. just north of
the South Athens Bypass.

Proclaimed "Best BBQ south of Tennessee" by ABC sportscasters at a recent
Georgia-Alabama football game. It's close to the university, so don't be surprised
if you find a room full of Dawgs chewing on bones inside this bright red
cinderblock building. Following the custom in Athens, Carithers' has hash
instead of stew. Other items include beans, cole slaw, potato salad, and pork
skins (not the same as pig skins). Dine in, table service, seats 28. Opened 1984.

Date visited _____ *Remarks* _____

Carter's Bar-B-Que (88)

700 McIntosh St.
Vidalia, Ga. 30474
912/537-2524
County: Toombs

Mon - Sat 11 a.m.- 8:30 p.m.
Carter's is at the corner of Hwys. 297 and 292
on the north side of Vidalia.

A yellow/orange vinegar-based sauce is lightly added to the wonderful barbecue
at this take-out-only establishment housed in a little white cinderblock building
in Vidalia. The crinkle-cut fries are tasty, too.

Date visited _____ *Remarks* _____

Carter's Grill & Restaurant (89)

321 W Highland Ave.
Albany, Ga. 31701
912/432-2098
County: Dougherty

Mon - Sun 6:30 a.m. - 9 p.m.
From Hwy. 82 Bus. and Jefferson St. (Hwy. 133) in
downtown Albany, go south one block on Jefferson.
Highland Ave. is at the first corner.

Carter's is in a big blue building. They serve beer. They play the blues on the
jukebox. So, naturally they invite you to "eat 'que, listen to blues, and kick back
some brews." To go with the meat they have a homemade sweet and tasty "Oh
Yes" red sauce. Soul-food specialties such as collards and peas and sweet potato
pie are popular items. Dine in or take-out. Owners Eddie and Sylvia Carter.

Date visited _____ *Remarks* _____

Chad's Bar-B-Que (90)

369 Hammonds Crossing
Cumming, Ga. 30130
770/887-6256
County: Forsyth

Mon - Sun 11 a.m.- 7 p.m. (Open til 9 in warm season.)
From Hwy. 19/400, take exit 17. Go one mile northeast
on Hwy. 306 to Hwy. 369 (Browns Bridge Rd.).
It's on the right.

Tender, flavorful chopped meat is cooked with hickory in a smoker next to this
little brown shack. Sides are Brunswick stew, beans, cole slaw, and potato salad.
Homemade fried pies, too. Take-out only, order at outside window. Thirty or so
seats at picnic tables in an adjacent screened-in dining shed.

Date visited _____ *Remarks* _____

Champ's Bar-B-Q (91)

2300 S Cobb Dr. SE
Smyrna, Ga. 30080
770/438-6618
County: Cobb

Mon - Thu 11 a.m. - 10 p.m., Fri 11 a.m.- 11 p.m., Sat
11 a.m.- 10 p.m., Sun 12 p.m. - 10 p.m..
From I-75, exit at Windy Hill Rd. Go west 4 miles, turn
right on South Cobb Dr.; it's on the left.

Good food grows a good business. Brothers Martin and Tom Jeneff opened this place on July 4, 1990. Five years ago they had to move to a larger building to handle the crowds. A specialty is hickory-smoked charbroiled beef brisket. Hearty, meaty Brunswick stew is lovingly made with pork, beef, chicken, tomatoes, corn, onions, and bell pepper. Real mashed potatoes, baby back ribs, hickory-smoked hot wings, baked hickory potatoes, and BBQ salad with choice of topping. Homemade beer-battered onion rings. Baked onions are also a specialty. Table service, 140 seats.

Date visited _____*Remarks* _____

Chandler's Bar-B-Q (92)

1285 Danielsville Rd.
Athens, Ga. 30601
706/354-1122
County: Clarke

Mon - Fri 11 a.m. - 2:30 p.m.,
Tue - Fri 4:30 p.m. - 9 p.m., Sat 11 a.m.- 9 p.m..
Chandler's is on Danielsville Rd. a mile north of the
Athens Bypass.

Roy Chandler bought, remodeled, and reopened Chandler's in 1996, after six years of ownership outside of the family. His uncle had started the place in 1944, and the Chandler family had owned and operated it most of the time since then. He cooks hams in a closed pit/smoker with oak and hickory. Country-style ribs are basted with sauce just before they come off the fire. A Carolina-style vinegar and pepper sauce and a sweet tomato-based sauce are available. He serves hash instead of Brunswick stew. Weekday country-cooking lunch buffet. Dine in, table service, seats about 75. Nonsmokers' area.

Date visited _____*Remarks* _____

Charlie's Pig Out (93)

123 Moultrie Rd. SE
Doerun, Ga. 31744
912/782-5058
County: Colquitt

Mon - Sat 11 a.m.- 2 p.m. & 5 p.m.- 8 p.m.
From Albany, go southeast 20 miles on Hwy. 133 to the
town of Doerun. It's on the right.

Charlene James' place is a small restaurant in a small town with small prices and a big taste. The only barbecue item is pork. It comes mixed with a homemade mustard/vinegar–based sauce. Sides include beans, cole slaw, fries, potato salad, onion rings, and vegetables. Several fast-food items are also on the menu. Wash it down with "the best iced tea in town." Dine in or take-out.

Date visited _____*Remarks* _____

Bar-B-Fact

Hudson's Hickory House in Douglasville opened in 1971,
the year of Atlantan Jerry Reed's No. 1 country song,
"When You're Hot, You're Hot."

Chattahoochee BBQ (94)

9719 Hwy. 75 N
Helen, Ga. 30545
706/878-1952
County: White

Tue - Sun 11 a.m.- 8 p.m.
In an old Pure Oil filling station next to the little
Robertstown courthouse at the intersection of Hwys. 75 and
356. Across from turn-off to Unicoi State Park.

A combination convenience store and BBQ place serving ample portions of
hickory-smoked pork, beef, chicken, and turkey. Baby back ribs, too. The meats
are cooked out front in a stone smoker stoked with green hickory. Choice of
mild or hot tomato-based sauce. The beans are excellent, as are the Cajun rice
and pasta salad. Eat inside or out on a deck overlooking the river.

Date visited _____ *Remarks* _____

Choo Choo Bar-B-Q (95)

4519 Hugh Howell Rd.
Tucker, Ga. 30084
770/496-0990
County: DeKalb

Mon - Sat 11 a.m. 'til 2 p.m. (Call ahead.)
On Hugh Howell Rd. a block west of Mountain Industrial
Blvd., between Tucker and Stone Mountain.

Choo Choo is a take-out place featuring closed-pit, hickory-smoked, chopped
'cue sandwiches in regular and jumbo sizes. Try the pork (or beef) stuffed potatoes. Sides are Brunswick stew, beans, cole slaw, potato salad, pickles, and
chips. Homemade cookies for dessert. Opened 1986.

Date visited _____ *Remarks* _____

Choo-Choo Bar-B-Q (96)

2058 Dover Bluff Rd.
Waverly, Ga. 31565
912/264-1822
County: Camden

Mon - Sun 9 a.m. - 9 p.m.
From I-95 southbound, take exit 5. Turn left; it's on the
right next to the Shell station/gift shop.

This little place off I-95 is known for its unique datil pepper barbecue sauce.
Winner of the Kansas City BBQ Sauce Cookoff, the concoction is made by owners Steve and Sharon Rawl, using their home-grown datil peppers. Other ingredients include fresh tomatoes, Worcestershire sauce, garlic, brown sugar, and
vinegar. It's good on seafood, too. Dine in, order at counter, 25 seats.

Date visited _____ *Remarks* _____

The Chop House (97)

Turner Field
Hank Aaron Drive
Atlanta, Ga. 30312
County: Fulton

Open during Braves games.
From the State Capitol, take Capitol Ave./Hank Aaron Dr.
south to Turner Field, the Atlanta Braves' ballpark.

The Atlanta Braves' own barbecue place looks out over left field at the ballpark.
It seats about 350 at picnic tables and at a bar downstairs. A separate take-out
stand nearby, Braves Barbecue, sells pork and beef sandwiches and other quick
bites. By the way, the secret ingredient in the barbecue sauce is walnut vinegar.

Date visited _____ *Remarks* _____

Col. Poole's

Name/Map ID   **Hours/Directions**

Cleve's Barbecue Kitchen (98)

1155 Hwy. 9/52
Dahlonega, Ga. 30533
706/864-4673
County: Lumpkin

Mon - Sat 10 a.m.- 6 p.m.
From the city square and Gold Museum, take W. Main St.
(Hwy. 9/52 Bus. S.) and turn right onto Hwy. 9/52.
Cleve's is a half mile on the left.

Originally opened in 1968, but closed for many years, Cleve's is a couple of cinderblock buildings hanging on the mountain slope by the old highway to Dawsonville. The barbecue is made from Boston butts cooked with hickory in an open pit. The ribs are baby back. Take-out only. Drive-thru.

Date visited _____*Remarks* _____

Col. Poole's Georgia Bar-B-Q (99)

P.O. Box 690
East Ellijay, Ga. 30539
706/635-4100
County: Gilmer

Tue - Sun 11 a.m.- 7 p.m.
On east side of Hwy. 515 (the Zell Miller Pkwy.) in East
Ellijay. Look for thousands of pig signs.

You'll just have to see it to believe it. Some 3,000 plywood pigs stand on a steep hillside behind this quirky place. Each pig-shaped sign bears the name of a patron who paid for the honor. And honor is important, because Col. Oscar Poole requires that you have "good intentions, an honest face, and five dollars" to put your name on the Pig Hill of Fame. The food's good, too. Honest! Dine in or take-out.

Date visited _____*Remarks* _____

Corky's Ribs & BBQ (100)

1605 Pleasant Hill Rd.
Duluth, Ga. 30136
770/564-8666
County: Gwinnett

Sun - Thu 11 a.m.- 10 p.m., Fri & Sat 11 a.m.- 11 p.m.
From I-85 northbound, take exit 40, turn right, go a half
mile to Sweetwater Road. Corky's is on the right.

Begun in Memphis, Corky's is now a small chain with restaurants in New
Orleans, Nashville, Knoxville, Tunica, and here. It was voted #1 in Memphis
nine years in a row, chosen #1 in a *Southern Living* poll, and voted Gwinnett's
best pork sandwich and best ribs. Dine in, take-out, drive-thru. Table service.
Nonsmokers' section. Full bar. Opened in the mid-1990s.

Date visited _____ *Remarks* _____

Country Corners Bar-B-Q (101)

1601 W Poplar St.
Griffin, Ga. 30223
770/467-9522
County: Spalding

Mon & Tue 11 a.m.- 2 p.m.,
Wed 11 a.m.- 7 p.m., Thu - Sat 11 a.m.- 8 p.m..
From downtown Griffin, take Hwy. 16 west; turn left onto Carver Rd.
It's just ahead at the corner of Carver and West Poplar St.

Country Corners serves not only smoked pork and baby back ribs, but also
mesquite chicken. Their barbecue sauce is red and a little sweet. Other items on
the menu include burgers, hot dogs, ham steaks, shrimp, and chicken. It's a
dine-in place with table service and 50 or so seats.

Date visited _____ *Remarks* _____

Country Store Bar-B-Q (102)

201 Hwy. 362 W
Williamson, Ga. 30292
770/229-5952
County: Pike

Wed 11 a.m.- 7 p.m., Thu - Sat 11 a.m.- 8 p.m.
From Griffin, take Hwy. 362 6 miles to the tiny town of
Williamson. It's in the old country store on the left.

Williamson was once a thriving little town at a railroad junction. The rails and
locomotives are long gone, but there's still a smokin' contraption here. It burns
mostly hickory and a bit of oak and makes some fine barbecue. To go with its
meaty output, there's a thick, smoky, mild sauce and several sides. Desserts,
too. Dine in, table service, seats about 70. Nonsmokers' area. Opened 1987.

Date visited _____ *Remarks* _____

Country's Barbecue (103)

3137 Mercury Dr.
Columbus, Ga. 31906
706/563-7604
County: Muscogee

Sun - Thu 10:30 a.m.- 10 p.m.,
Fri & Sat 10:30 a.m.- 11 p.m.
From I-185, take exit 4, go west. It's on the right across
Macon Road (Hwy. 22) from Columbus Square mall.

Country's pork with the mustardy sauce is as good as you will find anywhere.
The ribs are premium lean St. Louis–style cuts. Also pork tenderloin, BBQ
turkey, wings, grilled chicken, salads, and sandwiches. Try the "barbecue slaw."
Excellent beer selection. Wine, too, including Country's own "Swinefandel."

Date visited _____ *Remarks* _____

Country's North (104)

Veterans Pkwy.
Columbus, Ga. 31909
706/660-1415
County: Muscogee

Sun - Thu 11 a.m.- 10 p.m., Fri & Sat 11 a.m.- 11 p.m.
From I-185 and U.S. 80, take 80 east to the first exit. Go
south on Veterans Pkwy. At first traffic light
(Weems Rd.), turn left into Main Street Village.

Again, the same menu in a different setting. This Country's location is slick and contemporary in style.

Date visited_____Remarks _____

Country's
on Broad

Country's On Broad (105)

1329 Broadway
Columbus, Ga. 31901
706/596-8910
County: Muscogee

Mon - Sun 11 a.m.- 10 p.m.
Country's downtown location is in the old Trailways bus
station at Broadway and 14th Street.

Pretty much the same fine menu but a very different building. This old bus station has been carefully rehabilitated by Country's into a pleasant and interesting place to dine. They've even parked a vintage bus outside.

Date visited_____Remarks _____

Covered Wagon (106)

1532 S Broad St.
Monroe, Ga. 30655
770/267-7334
County: Walton

Mon - Fri 7 a.m. - 5 p.m., Sat 7 a.m.- 3 p.m..
From downtown Monroe, go south on S. Broad St.
(Hwy. 11) about a mile. It's on the right, behind Circle K.

Although Covered Wagon offers a variety of home-cooked food, barbecue is the specialty. Hams are pit-cooked with charcoal and served chopped. The Wagon's secret-recipe sweet red sauce accompanies it. Dine in, table service, 50 seats. Opened 1970.

Date visited_____Remarks _____

Cross Roads Barbecue (107)

Hwy 171 N
Gibson, Ga. 30810
706/598-3324
County: Glascock

Fri & Sat 8 a.m.- 9 p.m.
From I-20, take exit 56, 57, or 58 and go south through
Warrenton to Hwy. 171. Go 13 miles to Gibson.
It's on the left.

Cross Roads offers chopped or sliced BBQ, with the red vinegar-based sauce (hot or mild) served separately. On the side there's Brunswick stew, beans, cole slaw, and potato salad. Dine in, table service. Opened 1991.

Date visited _____*Remarks* _____

Crowe's Open Air Bar-B-Que (108)

1320 Eatonton Rd.
Madison, Ga. 30650
706/342-7002
County: Morgan

Mon - Sat 11 a.m.- 3 p.m.
From I-20, take exit 51. Go north on U.S. 441 toward
Madison. It's a mile and a half on the right.

Open-air style hickory-smoked barbecue. People come from many miles around to feast on Crowe's ribs. Plenty of pork is consumed here, and taken out too. Smoked turkey is an option. The homemade red sauce (not sweet, not hot, not ketchupy) gets good reviews. Sides include Brunswick stew, beans, cole slaw, and fries (and lots of potato chips). Hot dogs for the kids. Dine in, 70 seats.

Date visited _____*Remarks* _____

Cuz Bar-B-Q (109)

Rt. 8, Hwy. 257
Dublin, Ga. 31021
912/272-8391
County: Laurens

Mon - Sat 5 a.m. - 10 p.m., Sun 6 a.m. - 9 p.m.
From I-16, take exit 13 and follow Hwy. 257 north
toward Dublin. Cuz is a little over a mile on the right.

It's take-out only at this convenience store with a cooking shack next door. Owner Bobby Howell says he has been smoking meat all his life (or 45 years of it, anyway). He cooks hams, butts, and shoulders in a smoker using oak and hickory. The ribs are extra tender. The sauce is a mustard and ketchup mix. It's a bit spicy, but not too much for most tastes. Opened 1982.

Date visited _____*Remarks* _____

D.K.'s Barbeque (110)

701 Pittman St.
Waycross, Ga. 31501
912/283-9898
County: Ware

Mon - Sat 8:30 a.m. - midnight.
From the intersection of U.S. 1 and U.S. 84, go north
(toward Alma) 3 or 4 blocks and turn right on Folks St.
It's a half block on the left.

D. K. Moses' three-booth hole-in-the-wall barbecue place was established in 1960. Since then, a lot of mighty fine food has been pulled off his pit. To go with the peerless pork, chicken, and ribs, D.K.'s offers beans, cole slaw, fries, onion rings, potato chips, sausage sandwiches, sausage dogs, steak sandwiches, and a few non-BBQ items. For dessert, try the sweet potato pie. Dine in, table service.

Date visited _____*Remarks* _____

D.K.'s

Daddy D'z: The Bar-B-Que Joynt (111)

264 Memorial Dr. SE
Atlanta, Ga. 30312
404/222-0206
County: Fulton

Mon - Thu 11:30 a.m.- 10:30 p.m.,
Fri & Sat noon - 1 a.m., Sun 12 p.m.- 9:30 p.m.
On Memorial Drive at Hill St., four blocks east of the
Georgia state capitol.

DD'z won the 1995 *Creative Loafing* Critic's Choice for "Best Bar-B-Que Beef Sandwich" and was recommended "No. 1 Bar-B-Que and Blues" by the *NY Times*. Ribs are the house specialty. In the words of Daddy D, "You haven't tasted spare ribs until now! Super tender and flavorful. They're 'Bad' to the bone!" Also rib tips, BBQ turkey, stew, beans, slaw, fries, mac-and-cheese, collards, black beans and rice, other vegetables. Live blues Fri., Sat., and Sun. on enclosed deck. Table service. Nonsmokers' area. Opened 1993.

Date visited _____ Remarks _____

Daddy D'z

The Dairylane (112)

839 South Harris St.
Sandersville, Ga. 31082
912/552-2482
County: Washington

Mon - Thu 8 a.m.- 10 p.m., Fri & Sat 8 a.m.- 11 p.m.,
Sun 9 a.m.- 10 p.m.
On Hwy. 15 (S. Harris St.) between
Sandersville and Tennille.

The Dairylane opened in 1954 selling ice cream and hamburgers. Barbecue was added in the mid-1960s to diversify the menu. And what a successful diversification it was. The pork served here comes from hams carefully cooked with hickory in a closed pit. A tasty thin, vinegar-based sauce goes well with it. Savory Brunswick stew and various sides round out your meal. Dine in, table service, 125 seats. (The Dairylane was voted one of middle Georgia's favorite BBQ places in a *Macon Telegraph* poll.)

Date visited _____*Remarks* _____

Damon's (113)

2463 Demere Rd.
St. Simons Island, Ga. 31522
912/638-4461
County: Glynn

Mon - Sun 11:30 a.m.- 2:30 p.m. and 5 p.m.- 10 p.m.
From Brunswick take Torras Causeway to the island.
Straight onto Demere Rd. At 7/10 mile,
turn right into The Shops at Demere.

Damon's, which began in Columbus, Ohio, in 1979, now has over a hundred locations throughout the United States and Great Britain. Their barbecued ribs and onion loaf have won awards in cities all over the country. The smoked pulled pork is superb. Other tasty foods on the menu include Brunswick stew, beans, cole slaw, fries, prime rib, steaks, char-grilled chicken, sandwiches, salads, and desserts. Dine in, table service. Full bar.

Date visited _____*Remarks* _____

Damon's (114)

3064 Washington Rd.
Augusta, Ga. 30907
706/860-7427
County: Richmond

Sun - Thu 11 a.m.- 10 p.m., Fri & Sat 11 a.m.- 11 p.m.
From I-20, take exit 65. Go west (away from Augusta) a
quarter-mile. It's next to Burger King.

Damon's Augusta location offers the same famous lean, meaty barbecued ribs and other delicious foods as the others.

Date visited _____*Remarks* _____

Bar-B-Fact

Mary's Flying Pig was designed by Gainesville architect Garland Reynolds. He also designed the Savannah Hyatt Hotel and Atlanta's Civic Center MARTA station.

Damon's (115)

401 Mall Blvd.
Savannah, Ga. 31406
912/354-3331
County: Chatham

Mon - Sun 11 a.m. - 3 p.m., Sun - Thu 5 p.m. - 10 p.m.,
Fri & Sat 5 p.m. - 11 p.m.
On Mall Blvd. near Oglethorpe Mall on the
south side of town.

Ditto for the Savannah location. Smoked pulled pork and delectable ribs are found here, too.

Date visited _____ *Remarks* _____

Darien Texaco/ Andy Grinstead BBQ (116)

U.S. 17
Darien, Ga. 31305
912/437-4615 (Texaco)
County: McIntosh

Mon - Sat 11 a.m.- 8:30 p.m.
Next to the Texaco Station at the foot of the U.S. 17 bridge
in downtown Darien.

Andy Grinstead learned his barbecue-cooking skills from an old fellow on Sapelo Island who cooked his meat over a real pit (a hole in the ground) using bed-springs for a grill. Andy uses a more modern arrangement, but he still cooks meat 16 to 20 hours with oak, the old fashioned way. He offers barbecue plates and sandwiches and side orders. Order at a window; there's seating for eight in the station and three picnic tables outside.

Date visited _____ *Remarks* _____

Dave's BBQ & Soul Food (117)

114 Frobel St.
Monticello, Ga. 31064
706/468-0213
County: Jasper

Mon - Sat 6:30 a.m. - 7 p.m., Sun 7 a.m. - 4 p.m.
From the courthouse go one block east on Hwy. 16
(Greene St.). It's on the left at Frobel St.

Dave cooks hams with hickory in a closed pit. His homemade sauce is dark red and adds to the meat nicely. All kinds of good old Southern soul food are found here: collards, turnips, fried green tomatoes, okra, and squash, to name several. Brunswick stew is an occasional item. Dine in. Served cafeteria style.

Date visited _____ *Remarks* _____

David's Bar B-Q (118)

Watkinsville-Wolfskin Rd.
Crawford, Ga. 30630
706/742-7552
County: Oglethorpe

Mon - Sat 10 a.m.- 9 p.m.
From Athens, take U.S. 78 east to Oglethorpe County.
Turn right on Watkinsville-Wolfskin Rd. Go 5 miles
to David's, on the left.

Hash, not Brunswick stew. That's a tip-off that this out-of-the-way place is near either Athens or Augusta, the two hash centers of Georgia. As for the barbecue, it's slowly pit-cooked with hickory wood. The ketchup/vinegar–based sauce is not sweet. Besides barbecue, the menu includes fish sandwiches, steak sand-wiches, burgers, and hot dogs. Dine in, order at counter, 50 seats.

Date visited _____ *Remarks* _____

Davis Bar-B-Que (119)

3858 Refuge Rd.
Jasper, Ga. 30143
706/692-3717
County: Pickens

Fri - Sun 11 a.m.- 9 p.m.
Take I-575 north to Hwy. 515; turn right on Hwy. 108;
take first left at Antebellum House Furniture.

The stew is so good you will want to take a lot of it home. This place sells it in pints and gallons. Barbecue by the pound is a big seller, too. It's cooked on a wood-burning cooker built by father and son Jerry and Chip Davis. Whether by the pound, sandwich, or plate, it's some good eating. Dine in or take-out.

Date visited _____*Remarks* _____

Dean's Barbecue (120)

9480 S Main St.
Jonesboro, Ga. 30236
770/471-0138
County: Clayton

Wed - Sat 10:30 a.m.- 7:30 p.m.
On S. Main St., 1.5 miles south of downtown Jonesboro.

Roger Dean's place now has inside seating and a phone; for years it only had picnic tables under shade trees. Family owned since 1947, it has a limited menu with pork as the only meat. A note on the menu reads, "We sell pork BBQ only. If you want beef, let Roger sell you pork and shoot you the bull and you'll probably never know the difference." Very thin, mild red sauce. Only sides are stew, cole slaw, pickles, and chips. Picnic tables outside, still under the big trees.

Date visited _____*Remarks* _____

Delmonico Steak & Barbeque (121)

3799 Hwy. 81 SW
Loganville, Ga. 30249
770/466-8898
County: Walton

Mon - Thu 11 a.m.- 9 p.m., Fri & Sat 11 a.m.- 10 p.m.
From Atlanta, take U.S. 78 east about 35 miles to
Loganville. Turn right on Hwy. 81.
It's a quarter mile on the left.

Delmonico serves hickory-smoked meats cooked with care in a closed pit, then chopped, pulled, or sliced. On the side are stew, beans, slaw, fresh-cut fries, potato salad, and onion rings. Delmonico serves real tea (not machine-brewed). Dine in, table service, 65 seats, nonsmokers' area. Opened 1990.

Date visited _____*Remarks* _____

Dillon's, The Rib Specialist (122)

850 Dogwood Rd. SW
Lawrenceville, Ga. 30244
770/978-4887
County: Gwinnett

Mon - Thu 11 a.m.- 10:45 p.m.,
Fri & Sat 11 a.m.- 11:45 p.m., Sun 12 p.m.-9:45 p.m.,
Take Pleasant Hill Rd. to Ronald Reagan Pkwy., exit at
Five Forks–Trickum Rd. Turn right; then take first right.

Dillon's signature baby back ribs are served "dry" or with a sweet and tangy red sauce. There are several other entrees including seafood and pasta dishes. Chocolate and peanut butter lovers will love the desserts. Full bar. Dine in, table service, over 100 seats, nonsmokers' area.

Date visited _____*Remarks* _____

The Divine Swine Barbeque (123)

204 Roswell St.
Marietta, Ga. 30060
770/424-2800
County: Cobb

*Mon - Thu 11 a.m.- 3 p.m., Fri & Sat 11 a.m.- 9 p.m.
From The Big Chicken at U.S. 41 and Roswell St. (Hwy.
120), go west on Roswell St. towards the city square. It's
just before you get there, on the left.*

Owner Jack Mitchell was a caterer for many years. He opened his first Divine
Swine on Sandy Plains Rd. about four years ago, but moved it to downtown
Marietta in early 1996. Jack cooks his meats with hickory wood in a smoker and
completes the conversion of meat to barbecue with a hot, sweet homemade barbecue sauce. On the side are cole slaw, beans, potato salad, and a tasty black-
eyed pea and corn salad. Also caesar salad, with or without chicken, and barbecue salad. Fries and rings should be available, too, by the time you read this.
Dine in, table service, 44 seats.

Date visited _____ *Remarks* _____

Dixie-Q Bar-B-Que (124)

1604 Maple Ave.
Rome, Ga. 30161
706/291-8960
County: Floyd

*Mon - Sat 10 a.m.- 6 p.m.
From I-75, take U.S. 411 to the south side of Rome. Get
off 411 at Maple Ave exit. Look for the sign.*

A tiny take-out place with a walk-up window. It's barely big enough for one per-
son, so they can't cook in large volumes. But they will fix up plenty of plates if
you call ahead. Boston butts are cooked with hickory and sometimes pecan and
various fruit-tree woods. Dixie-Q has three pits: a slow one, a slightly faster
model, and a speed demon.

Date visited _____ *Remarks* _____

Don's Famous Bar-B-Q (125)

217 East U.S. Hwy. 80
Pooler, Ga. 31322
912/748-8400
County: Chatham

*Mon - Sat 11 a.m.- 10 p.m.
From Savannah, take U.S. 80 west to Pooler.
It's on the left.*

Lexington, N.C., native Don Yates cooks and serves barbecue as it is done in his
hometown. He cooks Boston butts with oak and hickory in a closed pit for 8
hours or more (depending on the size of the hog involved, of course). He chops
the meat by hand as it's ordered, and his tangy and spicy sauce is vinegar-based
with some ketchup. Bar-B-Q slaw, too. Also hamburgers, wings, and salads. Eat
in or take-out. Opened 1989.

Date visited _____ *Remarks* _____

Bar-B-Fact

*The Pink Pig in Cherry Log opened in 1967, the year
Atlanta's Gladys Knight and the Pips reached No. 2 on the
charts with "I Heard It through the Grapevine."*

Dr. B. S. Muthers' Old Timey BBQ (126)

4608 Augusta Rd.
Garden City, Ga. 31408
912/964-2845
County: Chatham

Mon - Sat 10 a.m.- 9 p.m.
From Savannah, take Hwy. 21 west to Garden City. It's on
the right as Hwy. 21 turns into Augusta Road.

Boston butts are smoked with oak and hickory in an open pit "the good old Georgia way" at Muthers' BBQ. To go with the resulting smoke-caressed meat, there's Muther's own sauce, a spicy red concoction, bottled and sold here. People have told Muther 'n' them that their Brunswick stew is the best in Georgia. Also on the menu are shrimp, catfish, vegetables, and the usual barbecue-related sides. Brownies and cookies for dessert. Dine in.

Date visited _____Remarks _____

Drake's Place Bar-B-Q (127)

106 Stuart Rd.
Brunswick, Ga. 31525
912/262-0867
County: Glynn

Mon - Sat 10:30 a.m.- 7 p.m.
From U.S. 17 at Torras Causeway, go north on 17 about
5 or 6 miles. Turn right on Stuart Rd.

"The Best in Town" is how Drake's Place owners Marian and James Drake describe the food at the place they opened a couple of years ago. Many of their customers agree so much that they eat there several times a week. The meats are cooked on a wood-burning open pit/grill, using mostly white oak. Drake's "Best-in-the-World" sauce is a sweet, but not too sweet, mustard sauce. It's usually put on the bun for sandwiches and on the side for plates. The hand-battered french fries are special. Great homemade desserts, including pies and fresh-from-the-oven cobblers daily. Dine in, order at window.

Date visited _____Remarks _____

Du-Roc Cafe Pit Bar-B-Q (128)

115 Marquis Dr.
Fayetteville, Ga. 30214
770/719-1744
County: Fayette

Tue - Thu 11 a.m.- 8:30 p.m., Fri & Sat 11 a.m.- 9:30 p.m.
From the old courthouse, take Ga. 54 west a mile and a
half. It's on the right, past the medical center.

Du-Roc serves up "taste bud addictive," authentic pit barbecue. It opened in early 1994 and won the Fayette Consumers' Choice award that year and again in 1995. The meats are cooked all night in a closed pit and served chopped, pulled, sliced, or chunked. (You can choose inside or outside chunks.) Choose a red sauce or a Carolina-style vinegar sauce. Also baby back ribs, BBQ turkey, stew, beans, slaw, fries, rings, baked potatoes, and cracklin' cornbread. Buttermilk available, too. Dine in, 220 seats, nonsmokers' area, banquet room.

Date visited _____Remarks _____

Bar-B-Fact

Pappy Red's may be the only barbecue restaurant in the nation
with a crashed plane on its roof.

Dunbar's BBQ. (129)

1984 Smith Ave.
Thomasville, Ga. 31792
912/225-1085
County: Thomas

Mon - Thu 10 a.m.- 7:30 p.m., Fri & Sat 10 a.m.- 9:30 p.m.
From Hwy. 19/300, go west on U.S. 84 Bus. It's on the left
as you come into town.

Dunbar's cooks preseasoned meats in a closed pit with charcoal. The sauce is a sweet and tangy "homegrown" brown mixture. Vegetables include okra, collards, peas, corn, and mac-and-cheese. Desserts include banana pudding. Dine in, table service, 75 seats, nonsmokers' area. Opened about five years ago.

Date visited _____*Remarks* _____

Dunbar's BBQ (130)

532 W Jackson St.
Thomasville, Ga. 31792
912/225-9697
County: Thomas

Call for hours of operation.
From Broad St. in the center of Thomasville, turn onto
Hwy 319 Bus. (W. Jackson St.).

Dunbar's newly opened second location in downtown offers the same menu plus burgers, fried chicken, and other items.

Date visited _____*Remarks* _____

Dusty's Barbecue (131)

1815 Briarcliff Rd. NE
Atlanta, Ga. 30329
404/320-6264
County: DeKalb

Sun.-Thu. 11 a.m.-9 p.m., Fri. and Sat. 11 a.m.-10 p.m.
On Briarcliff Road at Clifton Road in
north DeKalb County.

For three years, winner of the Taste of Atlanta award, as well as winner of the 1995 *Creative Loafing* Reader's Choice award, Dusty's does barbecue North Carolina style. The sauces are vinegary and red. The pork is served with a little slaw on top the way they do it in N.C., if you like. Hushpuppies are a side item. The stew is made using an old family recipe with lima beans and big chunks of potatoes in a thin (but flavorful) tomato base. Also available are wings, barbecue salad, vegetables, and pork rinds. Wide selection of desserts. Beer and wine.

Date visited _____*Remarks* _____

Dye's Barbecue (132)

104 Old Quaker Rd.
Wrens, Ga. 30833
706/547-0690
County: Jefferson

Mon - Wed 10:30 a.m.- 3:30 p.m.,
Thu - Sat 10:30 a.m.- 8 p.m.
From Augusta, take U.S. 1 to Wrens. Turn right at Lloyd
and Sons Auto Parts.

Dye's is just off U.S. 1, America's first Main Street. Today, the road affords a route to true barbecue. Dye's open-pit, chopped pork is anointed with a flavorful ketchup/vinegar–based sauce and served with a variety of delicious sides, including Brunswick stew, beans, cole slaw, potato salad, and macaroni salad. Dine in, table service, 85 seats, nonsmokers' area.

Date visited _____*Remarks* _____

Dye's Barbecue (133)

111 E Haynes St.
Sandersville, Ga. 31082
912/552-9246
County: Washington

Mon - Wed 10:30 a.m.- 3:30 p.m.,
Thu - Sat 10:30 a.m.- 8 p.m.
From the courthouse in the center of Sandersville,
go east on Haynes St.

This second Dye's location also offers e-pig-urean delights in a pleasant setting.
Dine in, table service, 45 seats, nonsmokers' area. Opened 1992.

Date visited _____ *Remarks* _____

Dynasty's Bar-B-Que (134)

615 Fourth Ave.
Columbus, Ga. 31901
706/322-9385
County: Muscogee

Mon - Wed 11 a.m.- 3 p.m., Thu - Fri 11 a.m.- 6 p.m.
From I-185, take exit 5, go west toward downtown on
Veterans Pkwy./4th Ave about 7 miles. It's on the right.

Call ahead for the chicken at Dynasty's. It's cooked by special request. Of
course, the hog-noscenti know that chicken is just something you eat while waiting for the pork to come off the pit. Here it's Boston butts cooked with hickory
or pecan in the open pit. The sauce is a homemade mustard and ketchup mix,
and is available in mild or hot. Like several other places in the Columbus area,
Dynasty's has barbecue slaw. Vegetables and hamburgers are served, too.
Desserts: sweet potato pie and egg custard. Eat in or carry out.

Date visited _____ *Remarks* _____

Earnie's Bar-B-Q and Steakhouse (135)

Hwy. 203
Alma, Ga. 31510
912/632-8507
County: Bacon

Mon - Sat 9 a.m.- 9 p.m.
From Alma, take Hwy. 32 east about 6 miles, then Hwy.
203 toward Jesup. It's several miles down on the left.

Guys, you may have to stop and ask for directions to this place, but it's worth it.
Think about open-pit-cooked meats, juicy whole slabs of ribs, tangy red barbecue sauce, beer, and homemade pecan pie or layered pound cake. Earnie's plans
to expand seating from 35 to 75 and to add a nonsmokers' section and a game
room. During the summer, there are live bands. In winter, turkey shoots.
Opened Feb. 1996. (Brunswick stew available in winter months or by special
order.)

Date visited _____ *Remarks* _____

Bar-B-Fact

Melear's Barbecue in Fayetteville opened in 1957, the year
jet airliners first flew out of the Atlanta airport.

Eastway Barbeque & Grill (136)

5552 Luna Dr.
Columbus, Ga. 31947
706/568-1935
County: Muscogee

Mon - Thu 11 a.m.- 7 p.m., Fri & Sat 11 a.m.- 11 p.m.
From I-185 at exit 3, go east on Buena Vista Rd. about a
mile and a half. Turn left onto Floyd Rd. Go about a mile
and turn right on Luna Dr. It's on the right.

Opened in 1996 by Adolphus Lakes, who was a fireman for 26 years. He cooked
as a hobby and then started up this place last year. Pork shoulders cooked with
hickory wood in a closed pit is his specialty. All of the heat in the pit comes from
wood, not gas or electricity. The homemade red sauce is sweet and hot, and is
served on the meat.

Date visited _____ *Remarks* _____

Echota Smoke House (137)

1214 N Wall St.
Calhoun, Ga. 30701
706/629-5660
County: Gordon

Mon - Sat 6 a.m. - 9 p.m.
On U.S. 41, just south of its junction with Hwy. 225, near
the Confederate monument.

Located near New Echota, the site of the capital of the Cherokee Nation, Echota
Smoke House serves closed-pit, hickory-smoked barbecue, available pulled or
sliced, and served with a tomato-based sauce. On the side are stew, beans, slaw,
fries, baked potatoes, potato salad, vegetable soup, and tossed salad. Indian arti-
facts on display. Dine in, table service, 95 seats. Opened 1985.

Date visited _____ *Remarks* _____

Edmunds' Bar-B-Que (138)

3935 Washington Rd.
Martinez, Ga. 30907
706/863-4277
County: Columbia

Mon – Thu 10 a.m. – 8 p.m, Fri & Sat 10 a.m. – 8:30
p.m., Sun 11 a.m. – 7 p.m.
From central Augusta, take Washington Rd. north.
It's on the right, about 5 or 6 miles beyond I-20.

Edmunds' has two locations, the original place across the river in Belvedere,
S.C., which opened in 1951, and this much newer restaurant. Both offer chipped
pork, ribs, chicken, and hash and rice. Order at the counter and take a seat in
the roomy dining area. Loaves of white bread and jars of sweet pickles are
already on the tables.

Date visited _____ *Remarks* _____

Fallin's Real Pit Bar-B-Q (139)

2614 E Pine Tree Blvd.
Thomasville, Ga. 31792
912/228-1071
County: Thomas

Sun - Thu 11 a.m.- 9 p.m., Fri & Sat 11 a.m.- 10 p.m.
One block west of U.S. 19 and just south
of Remington Ave.

In business since 1977, Fallin's serves old-fashioned barbecue made with meat
cooked on an open pit, then stewed in a red sauce. The stew is thin and mild,
and the cole slaw is creamy. There's a selection of country-style vegetables. All-
you-can-eat ribs and chicken every day. Dine in, table service, nonsmokers' area.

Date visited _____ *Remarks* _____

Fat Freddie's Bar-B-Q (140)

4170 Buena Vista Rd.
Columbus, Ga. 31907
706/561-2977
County: Muscogee

Sun - Wed 7 a.m.- 9 p.m., Thu - Sat 7 a.m.- 10 p.m.
From I-185 southbound, take exit 3, turn left.
It's on the left.

"It's the best barbecue in town, so if you leave hungry, it's your own fault," they say at Fat Freddie's. In business eighteen years, Fat Freddie's cooks Boston butts with hickory in a rotisserie smoker and adds a homemade mustard/ketchup sauce. It's available in mild, hot, and extra hot. Dine in, order at counter, 50 seats.

Date visited _____*Remarks* _____

Fat Freddie's Bar-B-Q (141)

3724 Hamilton Rd.
Columbus, Ga. 31904
706/323-0907
County: Muscogee

Mon - Sat 7 a.m. - 8 p.m.
From I-185 southbound, take exit 5. Turn right and go
west toward Alabama. Turn left on Hamilton Rd.

Try the house special at Fat Freddie's Hamilton Road location. It's a big pork sandwich, fries, and a drink for a very reasonable price. Dine in, order at counter, seats 48.

Date visited _____*Remarks* _____

Fat Man's Bar B Q (142)

3605 Campbellton Rd. SW
Atlanta, Ga. 30331
404/349-6600
County: Fulton

Thu - Sat 12 p.m.- 8:30 p.m.
From I-285 go west on Campbellton Rd. a quarter mile.
It's on the right. (Sign reads "St. Mark's Barbecue.")

Both pork and beef ribs are sold at Fat Man's. The barbecue is made from Boston butts cooked in a smoker. The sauce is sweet and red and comes in a choice of hot or mild. On the side are stew, beans, slaw, potato salad, collards, yams, and chitterlings. Desserts include homemade banana pudding and pound cake. Take-out only, except for 8 or so seats at picnic tables inside.

Date visited _____*Remarks* _____

Fat Matt's Rib Shack (143)

1811 Piedmont Rd. NE
Atlanta, Ga. 30324
404/607-1622
County: Fulton

Mon - Thu 11:30 a.m.- 11:30 p.m.,
Fri & Sat 11:30 a.m.- 12:30 p.m., Sun 2 p.m.- 11:30 p.m.
From I-85, take Piedmont Road south past Cheshire
Bridge Road. It's on the left.

Blues, brews, and barbecue have made Fat Matt's one of Atlanta's most popular rib houses. Live bands play frequently, there's a wide selection of beer, and the barbecue is quite good. It's hickory-smoked, chopped, and served with a tomato-based sauce. Sides are Brunswick stew, beans, cole slaw, and potato salad. No fried food. Dine in, order at counter, 42 seats inside, more seats outside. Voted No. 1 BBQ and No. 1 Ribs in Atlanta. Opened 1990. All nonsmoking.

Date visited _____*Remarks* _____

Fat Matt's

Name/Map ID   **Hours/Directions**

Feeder's For BarBQ (144)

248 Pharr Rd. NE
Atlanta, Ga. 30305
404/869-8979
County: Fulton

Sun.-Thu. 11 a.m.-10 p.m., Fri. & Sat. 11 a.m.-2 a.m.
From downtown Atlanta, go north on Peachtree St. about
5 miles. Turn right on Pharr Rd.

Some like it hot, some like it hotter, and some can't get it hot enough. Marty Boyd accommodates all three. He holds a "Hall of Flame" on Tuesday nights featuring hot and spicy cuisine from around the world (by reservation only), and he offers a very hot habanero sauce every day. Liquid heat aside, the barbecue here is excellent. Try the deluxe pork sandwich; it comes on a toasted hoagie roll. Dry-rub pork or beef ribs are also a good choice. Dine in, table service. Full bar.

Date visited _____ *Remarks* _____

Feeder's

Ferguson's Meat Market (145)

3315 Browns Bridge Rd.
Cumming, Ga. 30130
770/844-9517
County: Forsyth

Mon - Sat 9:30 a.m.- 7 p.m.
Ferguson's is in the Coal Mtn. community at Hwy. 9 and
Hwy. 369 (Browns Bridge Rd.), 5 miles
north of Cumming.

Ferguson's is a butcher shop that makes and sells barbecue for take-out. The sauce is tangy and tomato/vinegar–based. Sides include cole slaw, green beans, mac-and-cheese, and beans. Baby back ribs are a specialty. For dessert, Ferguson's has fruit cobblers and pies. Owner John Will.

Date visited _____*Remarks* _____

Fincher's Barbecue (146)

3947 Houston Ave.
Macon, Ga. 31206
912/788-1900
County: Bibb

Sun - Thu 9 a.m.- 9:30 p.m., Fri & Sat 9 a.m.- 10:30 p.m.
From I-75 southbound, take exit 49B. Turn left on Rocky
Creek Rd. which ends at Houston Ave.
Turn left, go four blocks.

Fincher's was the first barbecue to go up into space, traveling on the space shuttle with astronaut Sonny Carter on Nov. 22, 1989. (Don't believe any contrary claims made by any Alabama barbecue guidebooks.) Out-of-this-world-good barbecue is what Fincher's does so well. The open, pit, pulled and chopped pork is served with a tangy brown sauce made of tomato, vinegar, and mustard. Sides include Brunswick stew, cole slaw, fries. Fried apple tarts for desserts. Dine in, order at counter. Opened 1935.

Date visited _____*Remarks* _____

Fincher's Barbecue (147)

519 N Davis Dr.
Warner Robins, Ga. 31093
912/922-3034
County: Houston

Sun - Thu 9 a.m.- 9:30 p.m., Fri & Sat 9 a.m.- 10:30 p.m.
From Robins Air Force Base, go west on Watson Blvd.
(Hwy. 247C). Turn right onto North Davis Dr.

Same out-of-this-world barbecue fresh from the open pit, served with Fincher's tangy brown sauce. Dine in, order at counter.

Date visited _____*Remarks* _____

Fincher's Barbecue (148)

891 Gray Hwy.
Macon, Ga. 31211
912/743-5866
County: Bibb

Mon - Thu 9 a.m.- 9 p.m.,
Fri & Sat 9 a.m.- 10 p.m., Sun 11 a.m.- 7 p.m.
From I-16, take exit 2 (Spring St.). Go north, away from
town, on U.S. 129 (Gray Hwy.) It's on the right.

This Fincher's location offers the same succulent pork, tangy sauce, and most of the other items served at other Fincher's barbecue places. Dine in, order at counter.

Date visited _____*Remarks* _____

Fincher's Pit Barbecue (149)

3057 Columbus Rd.
Macon, Ga. 31204
912/742-2220
County: Bibb

Tue - Sat 9 a.m. - 6 p.m.
From I-75, take exit 51. Go west on Mercer Univ. Dr.
about 13 blocks and turn right onto Columbus Rd.
It's just ahead.

This Fincher's has no inside dining. You can go in and get it to go, or you can get curb service instead.

Date visited_____Remarks _____

Flaming Grill & Barbeque (150)

999 Cassville-White Rd.
Cartersville, Ga. 30120
770/606-8008
County: Bartow

Mon - Thu 11 a.m.- 8 p.m., Fri & Sat 11 a.m.- 9 p.m.
At I-75 exit 127 (Cassville-White Rd.).

Flaming Grill cooks Boston butts on a smoker with hickory. The specialty is flaming chicken covered with peppers and onions. Baby back ribs are available in full or half racks. The sauce is mild and red. Take-out mostly. About 18 seats at picnic tables. Opened 1994.

Date visited_____Remarks _____

The Flying Pig (151)

856 Virginia Ave.
Hapeville, Ga. 30354
404/559-1000
County: Fulton

Tue - Sat 10:30 a.m.- 8:00 p.m.
On north side of Hartsfield Airport. From I-85, take exit
19 and go east. It's on the right.

The Flying Pig has been serving up hickory-smoked pork to airport-area workers since 1957. It's cooked on an open pit, then served chopped or sliced with a vinegar-based sauce mixed in. Also available are Buffalo wings, barbecue wings, and chicken tenders. Sides include Brunswick stew, beans, cole slaw, home fries, onion rings, potato salad, and jalapeño peppers stuffed with cheddar cheese. Dine in, table service, 35 seats inside and 35 outside, nonsmokers' area. Opened 1957.

Date visited_____Remarks _____

Bar-B-Fact

Old South Bar-B-Q in Smyrna opened in 1968, the year the
C-5 Galaxy, the world's largest airplane, first rolled out of the
nearby Lockheed-Georgia factory.

411 Bar-B-Que (152)

1451 Tennessee Hwy. NE
Cartersville, Ga. 30120
770/382-4161
County: Bartow

Mon - Fri 7 a.m.- 2:30 p.m.
From I-75, take exit 126 (U.S. 411).

The barbecue is made from hams cooked in a smoker with hickory. The thick, spicy tomato-based sauce is served on the meat or on the side. BBQ turkey is available, as are Brunswick stew, beans, cole slaw, fries, potato salad, onion rings, vegetables, and short orders. For dessert, there's homemade pound cake. Dine in, table service, 15 seats. Opened 1995.

Date visited _____*Remarks* _____

4-N-One Bar-B-Que Restaurant & Catering (153)

3119 Victory Dr.
Columbus, Ga. 31903
706/683-9200
County: Muscogee

Mon - Sat 11 a.m.- 8 p.m.
From I-185, take exit 1, go west on Victory Dr.
It's on the right.

Four guys got together and opened this restaurant up in 1996 to serve eastern North Carolina barbecue, with a little soul food. Whole hogs are cooked in a closed pit with charcoal. After cooking, the meat is chopped and served. Add some homemade Carolina 'Q vinegar sauce (it's a little hot) and enjoy. That's 4-N-One, "Where you get a meal, not a portion."

Date visited _____*Remarks* _____

Frank's Barbecue (154)

1134 Main St.
Forest Park, Ga. 30050
404/361-3644
County: Clayton

Mon - Fri 11 a.m.- 7 p.m.
At Jonesboro Rd. and Main Street in Forest Park.

A take-out-only place that opened in 1996, Frank's everyday items are barbecued pork made from Boston butts cooked in a smoker, along with smoked ribs. Beef is available occasionally. Chicken is not sold every day, but most of the time. The homemade barbecue sauce is red and sweet. All kinds of vegetables.

Date visited _____*Remarks* _____

Freddie Mac's Ribs and Cuisine (155)

2818 Camp Creek Pkwy.
College Park, Ga. 30337
404/763-3606
County: Fulton

Mon - Sat 9 a.m.- 9 p.m., Sun 12 p.m.- 7 p.m.
From I-85 at Hartsfield Airport, take Camp Creek Pkwy.
west. At 3rd light, turn left into Hampshire Plaza.

The mouth-watering pork ribs are the specialty, but this is also a great place for home-style vegetables. The greens are particularly good. Hickory-smoked butts and hams and a thick, semi-sweet, tangy red sauce make some fine barbecue pork. Dine in, seats 66.

Date visited _____*Remarks* _____

Fresh Air, Flovilla

Name/Map ID	Hours/Directions

Fresh Air Bar-B-Que (156)

1164 Hwy. 42 S
Flovilla, Ga. 30216
770/775-3182
County: Butts

Mon - Thu 7 a.m. - 7:30 p.m., Fri & Sat 7 a.m. - 8:30 p.m., Sun 7 a.m. - 8 p.m.
From Jackson, take U.S. 23/GA 42 south toward Flovilla and Indian Springs. It's on the right.

The mother church of rural Georgia Bar-B-Que opened in January 1929 and has been in operation since. Old-timer John Bassett of Marietta says of Fresh Air, "The paper plates are now styrofoam, and the Cokes come in cups rather than bottles, but other than that, it's hardly changed since I was a kid." The meat is hickory-smoked in an open pit, then chopped and served with a delicious thin, tomato/vinegar sauce. The menu is short: pork, Brunswick stew, cole slaw, chips, and pickles are the only items. Chosen Georgia's Best Barbecue by Atlanta media. Dine in, order at counter, 155 seats.

Date visited _____ Remarks _____

Fresh Air Bar-B-Que (157)

3076 Riverside Dr.
Macon, Ga. 31210
912/477-7229
County: Bibb

Sun - Thu 11 a.m.- 8 p.m., Fri & Sat 11 a.m.- 9 p.m.
From I-75, take exit 54 (Pierce Ave.). Go north on Riverside Dr. It's on the left in Northgate Plaza.

Fresh Air's Macon operation has a slightly larger selection than the original place near Jackson, offering chicken, pork ribs, and baked beans in addition to the pork and Brunswick stew. Located in a nondescript space in a strip shopping center, it doesn't have the historic character of the venerable original, but it does have the same good eating, and it's closer to the interstate. Dine in, order at counter, plenty of seats. Drive-thru.

Date visited _____ Remarks _____

Frix's Pit Cooked Bar-B-Que and Catfish (158)

2545 East Hwy. 36
Jackson, Ga. 30233
770/775-1226
County: Butts

Mon - Thu 11 a.m.- 7:30 p.m.,
Fri & Sat 11 a.m.- 9:30 p.m.
In a little brown building beside Hwy. 36 at South River,
11 miles north of Jackson.

Conveniently located for Jackson Lake boaters and fishermen, Frix's offers a wide selection of meats and fish, vegetables, hamburgers, and other items to go. Barbecued pork, Brunswick stew, and smoked chicken are the main barbecue items. Choose a hot or mild sauce. Also fried chicken, catfish, flounder, shrimp, and steak. No beer (and a sign outside indicates that none is allowed on the premises). Limited seating.

Date visited _____ *Remarks* _____

Bar-B-Quote

"There is no flavor comparable, I will contend, to that of the crisp, tawny, well-watched, not over-roasted, crackling, as it is called..."
Charles Lamb in "A Dissertation Upon Roast Pig."

G&G Bar-B-Que (159)

2529 Gresham Rd. SE
Atlanta, Ga. 30316
404/241-0858
County: DeKalb

Tue - Sun 6 a.m. - 7:30 p.m. (Sat til 9 p.m.).
From downtown Atlanta, take I-20 east, exit at Gresham
Rd. Turn right and it's on the right in Gresham Plaza.

"Bar-B-Que and chicken fit for a king" is G&G's slogan. The barbecue here comes with a sweet and tangy red sauce and is available chopped or sliced. Brunswick stew, beans, cole slaw, and fries are on the side. Also catfish, whiting, fresh vegetables, and soul food. Vegetable stir-fry items are available for the health-conscious. Homemade cakes, bread pudding, sweet potato pie, and banana pudding.(It's good to be the king.) Dine in, table service, seats 22, all nonsmoking.

Date visited _____ *Remarks* _____

G.T.'s Bar-B-Que (160)

1925 W Washington Ave.
East Point, Ga. 30344
404/669-9494
County: Fulton

Tue - Thu 11 a.m.- 8 p.m., Fri & Sat 11 a.m. - 11 p.m.
From Main St. in downtown East Point, go west on
Washington Ave. It's about 7 blocks on the right, at 8th St.

Closed-pit, hickory-smoked, chopped or sliced barbecue to go. That's probably the fabulous aroma you noticed while driving down Washington Ave. G.T. serves his smoked meat with or without the sauce. Brunswick stew, beans, cole slaw, and potato salad are also available. Take-out only, one picnic table outside. Opened 1988.

Date visited _____ *Remarks* _____

Garrison's Bar-B-Q (161)

615 Clarkesville St.
Cornelia, Ga. 30531
706/776-1424
County: Habersham

Wed 11 a.m.- 2 p.m., Thu, Fri & Sat 11 a.m.- 8:30 p.m.
From Hwy. 365 northbound, take the second of the three
Cornelia exits. Turn right onto Old Hwy. 441, go past the
first light. It's a half mile on the right.

Take the old highway to Garrison's and get some old-style hickory-smoked, pit-cooked, chopped barbecue. The smoked chicken is especially good. Burgers, hot dogs, and chicken fillet are available for non-BBQ tastes. Homemade pies. Dine in, order at counter, seats 60. Opened 1993.

Date visited _____Remarks _____

The Georgia Pig (162)

U.S. 17 S
Brunswick, Ga. 31525
912/264-6664
County: Glynn

Mon - Sun 11 a.m.- 8 p.m., (Sat til 9 p.m.).
From I-95 southbound, take exit 6 (Jekyll Island). Turn
left onto U.S. 17. It's on the left next to the Texaco station.

Look carefully or you might miss this authentic old shack set back among the pines. Georgia Pig cooks Boston butts with oak, hickory, pecan, or other fruit woods in an open brick pit. A sweet 'n' tangy tomato-based sauce complements it well, and there's Tabasco sauce on the tables. "Traveling salesmen and tourists say we have the best barbecue in the country," is the slogan at Georgia Pig. Dine in, order at counter, 50 seats inside and several picnic tables outside. Since 1977.

Date visited _____Remarks _____

The Georgia Pig (163)

1072 Green St.
Roswell, Ga. 30075
770/642-6668
County: Fulton

Mon - Sat 11 a.m.- 9 p.m.
From historic downtown Roswell, go north on
Alpharetta St., turn left on Woodstock St. and
left again on Green St. past the fire station.

Georgia Pig's Roswell location also serves open-pit barbecue and tasty sides. Try the hickory salad topped with chicken, pork, or beef. For dessert, there's fruit cobbler, sweet potato pie, or ice cream. Beer and wine, too. Live country music Friday and Saturday nights. Lunch specials ("Squeal meal deals"). Dine in, table service, seats 120, nonsmokers' area. Lots of big tables. Opened 1987.

Date visited _____Remarks _____

Gilley's BarBQ (164)

342 W Bankhead Hwy.
Villa Rica, Ga. 30180
770/459-5543
County: Carroll

Mon - Sat 11 a.m.- 9 p.m.
On U.S. 78 just west of downtown Villa Rica.

In business over ten years, Gilley's barbecue place serves a savory barbecue made from hams cooked in a smoker with hickory. The baby back ribs and delicious Brunswick stew are other reasons to stop in. Frequent special deals on sandwich combos. Dine in, order at counter, seats 7.

Date visited _____Remarks _____

Glenn's Open-Pit Bar-B-Q (165)

1745 Hwy. 138
Conyers, Ga. 30208
770/929-0196
County: Rockdale

Sun - Thu 11 a.m.- 9 p.m., Fri & Sat 11 a.m.- 10 p.m..
From I-20, take exit 42 (Hwy. 138). Go south on 138
about a mile. It's on the right in the Kroger center.

Glenn and Jean Yontz opened this restaurant about ten years ago and eventually expanded to Snellville and Lilburn. They recently franchised the two expansion locations, but the menus remain essentially the same. The barbecue is tender, sweet, and smoky. Choose a thick, mild, sweet tomato-based sauce or a thinner hot sauce. Non-BBQ items include hamburgers, chicken sandwiches, and fried chicken. Dine in, table service, seats 175 – 200, nonsmokers' section. Drive-thru.

Date visited _____ *Remarks* _____

Glenn's Open-Pit Bar-B-Q (166)

4095 Lawrenceville Hwy. NW
Lilburn, Ga. 30247
770/925-8978
County: Gwinnett

Mon - Thu 11 a.m.- 9 p.m., Fri & Sat 11 a.m.- 10 p.m.
From I-85, take Beaver Ruin Rd.
southeast to Hwy. 29, turn left. Glenn's is a
half mile on the left.

Glenn's Lilburn location offers the same tender and smoky barbecue and other delectable goodies as found at the Conyers place. Dine in, seats about 140, nonsmokers' area. Drive-thru.

Date visited _____ *Remarks* _____

Glenn's Open-Pit Bar-B-Q (167)

2671 Hwy. 124 SW
Snellville, Ga. 30278
770/978-4700
County: Gwinnett

Tue - Thu 11 a.m.- 8:30 p.m.,
Fri & Sat 11 a.m.- 9:30 p.m., Sun 11 a.m.- 8 p.m.
From Atlanta, take U.S. 78 to Snellville, turn right on
Hwy. 124. It's about a mile on the right in a small mall.

A heap of prime pork, a bowl of meaty Brunswick stew, cole slaw, and iced tea. Let's eat. Dine in, table service, seats over 100, nonsmokers' section. No drive-thru at this location.

Date visited _____ *Remarks* _____

Gumlog Bar-B-Q Ranch (168)

106 Whitworth Sch. Farmer Rd.
Lavonia, Ga. 30553
706/356-4061
County: Franklin

Fri, Sat & Sun 11 a.m.- 10 p.m.
From downtown Lavonia, take Hwy. 328 towards Lake
Hartwell and Tugaloo State Park about three miles. Look
for the sign on the left, before Helen's Country Store.

This roomy establishment in the Gumlog community near Lake Hartwell sometimes fills up quickly even though it seats well over 100. In business since 1973, Gumlog Bar-B-Q Ranch prides itself on its consistency and good service. The pork is made from hams cooked with hickory in a homemade smoker. The sauce is ketchup and vinegar–based. Lemon and apple pie for dessert.

Date visited _____ *Remarks* _____

Gus' Barbecue (169)

Albany, Ga. 31707
912/883-2404
County: Dougherty

Mon - Thu 11 a.m.- 9:30 p.m., Fri & Sat 11 a.m. - 10 p.m.
From Albany Mall, go toward downtown on Dawson.
It's on the left, just past Whispering Pines Rd.

Gus does a fine closed-pit barbecue and serves it chopped or sliced. The meat is usually served with a tomato/mustard sauce. Among the sides are Brunswick stew, beans, cole slaw, and fries. Gus' menu also includes fresh vegetables and down-home country cooking. Dine in, 130 seats, table service. Nonsmokers' area. Take-out and catering, too. Opened 1979.

Date visited_____Remarks _____

Hamrick's Old Timey Town Bar-B-Q (170)

4912 Ogeechee Rd.
Savannah, Ga. 31405
912/234-9712
County: Chatham

Tue - Sun 11 a.m.- 9 p.m.
From I-516, exit at Ogeechee Road (Hwy. 17 South), go south about two miles. It's on the right.

"Old timey" is definitely the approach here. The barbecue sauce and Brunswick stew are made from old recipes from the 1920s; the building is constructed of century-old yellow pine; and old wagons and antiques are all around the place. The cooking methods are old-timey, too. The pork is cooked 8 to 10 hours over an open pit with oak and hickory. A sweet tomato-based sauce is served separately. Sides include Brunswick stew, baked beans, cole slaw, potato salad, and fries. Pecan pie for dessert. Root beer and Coke in bottles. Dine in, table service, 80 seats, nonsmokers' area. Opened 1995.

Date visited_____Remarks _____

Old sign on Milledge Road in Augusta. The place never opened for business. Originally located beside U.S. 1 at Deans Bridge Road, it was moved here in 1967.

Harold's, Atlanta

Name/Map ID	Hours/Directions

Harold's Barbecue (171)

171 McDonough Blvd. SE
Atlanta, Ga. 30315
404/627-9268
County: Fulton

Mon - Sat 10:30 a.m. - 8:30 p.m.
From Turner Field ballpark, take Hank Aaron Dr. south
to McDonough Blvd. Turn left. It's on the right.

Get here before noon. Otherwise, hungry hordes of Harold's devotees will be lined up out the door waiting to partake of the closed-pit, hickory-smoked, chopped or sliced goodness found within. Many come for the wonderful, marvelous, awe-inspiring Brunswick stew. Add some cracklin' cornbread, a sliced pork sandwich with outside meat, and iced tea, and you'll be in hog heaven. Dine in, table service, 100 seats. Nonsmokers' area. Opened 1947.

Date visited _____*Remarks* _____

Harold's Barbecue (172)

265 Hwy. 54
Jonesboro, Ga. 30236
770/478-5880
County: Clayton

Mon - Thu 10:30 a.m. - 9 p.m.,
Fri & Sat 10:30 a.m. - 9:30 p.m..
From Atlanta, take I-75 to exit 76; turn right on Hwy. 54.
Harold's is 2 1/2 miles on the right.

Opened in 1990 by Lee Hembree, one of Harold Hembree's sons, this second Harold's location offers the same pit-cooked perfection as the original Harold's in Atlanta plus a few extra menu items. Dine in, 180 seats, table service, nonsmokers' section.

Date visited _____*Remarks* _____

Harry's Barbecue (173)

U.S. 280
Hagan, Ga. 30429
912/739-4078
County: Evans

Mon - Thu 10 a.m.- 9:30 p.m., Fri & Sat 10 a.m.- 10 p.m.
Harry's is on U.S. 280 about two miles west of downtown
Claxton, next to Nesmith Chevrolet.

Lee Smith and his sister, Harriett Rice, preside over a family business established many years ago here. Beef ribs, which can be hard to find in Georgia, are a special treat. The sampler platter is a favorite, and the BBQ stuffed potato is very popular. The sweet corn comes out of the family garden. Dine in, table service (certain hours). Nonsmokers' area. Two big banquet rooms. Drive in.

Date visited _____*Remarks* _____

Hart's BBQ (174)

407 S Elm St.
Commerce, Ga. 30529
706/335-3728
County: Jackson

Mon - Sat 11 a.m.- 5 p.m.
From I-85 northbound, take exit 52, and turn right.
Follow Hwy. 98 into Commerce. It's on the right.

Hart's specializes in smoked pork and plenty more. A variety of vegetables are served on weekdays, including creamed potatoes, candied yams, butter peas, cabbage, and pinto beans. Among the non-BBQ items are baked chicken, pot roast, chicken livers, catfish, shrimp, sandwiches, and salads. Homemade cakes and ice box pies, too. Dine in, table service, 90 seats, nonsmokers' area.

Date visited _____*Remarks* _____

Hawes Bar-B-Q (175)

151 S Peachtree St.
Lincolnton, Ga. 30817
No phone
County: Lincoln

Open Saturday only, til the barbecue runs out.
On South Peachtree St. in downtown Lincolnton, next to
the telephone office. Look for an old red wooden building.

Mr. Hawes is planning to retire soon. He's cooked pork and hash at his downtown shack since the Eisenhower Administration, and a son will probably keep the business going, so he's decided it's about time to quit. He cooks hams over hickory and red oak coals. His sauce is a red vinegar-based mix. Take-out only.

Date visited _____*Remarks* _____

Hawkeye Barbecue (176)

307 West 12th St.
Tifton, Ga. 31794
912/382-6550
County: Tift

Mon - Wed 10 a.m.- 2 p.m., Thu - Sat 10 a.m.- 9 p.m..
From I-75 take exit 21 and turn onto U.S. 41 south
toward downtown. It's about a mile on the left.

The pork is a blend of hams and butts, cooked over oak in a closed pit. The homemade sauce is an orange mix of tasty ingredients, none of which dominates the taste. Slabs of ribs and half-chickens are popular take-out items. Also vegetables and non-BBQ items. Leave room for Mom's nine-layer chocolate cake, coconut cake, or pecan pie. Dine in, table service, 40 seats. All nonsmoking.

Date visited _____*Remarks* _____

Heavy's Bar-B-Que/Museum Dining Room (177)

2155 Sparta Rd. SE
Crawfordville, Ga. 30631
706/456-2445
County: Taliaferro

Fri - Sun 9 a.m. - 9 p.m.
On Hwy. 22, a mile south of I-20 (exit 55).

William F. "Heavy" Grant cooks with oak wood the old way. His chopped pork is served with a vinegar-based sauce. The food is the main attraction, but one should also visit this place to see Heavy's "unique museum and dining room." The rustic tin-roofed building is crammed full of antiques and curiosities. Scores of stuffed animals decorate the walls and ceilings. There's plenty to see outside, too, such as the kicking machine for anyone who has ever said, "I could just kick myself!" Dine in. Opened 1979.

Date visited _____*Remarks* _____

Heavy's

HHH Bar-B-Que (178)

4980 Hiram-Acworth Hwy.
Hiram, Ga. 31041
770/943-7616
County: Paulding

Mon - Sat 11 a.m. - 9 p.m.
From Atlanta, take I-20 west to Thornton Rd. It becomes
U.S. 278. At Hwy. 92, turn left. It's 2 miles on the right.

At HHH, a.k.a. Hiram Hickory House, the goal is to make the best barbecue possible. "The only way to cook a pig right is to cook it slowly," is the HHH pork philosophy. Beef briskets are marinated overnight before going on the Texas-built pit. The ribs are very lean and are cut in the St. Louis fashion. The Brunswick stew is made from scratch. Unbelievably good beans are made with ground pork. Desserts: fried pies and homemade moon pies. Dine in, order at counter, 50 seats. Drive-thru. Opened 1997.

Date visited _____*Remarks* _____

Hickory BBQ (179)

945 N Park St.
Carrollton, Ga. 30117
770/832-1803
County: Carroll

Mon 11 a.m.- 3 p.m., Tue - Sat 11 a.m.- 7 p.m.
From the city square in Carrollton, go north on Rome St.
about a mile to North Park St. (U.S. 27 N). It's on the left.

Hickory BBQ is a tiny shack with a big claim: "The Best BBQ in West Georgia."
Smoked pork is the specialty. The red barbecue sauce is available hot or mild.
Take-out only.

Date visited _____Remarks _____

Hickory Hut BBQ (180)

896 Hartwell Rd.
Lavonia, Ga. 30553
706/356-4113
County: Franklin

Mon - Thu 9 a.m.- 8 p.m., Fri - Sun 9 a.m.- 9 p.m.(or later).
From I-85, take exit 58, go one mile to Lavonia.
Turn left at the first traffic light. Go to Hwy. 77 and turn
right. It's about a mile ahead at the city limits.

Three tables full of trophies here attest to Hugh Thomas' success in barbecue
contests. He does a lot of catering and can cook a whole hog with the best of
them. Here, in a little take-out shack next to his house, he cooks mostly hams,
and sometimes Boston butts, in a rotisserie cooker with hickory wood. A
ketchup/vinegar sauce, served on the side, has Cajun seasonings, but isn't hot.
Even kids like it, says Hugh. Four large picnic tables outside seat 24 or so.

Date visited _____Remarks _____

Hickory Stick Bar-B-Q (181)

202 East Ave.
Cedartown, Ga. 30125
770/748-3896
County: Polk

Mon - Sat 11 a.m.- 10 p.m., Sun - 11 a.m.-4 p.m.
On East Ave. across from the City Auditorium.

The Dunn family serves a variety of open-pit-cooked barbecue items at their
roomy restaurant in downtown Cedartown, the county seat of Pork County
(oops, that's Polk County). Customers have a choice of chopped or sliced meat
and there's a wide selection of sides. The homemade sauce is vinegar-based and
mild. Homemade pies for dessert. Dine in, 100 seats. Drive-thru, too.

Date visited _____Remarks _____

Bar-B-Fact

"The first drive-in restaurant was the Pig Stand, a barbecue pork
place on the Dallas–Fort Worth highway in Texas. It opened in
September 1921. Within a decade, Pig Stands stood all over the
Midwest and as far away as New York and California."

—John Mariani, America Eats Out.

Fresh Air Bar-B-Que near Jackson opened in 1929, the year Georgia Tech beat California in the Rose Bowl.

Name/Map ID   **Hours/Directions**

Hickory Stick Bar-B-Que (182)

898 Southway Dr.
Jonesboro, Ga. 30236
770/477-6595
County: Clayton

Tue - Sat 11 a.m.- 5:30 p.m.
From I-75, take exit 77. Go south on U.S. 19/41 4 miles;
turn left on Hwy 138. It's 75 yards on the left.

This take-out-only place, which opened in 1990, is in a brightly colored carnival-trailer-like building with a six-foot corn dog sticking out of the roof. Despite that, Hickory Stick is known for its barbecue and Brunswick stew. The former is made from Boston butts cooked 12 to 16 hours with hickory in a smoker. The latter is thick and delicious. The sauce is homemade, sweet, and red. Also served are burgers, hot dogs, and sausages. Drive-thru, too.

Date visited _____ *Remarks* _____

Hill's Bar B Que (183)

1840 Hwy. 24 W
Louisville, Ga. 30434
912/625-8301
County: Jefferson

Wed 9 a.m.- 1 p.m., Thu - Sat 9 a.m.- 5 p.m.
From U.S. 1 at Louisville, go west through town on Hwy.
24 about 2 miles to the junction with Hwy. 171.
It's on the corner.

"The best barbecue you can find," they claim at Hill's. The open-pit, charcoal-cooked pig meat served here is some of the best in the area, especially for those who like their barbecue sauce red and spicy and unsweet. Ribs are available on occasion at Hill's. The desserts are homemade. Take-out only. Outside seating at picnic tables for 30 or so. Opened 1977.

Date visited _____ *Remarks* _____

Hilton's Restaurant/Sweat's Barbecue (184)

215 Main St. NW
Vidalia, Ga. 30474
912/537-3934
County: Toombs

Mon - Thu 10:30 a.m.- 8:45 p.m.,
Fri & Sat 10:30 a.m.- 9:30 p.m.,
Sun 10:30 a.m.- 2:30 p.m.
Hilton's/Sweat's is on Main Street in downtown Vidalia.

For years, Sweat's Barbecue sat just off the Soperton exit of I-16. It was closed some time ago, but now the name has returned in conjunction with Hilton's Restaurant, a popular Vidalia establishment. Sweat's barbecue is served with a thick red sauce, and Brunswick stew, potato salad, fries, cole slaw, and other items are on the side. A home-style buffet is offered at lunch and in the evening. On Friday and Saturday evenings, it's a seafood buffet. Dine in, table service, or order at counter, seats 200, nonsmokers' area.

Date visited _____ *Remarks* _____

Hodges' Country Bar-B-Que (185)

2141 Candler Rd.
Decatur, Ga. 30032
404/289-1804
County: DeKalb

Mon - Fri 10:30 a.m. - 11 p.m.,
Fri & Sat 10:30 a.m. - 1 a.m.
From I-20, take exit 33 and go north on
Candler Rd. (Hwy. 155) a little over a mile. It's on the left.

One of the best ways to make barbecue is to slowly cook it in an open pit with oak. This is how Hodges' makes some of the finest 'Q you'll find. A sweet, tomato-based sauce is served on the meat or on the side. Rib tips, stew, beans, cole slaw, and potato salad are other tasty items here. Dine in, order at counter.

Date visited_____Remarks _____

Hog Heaven (186)

2240 West Point Rd.
LaGrange, Ga. 30240
706/882-7227
County: Troup

Mon - Thu 11 a.m. - 9 p.m., Fri & Sat 11 a.m. - 10 p.m.
From I-85, take exit 4. Go straight through town. Beyond
the city square, go left at a fork onto West Point Rd. It's
about a mile on the right.

You know you're in Hog Heaven when you see the choice of sauces here: "Original Hog Heaven" (mild and mustardy), "Savannah" (half mustard/half ketchup), "Hog Heaven Hot" (ketchupy and hot), and "Lafayette" (vinegar-based and sweet/tangy). There's even a mustard-based sauce just for the hickory-smoked sausage. The big brick pit in the kitchen can be seen from the dining room, and blues and country music are played on the stereo. A bucket of peanuts is on each table. Dine in, table service, 95 seats, nonsmokers' section.

Date visited_____Remarks _____

Hog Mountain Store (187)

1953 Hwy. 324
Buford, Ga. 30518
770/932-2311
County: Gwinnett

Mon - Sat 6 a.m. - 2 p.m.
From I-85 northbound, take exit 47 (Hamilton Mill Rd.).
Turn right, then right again onto Hwy. 124. Go 2 miles to
Hwy. 324. It's at the junction.

The old Hog Mountain Store, built in the early 1900s, has been selling take-out barbecue for eighteen years. Whole loins are cooked 12 to 14 hours in a smoker using hickory. The sauce is red, sweet, and homemade. Take-out only, with tables under a shade tree. Try it before suburbia swallows it up.

Date visited_____Remarks _____

Hogsed Barbecue & Grill (188)

188 N Broad St.
Winder, Ga. 30680
770/307-0050
County: Barrow

Thu - Sat 10:30 a.m. - 8 p.m.
From May St. in downtown Winder, go north on Broad
St. (Hwy. 11). It's on the left, a little red and white trailer
next to a liquor store.

In business about six years, Hogsed Barbecue & Grill is a take-out and drive-thru place with picnic tables out front. The barbecue is made from Boston butts cooked in a smoker with hickory. The sauce is vinegar-based with tomato and mustard; it's available in hot or mild.

Date visited_____Remarks _____

Holcomb's Barbecue (189)

1260 E Main St.
White Plains, Ga. 30678
706/467-2409
County: Greene

Fri 8:30 a.m. - 10 p.m., Sat 8:30 a.m. - 8 p.m.
From I-20, take exit 54, go south a half mile to Siloam.
Turn left onto Hwy. 15. Go south 5 miles. It's on the left.

Like Fresh Air BBQ in Jackson, Holcomb's is a simple rural establishment serving barbecued pork and stew with slaw, pickles, and white bread. Potato chips are also available, but that's about it for the sides. There's no beef, no ribs, no beer, no cutesy menus, no frills whatsoever. The delectable pork, available chopped or sliced, is served at two long rows of picnic tables on a sawdust/woodchip floor. The vinegar-based sauce is a bit spicy. For dessert there's homemade cake. Dine in, table service, 100 seats, all nonsmoking. Opened 1971.

Date visited _____ *Remarks* _____

Holcomb's Barbecue (190)

Broad St. W
Greensboro, Ga. 30642
706/453-2577
County: Greene

Thu 9 a.m. - 7 p.m., Fri & Sat 9 a.m. - 8 p.m.
On Broad St./Madison Hwy. (U.S. 278) at GA 15, on the
west side of downtown Greensboro.

Holcomb's Greensboro place offers barbecue pork, cole slaw, chips, and white bread. Also homemade desserts. That's it. But ask yourself: what else do you really need? All cooking done at White Plains location. Dine in, table service 70 seats, all nonsmoking. Take-out window. Opened 1981.

Date visited _____ *Remarks* _____

Holt Bros. Bar-B-Q (191)

6359 Jimmy Carter Blvd.
Norcross, Ga. 30071
770/242-3984. Fax: 242-8279
County: Gwinnett

Mon - Thu 11 a.m. - 9 p.m., Fri & Sat 11 a.m. - 10 p.m.,
Sun 12 p.m.- 9 p.m.. (Drive-thru open til 11 on Fri & Sat).
From I-85 northbound, take exit 37. Turn left onto Jimmy
Carter Blvd., go 1.3 miles. On the right at Buford Hwy.

The thick, meaty Brunswick stew served here must be Georgia's tangiest. It's not spicy hot, but pungent instead. The barbecue is closed-pit-cooked with hickory, then chopped. The tomato-based sauce is dark, smoky, thick, and sweet. On the side are beans, slaw, collards, black-eyed peas, candied yams, fried okra, mac-and-cheese, corn on the cob, among others. Desserts include peach cobbler, pound cake, pecan pie, sweet potato pie, cheesecake, and banana pudding. Voted Gwinnett County's Favorite BBQ. Dine in, table service, 86 seats, nonsmokers' area. Opened 1993.

Date visited _____ *Remarks* _____

Bar-B-Fact

Twin Oaks Barbecue in Brunswick opened in 1943, the year
Georgia beat UCLA in the Rose Bowl.

Hometown BBQ (192)

2235 Atlanta Hwy.
Hiram, Ga. 31041
770/943-0969
County: Paulding

Mon - Thu 11 a.m. - 8 p.m., Fri & Sat 11 a.m. - 9 p.m.
From Atlanta, take I-20 west to exit 12 (Thornton Rd.).
Go north on Thornton Rd./U.S. 278 about 9 miles.
It's on the right.

Two hometown boys, Zeke Fitzgerald and Kenny Thomason, decided to come back and provide Hiram with good barbecue. Zeke smokes Boston butts and pork shoulders with hickory and makes the results available with a mild or hot red sauce. Pork ribs are served wet or dry and are available by the full rack. The Brunswick stew is divine. Dine in, order at counter, 15 seats. Opened 1994.

Date visited _____ *Remarks* _____

Hooked on Barbie-Q (193)

1510 Gloucester St.
Brunswick, Ga. 31520
912/261-8226
County: Glynn

Mon - Fri 11 a.m. - 6 p.m., Sat 11 a.m. - 3 p.m.
In downtown Brunswick at Gloucester St. and
Stonewall St., next to City Market.

This little take-out place in downtown Brunswick serves hickory-smoked pork sandwiches, ribs, wings, Brunswick stew, beans, cole slaw, and potato salad, among other items. Homemade desserts include peach cobbler and banana pudding. Cajun hot boiled peanuts, too.

Date visited _____ *Remarks* _____

Hooks' Barbeque (194)

N Hwy. 25
Millen, Ga. 30442
912/982-3440
County: Jenkins

Mon - Sat 6 a.m. - 8 p.m.
On U.S. 25. Go to second traffic light north of Hwy. 21.
Hooks is on the right near the Buy Rite store.

On December 3, 1864, much of Millen was burned by the army of General William T. Sherman. Nowadays, fire and smoke serve more beneficial purposes in this south Georgia town by helping Hooks' turn out some tasty barbecue. On the side is hash & rice instead of Brunswick stew.

Date visited _____ *Remarks* _____

Horace's Bar-B-Que Hut (195)

301 W Emory St.
Dalton, Ga. 30720
706/226-1953
County: Whitfield

Mon - Fri 10 a.m. - 2 p.m.
From I-75, take exit 136, go east. Turn left on Thornton
Ave. At first light, turn right on Emory St. It's on the right.

In business since 1984, Horace Smith's is a drive-thru and walk-up place with picnic tables outside for 12 or so. He cooks Boston butts with hickory in a closed pit. BBQ turkey is available, too. Sides include Brunswick stew, fries, slaw, and potato salad. Horace's homemade sauce is ketchup-based and a little spicy.

Date visited _____ *Remarks* _____

Hot Dog Cottage (196)

403 N Livington St.
Sylvester, Ga. 31791
912/776-3105
County: Worth

Mon - Wed 11 a.m. - 5 p.m.,
Thu - Fri 11 a.m. - 6 p.m., Sat 11 a.m. - 2 p.m.
From I-75 in Tifton, take exit 18. Go west 20 miles to
Sylvester. Turn right on N. Livingston St. It's on the left.

The barbecue at this little red cottage comes from Walker's Bar-B-Que Pit in nearby Sycamore, owned by the same family. Both barbecue plates and sandwiches are available, along with the standard side orders and vegetables. The sauce is tangy and red (also from Walker's). Dine in, 20 seats. Drive-thru.

Date visited _____*Remarks* _____

Hot's BBQ (Hot Thomas BBQ) (197)

3753 Hwy. 15 S
Watkinsville, Ga. 30677
706/769-6550
County: Oconee

Mon - Sat 9 a.m. - 7 p.m.
From Watkinsville, go south 5 miles on Hwy. 15.
It's on the left.

Pork, slaw, and Brunswick stew are the specialties at this peach orchard/barbecue place. Hot Thomas has been selling barbecue since the mid-80s and peaches for many years before that. Two types of sauce, a tomato-based mix and one of the vinegar variety, are available. Hamburgers served, too. Dine in.

Date visited _____*Remarks* _____

Howington's Bar B-Q (198)

1429 Thyatira-Brockton Rd.
Jefferson, Ga. 30549
706/367-8916
County: Jackson

Mon - Thu 11 a.m. - 2 p.m., Fri & Sat 11 a.m. - 9:30 p.m.
From Jefferson, take Hwy. 15 toward Commerce about
2 miles. Turn right just before C&D Groc.
It's 1.5 miles on the left.

Howington's Bar B-Q lies well off the beaten path, but it's worth the trip. Closed-pit-cooked pork is pulled and chopped and served with a flavorful homemade sauce. On the side are Brunswick stew, cole slaw, fries, tater tots, and onion rings. Dine in, order at counter, 40 seats. Opened 1986.

Date visited _____*Remarks* _____

Hudson's Hickory House (199)

6874 Bankhead Hwy.
Douglasville, Ga. 30134
770/942-4828
County: Douglas

Mon - Thu 9 a.m. - 10 p.m., Fri & Sat 9 a.m.- 11 p.m.
On U.S. 78 in downtown Douglasville.

Hudson's has been an institution in downtown Douglasville since 1971. The smoky-flavored meat is cooked in a closed pit with hickory, and served chopped or sliced with a thin, tangy red sauce. Along with the standard sides are hickory potatoes, beef or pork super salads, chick fillet, steaks, hot dogs, and hamburgers. Fried pies for dessert. Dine in, table service, plenty of seats.

Date visited _____*Remarks* _____

Leon's of Chicago

Name/Map ID	Hours/Directions

Hunter's Barbecue (200)

935 Douglas Hwy.
Ocilla, Ga. 31774
912/468-5770
County: Irwin

Tue - Fri 9 a.m. - 5:30 p.m.
On Hwy. 32, about 4 miles east of Ocilla, near Holt.

Look for the eighteen-wheelers parked by the road. Hunter's is a favorite of area truck drivers; plenty of local people stop by here, too. The place has no barbecue chicken, no fries, no onion rings, no desserts, no beer, and no character to speak of. But it does have some pretty good smoked pig meat. And that's really what it's all about.

Date visited _____ *Remarks* _____

Hurst's Real Pit Bar-B-Que (201)

206 Maddox Dr. E
Ellijay, Ga. 30540
706/276-2221
County: Gilmer

Mon - Thu 11:30 a.m. - 8 p.m., Sat 12 p.m. - 9 p.m., Sun 12 p.m. - 8 p.m.
From I-575, take Hwy. 515 (Zell Miller Pkwy.)
to the traffic light in East Ellijay. Turn left. It's on top of
the hill on the left at Clock Tower mall.

You know this is not your typical Georgia barbecue place when you see the specialties are mesquite chicken and corn nuggets (deep-fried creamed corn). The barbecue sauce is Ken's, a commercial sauce. Besides the corn nuggets, there's a nice selection of vegetables, including okra, squash, and corn on the cob. Dine in, table service, 60 seats, nonsmokers' section. Opened 1994.

Date visited _____ *Remarks* _____

If Pigs Could Fly BBQ & Wings (202)

5400 Hwy. 20
Loganville, Ga. 30249
770/466-8399
County: Walton

Wed & Thu 11 a.m. - 9 p.m., Fri & Sat 11 a.m. - 10 p.m.
From Loganville, go south on Hwy. 20 toward Conyers.
It's several miles down the road on the left, near BP.

Look for a winged pig in front of this take-out place between Loganville and
Conyers. IPCFBBQ&W cooks hams and Boston butts in a smoker with hickory
and pecan wood. The sauce is not too sweet and not too tangy. Hot dogs, wings,
and nachos are sold here, too. Picnic tables for 10 to 15. Opened 1996.

Date visited _____*Remarks* _____

J&E Country Barbecue & Snack Bar (203)

4090 Hwy. 85
Ellerslie, Ga. 31807
706/561-7442
County: Harris

Mon - Tue 11 a.m. - 10 p.m., Wed 11 a.m. - 3 p.m.,
Thu 11 a.m. - 8 p.m., Fri. & Sat. 11 a.m. - 10 p.m.
From I-185 in Columbus, take exit 5, go north on
U.S. 27Alt./85 16 miles to Ellerslie. It's on the right.

The barbecue sandwich at J&E comes with big, hickory-smoked chunks of tender pork fresh from the open pit. The thin, tomato-based sauce accents the
meat perfectly; it's available in a choice of hot or mild. Brunswick stew and
some side orders are served, too. Also short orders. Excellent desserts. Dine in,
order at counter. Seats 20 or so in a small, but pleasant dining room.

Date visited _____*Remarks* _____

J&J BBQ (204)

U.S. 27 N
Franklin, Ga. 30230
No phone
County: Heard

Wed - Sun. 11 a.m. - 7 p.m.
On U.S. 27 a quarter mile north of the river, on the left.

J&J sells sandwiches and plates to go at this little walk-up and take-out shack
alongside U.S. 27. It's rated highly by those who have eaten the 'que here. The
meats are cooked in a big smoker on the premises.

Date visited _____*Remarks* _____

Bar-B-Fact

*Some years ago, after losing an election, a Georgia politician
suggested that many among the hordes of voters who ate his
barbecue at campaign rallies didn't vote for him.
Augusta's Larry Sconyers fared better. Augustans have been eating
his barbecue since 1956. In 1995 they elected him mayor.*

J&R Ribshack (205)

1001 N Hill St.
Griffin, Ga. 30223
770/228-7539
County: Spalding

Mon - Thu 11 a.m. - 7 p.m., Fri & Sat 11 a.m. - 11 p.m.
From downtown Griffin, go north on Hill St.
It's on the left.

The secret sauce is red and spicy, and the ribs are tender and smoky at James
Ellis' place. Fried chicken, fish, wings, burgers, hot dogs, slaw, beans, and home-
style vegetables are served, too. Desserts are available occasionally. Dine in,
order at counter, 12 seats. Opened 1995.

Date visited _____ *Remarks* _____

J.B.'s Bar-B-Que and Grill (206)

2247 Hwy. 319 S
Thomasville, Ga. 31792
912/377-9344
County: Grady

Tue - Thu 11:30 a.m. - 9 p.m., Fri 11:30 a.m. - 10 p.m.,
Sat 12 p.m. - 10 p.m., Sun 12 p.m. - 9:30 p.m.
On U.S. 319, about 3 miles north of the Florida line.

Seats nearly 200 pork-lovers in a single large room. It's clean and well-lit inside
with a no-nonsense atmosphere that leaves cutesy pig decor to others. Plates
feature chopped pork or beef, barbecued chicken, ribs, or a combo. All plates
are served with bread and two of the following: baked beans, fries, potato salad,
or cole slaw. Try the sweet potato or apple pie for dessert.

Date visited _____ *Remarks* _____

J.C.'s Bar-B-Q (207)

4668 East Oglethorpe Hwy.
Hinesville, Ga. 30313
912/877-2687
County: Liberty

Mon - Sat 11 a.m. - 7 p.m.
From downtown Hinesville, take U.S. 84 east toward
Savannah. It's on the left just before the overpass.

There are three seats inside, but it's mostly take-out at this trailer-like building in
Hinesville. Ribs are sold by the slab or half slab or however you want them. Sides
include mac-and-cheese, and collard greens. Food other than barbecue varies;
sometimes fish is available and sometimes it's not. Cakes and pies for dessert.

Date visited _____ *Remarks* _____

J.J.'s Rib Shack (208)

2979 Campbellton Rd. SW
Atlanta, Ga. 30311
404/349-2717
County: Fulton

Wed 12:30 p.m. - 8 p.m., Thu 12:30 p.m. - 9 p.m.,
Fri & Sat 12:30 p.m.- 10 p.m.
From Hwy. 166 (Lakewood Frwy.), exit at Greenbriar Pkwy. Go north
one block, turn right on Campbellton Rd. It's a half mile on the left.

If you're driving on Campbellton Road looking for J.J.'s, just look for the smoke.
On Saturday nights look, too, for an already-packed parking lot, with even more
motorists waiting for a spot to open up. You might decide to drive on, but if the
divine aroma of smoked pork drifts out of the pit shelter at this busy establishment, you might not be able to pass it by. Barbecue beef available occasionally.
Also fresh vegetables, beans, cole slaw, mac-and-cheese. Mostly take-out.

Date visited _____ *Remarks* _____

J.L.'s Open Pit Bar-B-Q (209)

Eisenhower Pkwy.
Macon, Ga. 31206
912/788-1989
County: Bibb

Sun - Thu 11 a.m. - 9 p.m., Fri & Sat 11 a.m. - 9:30 p.m.
At U.S. 80 (Eisenhower Pkwy.) and I-475 (exit 1),
on the west side of Macon.

If you're looking for low-fat alternative meats, or if you want to taste something different, stop in at J.L.'s and try their ostrich fillet or ostrich burger. However, if you'd rather keep your head in the sand about ostrich meat, order the pork or pork ribs instead. You won't regret it. J.L. cooks his barbecue over red oak coals in an open pit and offers a fine brown ketchup-based sauce (hot or mild) or a sweet honey sauce to go on it. Dine in, table service, 200 seats. Mostly nonsmoking.

Date visited _____ *Remarks* _____

J.R.'s Barbecue (210)

836 Hazel St.
Macon, Ga. 31201
912/747-8678
County: Bibb

Mon - Sat 9 a.m. - midnight, Sun 1 p.m. - midnight.
From I-75, take exit 51. Go east on Mercer Blvd./Little
Richard Blvd. Turn left on Telfair. Go 3 blocks.
It's on the corner at Hazel St.

J.R.'s superb spare ribs were offered at a recent Macon Cherry Blossom Festival, and sold out in record time. The barbecued pork, made from marinated prime meats, is excellent without any sauce, but J.R.'s has several sauce options available if desired. Homemade pork rinds, too! Dine in, order at counter.

Date visited _____ *Remarks* _____

J.R.'s Log House Restaurant (211)

6601 Peachtree Industrial Blvd.
Norcross, Ga. 30092
770/449-6426
County: Gwinnett

Mon - Thu 7 a.m. - 9 p.m., Fri - Sat 7 a.m. - 10 p.m.,
Sun 8 a.m. - 9 p.m.
At Peachtree Industrial Blvd. and
Peachtree Corners Circle, 3 miles north of I-285.

J.R.'s is a big, roomy full-service restaurant specializing in open pit, hickory smoked barbecue. It's available sliced or chopped. The extensive list of sides includes J.R.'s Brunswick stew, a thick, rich mix of smoked meats, tomatoes, potatoes, corn, and onions. All-you-can-eat specials Sunday through Thursday. Wide selection of beer and wine. Fruit cobblers, pecan pie, and banana pudding for dessert. Dine in, table service, lots of seats, nonsmokers' area. Opened 1983.

Date visited _____ *Remarks* _____

J.R.'s Log House Restaurant (212)

10270 Medlock Bridge Rd.
Duluth, Ga. 30155
770/476-1766
County: Fulton

Mon - Thu 7 a.m. - 9 p.m., Fri - Sat 7 a.m. - 10 p.m.,
Sun 8 a.m. - 9 p.m.
Between Duluth and Alpharetta on Hwy. 141, one mile
north of State Bridge Rd., on the left.

J.R.'s second location is housed in a contemporary building quite unlike the log cabin structure at the Norcross original. The menu, however, is the same.

Date visited _____ *Remarks* _____

J.R.'s, Norcross

Name/Map ID	Hours/Directions

Jack Wingate's Fishing Lodge (213)

139 Wingate Rd.
Bainbridge, Ga. 31717
912/246-0658
County: Decatur

Mon - Sun 6 a.m. - 9 p.m.
From Bainbridge, go south on Hwy. 97 about 12 miles.
Turn right on Hutchinson Ferry Rd.

Wingate's is a local landmark serving "Fried Fish and Stuff." The stuff includes barbecued pork, beef, and chicken (all slow-cooked on a genuine oak fire and guaranteed to be "larruping good"), along with Brunswick stew, fries, salad, and rolls. Tangy, not sweet, red sauce. Tabasco sauce on the table. Also available are seafood, steaks, and country dinners. The dining room is a comfortable space festooned with antique sporting gear, arrowheads, and the like. Be sure to see THE Bass.

Date visited _____ Remarks _____

Jack's Little Store (214)

Hwy. 46 E
Metter, Ga. 30439
912/685-4177
County: Candler

Mon - Sat 9 a.m. - 10 p.m.
On Hwy. 46 between Metter and Pulaski.

It used to be a convenience store, now it's another kind of gathering place for a small community. On Wednesdays and Fridays, local folks sometimes provide music and entertainment for customers at Jack Daniel's place. The meats are cooked on an open pit and in a smoker. Oak is the wood of choice. Some folks say the red sauce is what makes the barbecue at Jack's; it has a little bite to it. There's also a sweet sauce. The ribs are so tender the meat falls off the bone when you pick them up. Dine in, order at counter, 30 seats.

Date visited _____ Remarks _____

Jack's Wood-Cooked Bar-B-Q (215)

2030 East 10th St.
Woodbine, Ga. 31569
912/576-4073
County: Camden

Mon - Sun 11 a.m. - 9 p.m.
(Closed only on Christmas and Thanksgiving.)
From I-95 southbound, take exit 4. Turn right onto
Hwy. 25 Spur; it's on the right.

Jack Sutton has two barbecue places here on the Georgia coast. He had a third location in downtown St. Marys, but he closed it when he decided he just couldn't keep up the quality at three places. He uses mostly live oak, mixed with hickory, in his smoker. He cooks with green wood after starting the fire with dry wood; he says it keeps the meat more moist. He's been cooking for thirty years, primarily at civic and family events, and has cooked commercially for five years. Dine in, order at counter, 50 seats inside. Drive-thru. Opened 1994.

Date visited _____ *Remarks* _____

Jack's Wood-Cooked Bar-B-Q (216)

Harriett's Bluff Rd.
Kingsland, Ga. 31548
912/729-1500
County: Camden

Mon - Sun 11 a.m. - 9 p.m.
From I-95 southbound, take exit 3. Turn left; it's on the
right next to the Shell station.

The Brunswick stew here (and at Jack's Woodbine location) is homemade with pork, beef, and vegetables; it's so thick you can eat it with a fork. This is also a good place to get a Georgia favorite—boiled peanuts. Dine in, order at counter, 30 seats inside and 20 outside.

Date visited _____ *Remarks* _____

Jackson's Barbeque Corner (217)

Lamb Ave.
Union Point, Ga. 30669
706/486-2592
County: Greene

Mon - Wed 6 a.m. - 9 p.m., Thu - Sun 9 a.m. - 11 p.m.
From I-20 eastbound, take exit 53. Go north to
Greensboro and take Hwy. 44 to Union Point. It's on the
left at the edge of town.

During the Civil War, the Wayside Home here in Union Point, operated by fourteen of the city's women, served more than one million meals to Confederate soldiers passing through town. Jackson's Barbeque Corner may not have served that quantity just yet, but they have quality down pat. The meat is cooked in an open pit with oak and charcoal and doused with Jackson's home-made sauce. Dine in.

Date visited _____ *Remarks* _____

Bar-B-Fact

While at Johnny Harris Restaurant in Savannah, ask to see a copy
of their 1936 menu (barbecue pork sandwich, 25¢, Schlitz, 20¢).
You might have to explain to the kids what that "¢" means.

Jarrard's Bar-B-Que (218)

402 E Second Ave.
Rome, Ga. 30161
706/235-1199
County: Floyd

Mon - Wed 11 a.m. - 3 p.m., Thu - Sat 11 a.m. - 7 p.m.
From Turner McCall Blvd. and Broad St. in Rome, go
through downtown to Second Ave., turn left, go four
blocks. It's on the right.

Hickory-smoked, closed-pit-cooked barbecued pork, both baby back and regular ribs, Brunswick stew, and all the sides are served at Chris Jarrard's place. For dessert, choose among fried pies, cobblers, and cakes. Non-barbecue items include burgers, sandwiches, and salads. Dine in, 80 seats, nonsmokers' area. Table service during evenings on Thursday through Saturday. Opened 1990.

Date visited _____ *Remarks* _____

Jesse James Pit Barbecue (219)

6083 Old National Hwy.
College Park, Ga. 30349
770/997-9921
County: Fulton

Mon - Thu 11:30 a.m. - 10 p.m., Fri & Sat 11:30 a.m. - 12 p.m.
From I-285, exit at Old National Highway (Hwy. 279).
Go south on Old Nat'l to the fourth light.
It's on the right at Flat Shoals Rd.

We've heard "Best in Georgia" and "Best in the South," but the all-time-record claim for best barbecue must be Jesse James' "Best 'que this side of heaven." Along with the usual sides, there are fresh greens, cornbread, and mac-and-cheese. Peach cobbler for dessert. The sauce is a ketchup and mustard mix. Dine in, table service, 120 seats. Owner Jesse James Spikes.

Date visited _____ *Remarks* _____

Jesse James Pit Barbecue (220)

Georgia Dome
Atlanta, Ga. 30303
No phone
County: Fulton

Open during most events.
The Georgia Dome is in downtown Atlanta at Martin
Luther King Jr. Dr. and Northside Dr.

Jesse James' pork, chicken, and sausage sandwiches are the only items served at the Dome location. (Please, no jokes about smoked falcons.)

Date visited _____ *Remarks* _____

Jim Day Bar-B-Que (221)

1101 N. Washington St.
Albany, Ga. 31701
912/435-9188
County: Dougherty

Mon - Sat 9 a.m. - 6 p.m.
At North Washington and Fourth Ave. on the north side of
downtown Albany, near the river.

Jim Day Bar-B-Que was closed for remodeling when we visited; it should be reopened by the time you read this. Essentially, it's a walk-up and mostly take-out place serving barbecue basics. "We cook it with care and love and time," is how they describe their approach to barbecue. It originally opened in 1947.

Date visited _____ *Remarks* _____

Fincher's Barbecue in Macon opened in 1940, the year Southern Railway announced it would replace the steam locomotives of its passenger train Southern Crescent *with diesel-electric units.*

Name/Map ID	Hours/Directions

Jimbo's Log Kitchen (222)

600 W Dame Ave.
Homerville, Ga. 31634
912/487-2142   912/487-5048
County: Clinch

Mon - Sat 5 a.m. - 9 p.m., Sun 7 a.m. - 2 p.m.
On U.S. 84, just west of downtown Homerville.

Barbecue-lovers in southeast Georgia recommend Jimbo's perhaps more than any other place in the area. The "hog-noscenti" know that, of all the places in the pines, Jimbo's is the best. It's been here since 1936. They cook Boston butts right at the door in an open pit, so you can see what you get. There are two sauces, the original ketchup-based mix and a sweet mustard-based sauce; both are homemade, and are served on the meat or on the side. Dine in.

Date visited _____*Remarks* _____

Jimmy's Smokehouse Barbecue (223)

Hwy. 124
Snellville, Ga. 30278
770/972-1625
County: Gwinnett

Fri 3 p.m. - 9:30 p.m., Sat 11 a.m. - 9:30 p.m.
From U.S. 78 in Snellville, go south on Scenic Highway
(Hwy. 124) 2 miles to Everson Road. It's at the corner.

This recently opened take-out shack in busy Snellville serves no food other than barbecue and fixings. Jimmy's specialties are ribs, chopped pork, Brunswick stew, and grilled chicken. The meats are cooked in a wood-fired smoker. Try the potato casserole, a hot potato salad, and Jimmy's "Soon to Be Famous Tangy Wang Sauce."

Date visited _____*Remarks* _____

Joe's Store & Bar-B-Que (224)

4481 Eatonton Rd.
Madison, Ga. 30650
706/342-9056
County: Morgan

Mon - Sun 8 a.m. - 9 p.m.
From I-20, take exit 51. Go south on U.S. 441/129 about
6 miles to Seven Islands Rd. It's on the right.

For more than a century, a country store of one sort or another has been here on Seven Islands Road. One of America's earliest "interstate" highways, it connected Philadelphia to the Mississippi River. The store has been selling barbecue, by the sandwich, plate, or pound, about twelve years. It's mostly for take-out, but there are eight seats inside. Hunters and truck drivers are among the biggest customers.

Date visited _____*Remarks* _____

John and Earl Dillard's Place (225)

U.S. 441
Dillard, Ga. 30537
706/746-5965
County: Rabun

*Sun - Fri 6:30 a.m. - 9 p.m., Fri & Sat 6:30 a.m. - 10 p.m. (Closes an hour earlier in winter.)
On U.S. 441 at the Best Western in downtown Dillard.*

The meats are cooked over wood coals (hickory, apple, and oak mostly) at John and Earl's place. A tomato/vinegar barbecue sauce is added. Besides barbecue, the menu includes fried chicken, steaks, seafood, as well as assorted vegetables at lunch. Try the barbecued turkey. Homemade pies and cobblers for dessert. Dine in, table service, 150 seats, nonsmokers' section. Opened in 1972.

Date visited _____ Remarks _____

Johnny Brown's Country Fixins (226)

410 Johnson Rd.
Hogansville, Ga. 30230
706/637-8808
County: Troup

*Thu - Sat 5 p.m. - 9 p.m.
From Hogansville, take Hwy. 29/100 north. Turn left to stay on Hwy. 100 and go 3 or 4 miles to a fork. Turn left onto Johnson Rd. It's a mile on the left.*

Look for two concrete pigs at the entrance to this rural place. Open-pit cooking and a vinegary brown barbecue sauce make Johnny Brown's barbecue pork special. The standard barbecue-related sides are served, as are steaks and hamburgers. Homemade desserts, including a fine chocolate chip pie. Dine in, table service, 70 seats. Opened 1987.

Date visited _____ Remarks _____

Johnny Harris Restaurant (227)

1651 E Victory Dr.
Savannah, Ga. 31404
912/354-7810
County: Chatham

*Mon - Thu 11:30 a.m. - 10:30 p.m.,
Fri & Sat 11:30 a.m. - 12:30 a.m.
From downtown Savannah, go south to Victory Drive (U.S. 80 East), turn left. It's on the right.*

Begun as a roadside barbecue stand, Johnny Harris has been a Savannah tradition for over seventy years. It was featured in the "Great Chefs" PBS series, "Great Barbecue Restaurants in the South." (Chef Wolfgang Pork, perhaps?). JH makes and bottles its own sauce and sells it throughout the South. It was chosen No. 1 by *Food & Wine* magazine and tied for first place in *Cooks Magazine*. Besides barbecue, Johnny Harris serves seafood, steaks, fried chicken, and other items. Dine in, table service, 275 seats, nonsmokers' area. Full bar.

Date visited _____ Remarks _____

Bar-B-Fact

The piggy bank can trace its ancestry back to the 1400s when people used to stash coins and money in a jar or pygg, as it was called in Old English.

Johnny Mac's Barbecue Restaurant (228)

1225 N Chase St.
Athens, Ga. 30601
706/549-3111
County: Clarke

Tue - Sat 10 a.m. - 9 p.m.
From the North Athens Bypass, exit at Chase St. and go
toward town. It's on the right.

The interior is decorated with lots of Bulldog memorabilia, but Tech fans are welcome, too, at Johnny Mac's, a place that gives you a choice of Brunswick stew, hash, or chicken mull (a unique chicken stew). Rumor has it that the chicken mull is made from South Carolina gamecocks. We don't know about that, but we do know the 'que comes from hams and butts cooked in a hardwood-burning smoker out back. The red sauce is available in hot, extra hot, and mild. A vinegar-based sauce is available, too. Dine in, 45 seats, drive-thru. Opened 1994.

Date visited _____*Remarks* _____

Johnny's Bar-B-Que (229)

1710 Park Hill Dr.
Gainesville, Ga. 30501
770/536-2100
County: Hall

Mon - Wed 11 a.m. - 8 p.m., Thu - Sat 11 a.m. - 9 p.m.
On Park Hill Dr. (Hwy. 129 Bus.), about 3 miles north of
downtown Gainesville, on the right.

The meats at Johnny's are hickory-smoked in a closed pit and complemented by a homemade red nonsweet sauce. The tasty sides are served in ample portions. And there are plenty of seats at tables and booths in the clean, well-lit dining room.

Date visited _____*Remarks* _____

Johnny's Steaks and Bar-B-Q (230)

4179 Marietta St.
Powder Springs, Ga. 30073
770/943-4500
County: Cobb

Tue - Sat 11 a.m. - 9:30 p.m.
At intersection of Hwy. 6 Bus. and Hwy. 176 (New
Macland Rd.), just east of downtown Powder Springs.

Barbecue by the plate, sandwich, or pound—it's all popular at Johnny's. Other favorites are hickory potatoes and onion rings. Johnny's also serves steaks, chick fillet (grilled or fried), and burgers. For dessert: pies (coconut, pecan, or lemon), cheesecake, ice cream, and apple or peach fried pies. Two sauces, one a hot mustardy sauce and the other a thin, spicy Worcestershire-flavored mix, are offered. Dine in, table service, plenty of tables and booths in a single large room.

Date visited _____*Remarks* _____

Johns Barbecue (231)

411 N. Glenwood Ave.
Dalton, Ga. 30721
706/226-1769
County: Whitfield

Mon - Fri 10 a.m. - 8 p.m., Sat 10 a.m. - 3 p.m.
From I-75, take exit 136. Go east on Walnut Ave. Turn
left on Glenwood. It's on the left after the 5th traffic light.

The Johns family has been cooking barbecue since the 1950s. Here, they cook hams in a smoker using hickory wood and serve it with a homemade red sauce. Baby back ribs and hot slaw are specialties. For dessert, try one of three home-made pies: coconut, chocolate, or peanut butter. Dine in, order at counter, 50 seats.

Date visited _____*Remarks* _____

Johnny Harris

Name/Map ID   **Hours/Directions**

John's Barbecue House (232)

95 Hwy. 53
Hoschton, Ga. 30548
706/654-3350
County: Jackson

Thu 10 a.m. - 8 p.m., Fri & Sat 10 a.m. -9 p.m., Sun 11 a.m. - 2 p.m.
From I-85 northbound, take exit 49. Go south about six miles on
Hwy 53. It's on the right, at
the Jackson/Barrow county line.

This local landmark next to the Mulberry River bridge between Braselton and Winder serves up barbecue, fried chicken, catfish, and other items. The barbecue is made from hams cooked with hickory in a smoker. The red vinegar–based sauce is available in hot or mild. Dine in, table service, 150 seats. Opened 1964.

Date visited _____Remarks _____

Jomax Bar-B-Q (233)

1120 S Lewis St.
Metter, Ga. 30439
912/685-3636
County: Candler

Mon - Sat 9 a.m. - 7 p.m.
From I-16, take exit 23 and go north towards Metter. It's
two blocks on the left.

Named for the owners, Maxine and Joe Hulsey. Their "world-famous sauce" is shipped "all over the planet." It's served on the meat or on the side. Meats are cooked in a closed pit with oak, hickory, or pecan. Barbecue turkey available. Dine in. Opened 1986.

Date visited _____Remarks _____

Jones Bar-Be-Cue (234)

202 Hwy. 78 W
Temple, Ga. 30179
770/562-4387
County: Carroll

Mon - Thu 6:30 a.m. - 9 p.m.,
Fri & Sat 6:30 a.m. - 10 p.m.
From I-20 take the Temple-Carrollton exit (exit 4). Go
north. At stoplight, turn left and follow the signs.

Pit-cooked barbecue (hams cooked in a smoker with hickory) is the main attraction. Two different sauces: one for the pork and beef, the other for the ribs and chicken. Mustard-sauce fans will want to try the hot sauce. Baby back ribs by the plate or the pound. Vegetable lunches Monday through Thursday. Dine in, table service and order at counter, 120 seats, nonsmokers' area. Opened in 1981.

Date visited _____Remarks _____

Jones Bar-Be-Cue (235)

8011 S Park St.
Carrollton, Ga. 30117
770/830-1217
County: Carroll

Mon - Thu 10:30 a.m.- 9 p.m., Fri - Sat 10:30 a.m.- 10 p.m.
From downtown Carrollton, take S. Park St. (U.S. 27)
about a mile south. It's on the right, across from
West Georgia Shopping Center.

"Be a wife saver" is the slogan at Jones. Hams cooked with hickory in a smoker, baby back ribs, and Jones' fine stew might save a wife from kitchen drudgery, but they won't save many waist lines. The sauce is brown and vinegary and available in hot or mild. Dine in, table service, 60 seats. Opened 1981.

Date visited _____ *Remarks* _____

Jones Barbecue (236)

403 St. Marys Dr.
Waycross, Ga. 31501
912/285-7991
County: Ware

Mon - Thu 11 a.m. - 7 p.m.,
Fri 11 a.m. - 8 p.m., Sat 11 a.m. - 7 p.m.
At Hwy. 520 and U.S. 1/23, across from Holiday Inn.

"We ain't nothing but a little brown building with a little bit of seating outside," we were told when we called for information on dining at Jones Barbecue. The facilities may be modest, but the food is fine. The meats are cooked out back. The sauce is mild and red. To go with the 'que are various barbecue-related sides and vegetables, including corn nuggets.

Date visited _____ *Remarks* _____

Jordan's Bar-B-Que (237)

2485 Carrollton–Villa Rica Hwy.
Carrollton, Ga. 30116
770/832-1606
County: Carroll

Tue & Wed 10:30 a.m. - 3 p.m.,
Thu - Sat 10:30 a.m. - 9 p.m.
At Hwy. 166 and Hwy. 61, on the east side of Carrollton.

Super Salads topped with barbecued pork, beef, or turkey are people-pleasers at Jordan's. Meats are cooked in a closed pit with hickory, then pulled and chopped, and served with or without the vinegar-based sauce. Also available are cracklin' cornbread, jalapeño peppers, and pickles. Dine in, table service, 40 seats.

Date visited _____ *Remarks* _____

Jus' Bar-B-Que (238)

Courthouse Square
Cusseta, Ga. 31805
706/989-0660
County: Chattahoochee

Mon - Thu 7:30 a.m. - 3 p.m.,
Fri 7:30 a.m. - 8 p.m., Sat 7:30 a.m. - 3 p.m.
On the courthouse square in Cusseta, just east of U.S. 27.

The courthouse is across the street and there might be a personal-injury lawyer around. That might be why they don't put the hot sauce on the table here. It's so hot, you have to ask for it. It's a mustard-based mix that, fortunately, also comes in mild and medium. It goes nicely with the meats, which are cooked with oak and hickory. Among the sides is corn on the cob. Table service, 45 seats.

Date visited _____ *Remarks* _____

K&L Bar B Q (239)

103 Luckie St.
Baxley, Ga. 31513
912/367-7373
County: Appling

Mon - Thu 10:30 a.m. - 8 p.m.,
Fri 10:30 a.m. - 9 p.m., Sat 10:30 a.m. - 6 p.m.
From the junction of U.S. 1 and U.S. 341, go south on U.S. 1. Cross
the RR tracks and turn right on Park St. It's 100 yards on the left.

Owner Tommy Taylor doesn't want the rat race of a big restaurant, he says. His place doesn't have inside dining; it's walk-up and take-out (drive-thru too) and strictly barbecue. Very tender ribs are among his specialties. The sauce is thick, sweet, and ketchup-based. The twelve-ounce stuffed potato is a meal for two. It comes with salt and butter and is smothered in chipped pork or chicken and cheese and barbecue sauce. Opened 1988.

Date visited _____ Remarks _____

K.C. Rib Company (240)

2217 Roswell Rd. NE
Marietta, Ga. 30062
770/971-6200
County: Cobb

Mon - Thu 4:30 p.m. - 10 p.m.,
Fri & Sat 4:30 p.m. - 11 p.m., Sun 4:30 p.m. - 9 p.m.
On Roswell Rd. (Hwy. 120) at Barnes Mill Rd., 3/4ths
mile east of Marietta Pkwy. (Hwy. 120 Loop).

Lamb and pork barbecued ribs are popular menu items at this suburban Atlanta establishment. The baby back ribs are award winners. The sauce is tangy and tomato-based. Also lamb chops, pork chops, steaks, chicken, burgers, vegetable of the day, beans, cole slaw, baked apples, potato au gratin, salads, appetizers, and desserts. Casual dining, table service, 200 seats, nonsmokers' area. Opened 1989.

Date visited _____ Remarks _____

Bar-B-Fact

Piggie Park opened its barbecue drive-in on the north side of Thomaston in 1965, the year John, Paul, George, and Ringo entertained some 50,000 fans in Atlanta Stadium.

K.D.'s Bar-B-Q & Cafe (241)

504 Elizabeth St.
Waycross, Ga. 31501
912/285-3300
County: Ware

Mon - Sat 11 a.m. - 2 p.m., Fri & Sat 6 p.m - 9 p.m.
From the center of downtown Waycross, go west on
Elizabeth St. "Use your eyes and your nose
and you'll find it quickly."

Owner Kevin Woods thinks barbecue is a blast. He can't believe he's making money at "sit-down" barbecue, he says. He uses a "Chinese water smoker," a contraption that looks like a big refrigerator, because he can't do outdoor smoking on this site. He stacks the meat with the chicken on top. Chicken juices drip onto the pork. Yum! No barbecue at night, but if Kevin likes you, he'll get it for you. Dine in, 80 seats. Opened 1995.

Date visited _____ Remarks _____

Kelly's BBQ (242)

P.O. Box 60
Walnut Grove, Ga. 30210
770/786-0585
County: Walton

Sun - Thu 11 a.m. - 9 p.m., Fri - Sat 11 a.m. - 10 p.m.
(Closes an hour earlier in winter.)
From Covington, go nine miles north on Hwy. 81 to the
junction with Hwy. 138. It's on the left.

The aroma that drifts across the parking area at this little place lets you know quickly that you've made the right choice for a meal. The chopped pork sandwich with Kelly's thin tomato-based sauce is a good start. To go with it, choose among Brunswick stew, cole slaw (choice of red or white), fries, onion rings, hushpuppies, and beans. For dessert, there's apple or pecan pie. Also burgers, hot dogs, and other sandwiches. Dine in, order at counter.

Date visited _____*Remarks* _____

Kelly's

Kemp's Ole Tymer Bar B Que (243)

1000 N Broad St.
Rome, Ga. 30161
706/234-8000
County: Floyd

Mon - Thu 6 a.m. - 8 p.m., Fri & Sat 6 a.m. - 9 p.m.
From downtown Rome, take Broad St. north, past Turner
McCall Blvd., to the Five Points area of town.
Look for the sign.

Top-quality, low-fat, hickory-smoked, hand-chopped barbecue is sold from this little drive-thru log cabin in northeast Rome. Other take-out treats are Brunswick stew, smoked turkey breast, beans, cole slaw, fries, potato salad, corn on the cob, salads, and "Slaw-B-Que." For dessert, there's lemon ice box pie. Kemp's also serves full breakfasts. Take-out only. Opened 1984.

Date visited _____*Remarks* _____

Ken's Barbecue (244)

204 24th Ave. W
Cordele, Ga. 31015
912/273-8251
County: Crisp

Mon - Sat 9 a.m. - 8 p.m.
From I-75, take exit 33, and go west towards town.Turn
left at Church's Fried Chicken. At 24th St., turn rigtht;
it's on the right.

Rib sandwiches are the specialty at Kenneth Campbell's establishment. Although it's a small place with only one table and a counter, it does have a drive-thru window. Ken's open-pit, hickory-smoked, chopped or sliced barbecue is served with a homemade, mildly spicy red sauce. Dine in, 10 seats, table service. Opened 1984.

Date visited _____ Remarks _____

Kendricks Q Bar B Q (245)

105 Macon Hwy.
Warrenton, Ga. 30828
706/465-2446
County: Warren

Thu 9 a.m. - 8 p.m., Fri 7 a.m. - 10 p.m., Sat 8 a.m. - 6 p.m.
(Closes earlier if the barbecue is sold out.)
From the courthouse in downtown Warrenton, take
Hwy. 16 west a quarter mile. It's on the left.

Owner James Kendricks serves hash and rice, but he calls it stew. (His place is on the border of hash country.) Tasty vegetables and desserts, too. Dine in, order at counter. Picnic tables under shade trees.

Date visited _____ Remarks _____

Kennedy's Kitchen (246)

3357 Sandhill Rd.
Eden, Ga. 31307
912/748-6909
County: Effingham

Tue - Thu 11 a.m. - 9 p.m., Fri & Sat 11 a.m. - 10 p.m,.
From Savannah, take U.S. 80 west to Eden.
It's at the Sandhill Rd. turn-off.

Owner James Kennedy says plenty of folks try to get his sauce recipe, but he's not going to divulge it. He says it has mustard and ketchup and "a whole lot of other things so people can't figure out what's in it." His barbecued pork is made from Boston butts cooked with hickory or pecan in indoor closed pits. Also served are Brunswick stew and the usual sides, along with seafood, catfish, grits, vegetables, and desserts. Dine in.

Date visited _____ Remarks _____

Kennesaw Bar-B-Que (247)

2196 Cobb Pkwy. NW
Kennesaw, Ga. 30152
770/422-6193
County: Cobb

Mon - Thu 10:30 a.m. - 9 p.m., Fri & Sat 10:30 a.m. - 10 p.m.
From I-75 N, exit at Chastain Rd., turn left, go 3 miles; past
airport, turn left at light onto S. Main St. Go south 2/3 mile.

Kennesaw Bar-B-Que is brought to you by the same folks who peddle the pork at Bar-B-Que House in Lithia Springs, so you can expect the same superior hickory-cooked barbecue and excellent Brunswick stew. They even have "Yellow Jacket Hot Dogs," too. Dine in, order at counter, 160 seats.

Date visited _____ Remarks _____

Kirkwood Rib Shack (248)

42 Howard St. SE
Atlanta, Ga. 30317
404/373-1873
County: DeKalb

Wed - Fri 4 p.m - 12 midnight, Sat & Sun 4 p.m. - 5 a.m.
From the State Capitol, take Memorial Dr. east about
3 miles. Beyond Crim High School, turn left on Howard
St. It's two blocks on the right.

Kirkwood was an incorporated place from 1899 until 1922, when it was absorbed into Atlanta. About four decades later, the rib shack opened up. We thought you might enjoy this short local history while you enjoy the delicious short end ribs served here. The 'que is made from Boston butts cooked in an open pit. Three sauces are available: mild, regular, and hot. Dine in, order at counter, 15 seats.

Date visited _____*Remarks* _____

Knowles' Bar-B-Que (249)

206 Telfair Ave.
McRae, Ga. 31055
912/868-2946
County: Telfair

Mon - Wed 7:15 a.m. - 2:30 p.m., Thu & Fri 7:15 a.m. -
9 p.m., Sat 7:15 a.m. - 2:30 p.m.
From downtown McRae, go south on Telfair Ave.
Look for the sign.

In three large dining rooms inside an old white house in McRae, Alice and Dennis Wood serve breakfast, home-cooked lunches, and their specialty—barbecue. They make it from hams cooked with oak in an outside closed pit. Their sauce is home-made, mustard-based, and spicy. Dine in, table service. In business twenty-one years.

Date visited _____*Remarks* _____

Kregg's Pit Barbecue (250)

1401 N Jefferson St.
Albany, Ga. 31701
912/431-0799
County: Dougherty

Mon - Fri 10:30 a.m. - 7 p.m., Sat 10:30 a.m. - 4 p.m.
At the corner of N Jefferson St. (Hwy. 133) and
Seventh Ave. in north Albany.

Pork and beef are cooked in a closed pit, marinated in a red home-made sauce, and served chopped. Owner Smokey Miller's BBQ beef, by the way, is excellent. Try it and you'll probably go back for more. Also smoked chicken, burgers, hot dogs, and delicious BBQ pinto beans. Take-out only.

Date visited _____*Remarks* _____

Lawrence's Country Store (251)

796 Madison Rd.
Eatonton, Ga. 31024
706/485-7537
County: Putnam

Mon - Sat 7 a.m. - 5 p.m.
From I-20, take exit 51. Go south on U.S. 441/129 about
17 miles to Eatonton. It's on the left,
just inside the city limits.

It's not really a country store; it's a barbecue place. The business is mostly take-out, but a few seats are inside. The meat (hams) is cooked in an open pit over oak and charcoal. Baby backs are the rib of choice. Homemade spicy red sauce. No food besides barbecue.

Date visited _____*Remarks* _____

Lee & Eddie's Bar-B-Q (252)

919 Pio Nono Ave.
Macon, Ga. 31204
912/745-5959
County: Bibb

Mon - Wed 11 a.m. - 7 p.m., Thu - Sat 11 a.m. - 9 p.m.
From I-75, take exit 54 (Pierce Ave). Cross Riverside Dr.
and go south on Pierce Ave., which becomes
Pio Nono Ave., about 2 miles.

The meat at Lee & Eddie's is cooked to perfection. "It comes right off the bone, and there's no bones about it!" they say. Brunswick stew and the usual sides are served, too, and the specialty is ribs. The homemade vinegar/mustard–based sauce is available in hot or mild. Dine in, seats 20. Opened 1974.

Date visited _____*Remarks* _____

Leon's Bar B Que (253)

414 E Taylor St.
Griffin, Ga. 30223
770/228-7950
County: Spalding

Tue & Thu 10:30 a.m. - 5:30 p.m.,
Fri 10:30 a.m. - 6 p.m., Wed & Sat 10:30 a.m. - 3 p.m.
From I-75, take exit 67. Go west 10 miles on Hwy. 16.
It's on the left just before you get to downtown Griffin.

Leon's has been in business seventeen years (twelve at the present location) serving closed-pit, hickory-smoked, chopped pork with a vinegar-based sauce on the 'que or on the side. Ribs and turkey are offered, too. A popular item is the smoked turkey sandwich (with or without barbecue sauce). Sides include Brunswick stew, beans, cole slaw, chips, and fries. Leon's Piggy Pie is chocolate and pecan pie with ice cream. A brownie-like fudge pie and French silk pie are other options. Dine in, table service, 43 seats (at tables and at counter).

Date visited _____*Remarks* _____

Leon's of Chicago (next page)

Leon's of Chicago Bar-B-Que & Grill (254)

157 North Ave. NE
Atlanta, Ga. 30308
404/607-0333
County: Fulton

Mon - Fri 11:30 a.m. - 10 p.m.,
Fri & Sat noon til midnight.
At Piedmont Ave. and North Ave., across from Rio Mall.

This cinderblock-and-slapdash building provides seating on a screened porch or deck (50 or so seats total). Order at a single small window. Short but sweet menu: Ribs, rib tips, chopped pork, chicken, wings, fries, slaw, potato salad. The pork is some of the best in town. A slab of ribs costs $14.00; a pitcher of beer $4.50. Leon Finney Sr. moved to Chicago from Yazoo City, Miss in the 1930s and opened the first of his Chicago places in 1942. This location opened in 1996.

Date visited _____*Remarks* _____

Lil' Mama's Bar-B-Q (255)

601 North Blvd.
Baxley, Ga. 31513
912/367-3333
County: Appling

Wed 10 a.m. - 7 p.m., Thu 10 a.m. - 8 p.m.,
Fri & Sat 10 a.m. - 9 p.m.
From the courthouse in Baxley, go north on U.S. 1.
It's across from Dairy Queen.

Owner Carlos Rooks' named his place for his grandmother, who was affectionately known as "Lil Mama." He cooks butts with oak on a closed grill. His sauce is red, vinegar-based, and spicy or regular. Other items include veggies, wings, and pork chops. It's take-out only, but up to eight people can eat on the porch.

Date visited _____*Remarks* _____

Lloyd's True Southern Bar-B-Q (256)

P.O. Box 362
Manchester, Ga. 31816
706/846-8234
County: Meriwether

Tue 11 a.m. - 7 p.m.; Wed - Sat 11 a.m. - 8 p.m.
At U.S. 27/GA 41 (Fifth Avenue) and
Main Street in downtown Manchester.

Ample portions of smoke-flavored pork and excellently prepared sides are served in this cozy little building. Lloyd's cooks hams and butts in a smoker. In addition to the usual sides, the menu includes okra and corn fritters. Among the desserts are banana pudding and bread pudding. Dine in, order at counter, 16 seats. Opened 1989.

Date visited _____*Remarks* _____

Log Cabin BBQ (257)

36 Hwy. 11
Social Circle, Ga. 30279
770/786-0912
County: Newton

Mon - Thu 11 a.m. - 8 p.m., Fri & Sat 11 a.m. - 9 p.m.
From I-20, take exit 47.
Go south on Hwy. 11 a half mile. It's on the left.

Pit-cooked pork and baby back ribs are the chief barbecue items on the extensive menu at this country-cooking establishment. The sauce is brown and vinegar-based; a honey-mustard sauce is also available. Many non-BBQ meats. Dine in, table service, 140 seats.

Date visited _____*Remarks* _____

Log Cabin Barbeque (258)

2184 Kingston Rd.
Rome, Ga. 30161
706/235-3242
County: Floyd

Mon - Sat 10 a.m. - 7 p.m.
From downtown Rome, go north on Broad St., turn right
on Calhoun Ave., then right again onto Kingston Rd.

Boneless hams are cooked in a hickory-fired closed pit and sliced to make some fine barbecue at this little log building on the east side of Rome. A sweet and tangy homemade ketchup-based sauce is added to the meat. Brunswick stew, the standard sides, and vegetables are served, too. Cake for dessert. Dine in.

Date visited _____*Remarks* _____

Luella Junction BBQ (259)

3200 Hwy. 155 S
Locust Grove, Ga. 30248
770/957-5496
County: Henry

Tue - Sat 11 a.m. - 7 p.m., Fri & Sat 11 a.m. - 8 p.m.
From I-75, take exit 69, and go southwest 4 miles to the
little community of Luella.

A quirky century-old building standing close by the highway houses Frenchie DeBald's barbecue emporium. Framed articles on local history, motorcycle stuff, and Vietnam War memorabilia decorate the walls. Hickory-smoked hams cooked in Frenchie's closed pit are the basis for his barbecue, along with a tangy tomato/vinegar/pepper sauce. Besides pork, ribs, Brunswick stew, and the usual sides, Frenchie serves hot dogs, hamburgers, club and sub sandwiches. Desserts are available occasionally. Try the chocolate cake if he has it. Dine in, order at counter, 48 seats. Since 1967.

Date visited _____*Remarks* _____

Luella Junction, Locust Grove

Lynn & Bob's Bar-B-Q Place (260)

303 Coleman St.
Swainsboro, Ga. 30401
912/237-2064
County: Emanuel

Mon - Thu 11 a.m. - 9 p.m., Fri & Sat 11 a.m. - 10 p.m.,
Sun 11 a.m. - 3 p.m.
From I-16, take exit 21, go north 14 miles to Swainsboro.
Turn right on Short St. It's at Short and Coleman.

It used to be a hole-in-the-wall; now it has 300 seats. A profusion of antiques dec-
orates the walls in this roomy place; there's also a game room with pool tables.
A big buffet forms the main attraction. As for barbecue, they cook hams in an
open pit with oak, and the Brunswick stew is made according to an old family
recipe from way back. For dessert, there are homemade cakes, cobblers, and
puddings. Drive-thru too.

Date visited _____ *Remarks* _____

Bar-B-Fact

Spruce's Bar-B-Q in Griffin opened in 1938, the year
Savannah's Johnny Mercer wrote
"You Must Have Been a Beautiful Baby."

Mack's Bar-Be-Que Place (261)

2809 Glynn Avenue (U.S. 17)
Brunswick, Ga. 31520
912/264-0605
County: Glynn

Mon - Sat 10:30 a.m. - 9:00 p.m.
On U.S. 17 between Torras Causeway (the road to St.
Simons Island) and Parkwood Dr.
Next to Jinright's Seafood House.

It doesn't look like a barbecue place, but the sweet aroma that greets you as you
enter says otherwise. The meats are wood-cooked in a closed pit, then served
chopped or sliced. You can also choose "inside" or "outside" meat. Lemonade
pie and cheesecake for dessert. Dine in, table service, 75 seats. Choice of tables,
booths, or counter stools. Opened 1990.

Date visited _____ *Remarks* _____

Macon Road Barbeque (262)

2703 Avalon Rd.
Columbus, Ga. 31907
706/563-0542
County: Muscogee

Mon - Sat 10 a.m. - 8 p.m.
From I-185, take exit 4 (Macon Rd.), and go east, away
from downtown. Turn right on Avalon Rd.

Although it's now on Avalon Road, this place continues to serve open-pit, all-
wood-cooked barbecue as it has done for over twenty-five years. You can often
smell it cooking before you get there. The homemade ketchup/mustard–based
sauce is very mild.

Date visited _____ *Remarks* _____

Mac's Bar-B-Q (263)

Spring St.
Warm Springs, Ga. 31830
706/655-2472
County: Meriwether

Mon - Sun 11 a.m. - 8 p.m.
On Hwy. 41 (Main St.) at Spring St. on south side
of downtown Warm Springs.

"Best barbecue in the region" is the claim at Mac's. Owner Mac Davis comes from a family of barbecue masters. He has relatives who own barbecue places in Tupelo, Mississippi, and Dadesville, Alabama. Mac himself has two places, this one and another in Pine Mountain. The secret-recipe red sauce is spicy and tangy; it comes in mild, medium, and hot. Cakes and pies for dessert. Dine in, table service, or order at counter. Plenty of tables inside, on a porch, and in the yard.

Date visited _____ Remarks _____

Mac's Bar-B-Q (264)

Atlanta Hwy. (U.S. 27)
Pine Mountain, Ga. 31822
706/663-8423
County: Harris

Mon - Thu 11 a.m. - 8 p.m.,
Fri & Sat 11 a.m. - 9 p.m., Sun 11 a.m. - 6 p.m.
In downtown Pine Mountain on west side of U.S. 27.

Mac's other location. Dine in, order at counter, 20 seats inside, 12 outside. Drive-thru too.

Date visited _____ Remarks _____

Mac's Barbecue (265)

8723 Ford Ave.
Richmond Hill, Ga. 31324
912/756-6555
County: Bryan

Tue - Sat 11 a.m. - 9 p.m.
From I-95 take exit 15; go north on U.S. 17 to Ford Ave.

How many Ford vehicles travel on I-95 each day? Richmond Hill is a good place to take a break from the road and ponder such questions. Henry Ford himself had a home nearby, and his ghost might whisper the answer while you're dining on brain food such as Boston butts and spare ribs pit-cooked over oak and hickory. Thin, tangy tomato/vinegar sauce. Dine in, table service, 60 seats.

Date visited _____ Remarks _____

Bar-B-Quote

"If bacon is the object desired, it is well to select the large and heavy variety [of hog]. If pork is the thing desired, choose the smaller varieties, such as arrive with greatest rapidity at maturity and are likely to produce the most delicate flesh."
—Georgia Department of Agriculture, 1901

> *"For if the love of barbecue is universal, its variations seem endless. The meat roasting above hardwood coals in one state may be a far cry from what's cooking in the next. Because from state to state, and even from one town to the next, barbecue is an incomparable, ever-changing combination of meats, sauces, and side dishes."*
>
> *—Gary D. Ford, "The South Burns for Barbecue,"*
> *Southern Living, May 1992*

Name/Map ID   **Hours/Directions**

Mad Dog's Legendary BBQ (266)

4489 Hwy. 20 S, Suite 2
Conyers, Ga. 30208
770/922-2272
County: Rockdale

Tue - Thu 11 a.m. - 8 p.m.,
Fri 11 a.m. - 9 p.m., Sat 12 p.m. - 9 p.m.
From I-20, take exit 42. Go south 6 miles on Hwy. 20 to
Winn-Dixie shopping center. It's on the south end.

Before opening this place in late 1996, Jerry and Pat Walker were in the catering business for a couple of years. "Mad Dog" is Jerry's nickname from his junior high school days. (Pat says he's bad, but not mad.) They serve pulled pork, sliced beef, and chopped chicken sandwiches. They make their pulled pork from Boston butts cooked with hickory in a closed pit. Try the St. Louis–style ribs. Sides are beans, slaw, chips, and pickles. For dessert there's lemon meringue pie. Dine in, order at counter, 20 seats.

Date visited _____ *Remarks* _____

Molden Tillman's
(See page 110)

Mary's Flying Pig

Name/Map ID   **Hours/Directions**

Mary's Flying Pig (267)

3087 Peachtree Industrial Blvd.   *Mon - Thu 5:30 a.m. - 9 p.m., Fri 5:30 a.m. - 10 p.m.,*
Buford, Ga. 30518   *Sat 6:30 a.m. - 10 p.m., Sun 6:30 a.m. - 9 p.m.*
770/932-1329   *On Peachtree Ind./McEver Rd. at Holiday Rd. (Ga. 347).*
County: Hall

Painted to look like a bus full of cartoon-character pigs, Mary's Flying Pig was designed by Garland Reynolds, architect for the Civic Center MARTA station and the Savannah Hyatt Hotel. The shredded pork sandwich is served on a big seeded bun. Mary's tomato-based sauce is semi-sweet and a little smoky; it's available in mild, medium, or hot. Besides the usual sides, Mary offers seasoned fries, corn on the cob, and sweet potato logs. For dessert, there's pie of the day. Order at window. Outside seating only at four concrete picnic tables.

Date visited _____*Remarks* _____

Mathis Bros. Bar-B-Q (268)

873 Barnetts Bridge Rd.   *Thu 11 a.m. - 8 p.m., Fri & Sat 11a.m. - 9 p.m.*
Jackson, Ga. 30233   *From Jackson, take Hwy. 36 toward Covington. After*
770/775-6562   *crossing RR, bear right onto Stark Rd. Go 4 miles, turn*
County: Butts   *left on Barnetts Bridge Rd. It's on the right.*

Although not as well known as the venerable Fresh Air Bar-B-Q a few miles away, Mathis Brothers can claim two decades in business. They cook hams and ribs in an open pit, and beef and turkey in a closed pit. The sauce is tomato-based and comes in hot and mild. Brunswick stew and chili are both home-made. Hot dogs and burgers served, too. Pecan pie for dessert. Dine in, order at counter, 50 seats. Drive-thru.

Date visited _____*Remarks* _____

Max's Bar-B-Que Place (269)

102 S First St.
Warner Robins, Ga. 31099
912/922-3595
County: Houston

Mon - Wed 11 a.m. - 8 p.m.,
Thu & Fri 11 a.m. - 9 p.m., Sat 11 a.m. - 8 p.m.
At Hwy. 247 Conn. (Watson Blvd.) and U.S. 129 (First
Street), across from Warner Robins AFB main entrance.

One of middle Georgia's favorite BBQ places in an October 1996 *Macon Telegraph* poll, Max's has been open a little over three years. Formerly A.B.'s, it serves hickory-smoked chopped pork with a tomato/mustard–based sauce. Brunswick stew, beans, cole slaw, fries, rings, corn nuggets, potato salad, and tossed salad are the sides. Also available are fried chicken, catfish, and other items. (The turkey salad sandwich is especially popular.) Dine in, order at counter, 84 seats, nonsmokers' section. Drive thru.

Date visited _____*Remarks* _____

McGhin's Southern Pit Bar-B-Que (270)

2964 North Expressway
Griffin, Ga. 30223
770/229-5887
County: Spalding

Wed - Thu 11 a.m. - 8 p.m., Fri & Sat 11 a.m. - 9 p.m.
On U.S. 41/19, about 4 miles north of Griffin and just
south of Birdie Road.

Griffin's discount textile outlets attract shoppers from far and wide, but an even better reason to drive to this thriving little city is barbecue. One of the best of several excellent places in town is McGhin's. Tomato-vinegar-mustard hot sauce and a mild sauce are served on the side. Among the sides is cracklin' cornbread. No beer, but you can get buttermilk. Chicken and ribs available Friday and Saturday nights only. Dine in, table service, 195 seats. Banquet room. Voted best barbecue place in *Macon Telegraph* readers' poll, 1996.

Date visited _____*Remarks* _____

McGhin's Southern Pit Bar-B-Que (271)

716 Hwy. 155 S
McDonough, Ga. 30253
770/957-8222
County: Henry

Wed - Thu 11 a.m. - 8 p.m., Fri & Sat 11 a.m. - 9 p.m.
From I-75, take exit 69, turn left, go under bridge; it's 200
yards on the left.

Same menu as the Griffin location. Same motto: "When I get hungry, I throw a fit if I can't eat at Southern Pit." Dine in, table service, 150 seats. Owners: Sharon and Earl Smith. Opened 1995.

Date visited _____*Remarks* _____

Bar-B-Fact

Brinson's Bar-B-Que near Millen opened in 1966, the year Macon's Otis Redding released his album "The Otis Redding Dictionary of Soul."

McNeal's Bar B Q (272)

1600 Broomtown Rd.
LaFayette, Ga. 30728
706/638-6555
County: Walker

Mon - Fri 8:30 a.m. - 8 p.m.
From the city square, go south to traffic light at Family
Dollar and turn right. At second light, turn left. Go 2
miles. It's on the left, across from S&S Groc.

McNeal's is housed in a small plain building seating about 20 at four tables and five or six stools. The barbecue is cooked out back on a "grill." The sauce is red, and (surprise, surprise) the ingredients are secret.

Date visited _____ *Remarks* _____

Melear's Barbecue (273)

6701 Roosevelt Hwy.
Union City, Ga. 30291
770/964-9933
County: Fulton

Mon - Thu 6 a.m. - 9 p.m.,
Fri & Sat 6 a.m. - 10 p.m., Sun 7 a.m. - 9 p.m.
Between Union City and Fairburn. From I-85, take exit 13.
Go west on Hwy. 138 and north on U.S. 29. It's on the left.

Fifty-year-old Melear's Barbecue has long served BBQ pork and beef. They added chicken and ribs as regular menu items recently. The pork plate comes with finely chopped meat, Brunswick stew, and sides on a school-lunch-like platter. Order a regular plate and, if you want more, you can upgrade to an all-you-can-eat plate. A nice deal, one which should be imitated by others. Impressive collection of commemorative plates displayed in the dining room. Friendly staff. Dine in, table service, 100 seats, nonsmokers' section.

Date visited _____ *Remarks* _____

Melear's Barbecue (274)

Hwy. 85
Fayetteville, Ga. 30214
770/461-7180
County: Fayette

Mon - Thu 6 a.m. - 9 p.m., Fri & Sat 6 a.m. - 10 p.m.
From the old courthouse in Fayetteville, go south on
Hwy 85. It's about four blocks, on the left.

"Good food since 1957." Melear's in Fayetteville serves barbecue sandwiches, platters, Brunswick stew, and the standard sides. For dessert, Edwards pies are available. Dine in, table service, plenty of seats. Banquet room available. Open for breakfast too.

Date visited _____ *Remarks* _____

Melear's Barbecue (275)

9 Ellis St.
Newnan, Ga. 30263
770/253-2726
County: Coweta

Mon - Wed 5 a.m. - 1:45 p.m, Thu - Sat 5 a.m. - 6 p.m.
From I-85 southbound, take exit 9, turn right, go 4 miles
to Hwy 16. Turn left onto Ellis St. It's on the right.

Melear's in Newnan has been in business fifty-four years. Meats are cooked in a closed pit with hickory. The barbecue sauce is red and spicy. The standard sides are joined by corn, peas, limas, okra, and green beans. Fried chicken, steaks, and meatloaf, too. Dine in, table service.

Date visited _____ *Remarks* _____

Michael's Gillionville Bar-B-Que (276)

2319 Gillionville Rd.
Albany, Ga. 31707
912/435-6199
County: Dougherty

Mon - Sat 11 a.m. - 8 p.m.
From Slappey Blvd. (U.S. 19/82 Bus.), just south of the
Dawson Rd. intersection, go west on Gillionville Rd.

Slow-cooking in an old-fashioned wood-burning cooker can turn out some mighty fine barbecue. Mel, the owner, loves to cook; he used to do it as a hobby. Be sure to try his pork ribs. No dog ever enjoyed a bone the way you will enjoy these. Drive-thru only.

Date visited _____*Remarks* _____

Michael's Original Bar-B-Que (277)

1607 Hwy. 19 S
Leesburg, Ga. 31763
912/436-9390
County: Lee

Mon - Fri 10:30 a.m. - 8:30 p.m.
From Albany, take U.S. 19 north toward Leesburg.
Michael's is on the left, about two miles south of town.

Country decor (checkered table cloths, old signs on the walls, and other Cracker Barrel–esque touches) makes Michael's a comfy place to stop. Hams are cooked with red oak in a cooker/grill. The sauce, served on the side, is mild, sweet, thick, and red. Vegetables and several non-BBQ meats are also available. For dessert, try the blackberry cobbler. Dine in, order at counter, 52 seats.

Date visited _____*Remarks* _____

Mickey Pigg's Bar-B-Que (278)

Hwy. 365
Alto, Ga. 30510
706/776-2267
County: Habersham

Sun & Wed 11 a.m. - 3 p.m., Thu, Fri & Sat 11 a.m. - 8 p.m.
From Gainesville, go north about 17 miles on Hwy. 365/23.
It's on the right in a small shopping center.

This little establishment has changed hands or names once or twice in the past few years, but they still lure mountain-bound travelers off the highway for baby back ribs and tender, smoky pork sandwiches. The pork is made from hams smoked over hickory wood. Freshly baked desserts. Dine in, order at counter.

Date visited _____*Remarks* _____

Mike & Ed's Bar-B-Que (279)

3930 Veterans Pkwy.
Columbus, Ga. 31904
706/323-8676
County: Muscogee

Mon - Sat 10:30 a.m. - 9 p.m.
From J.R. Allen Pkwy. (U.S. 80, the north bypass), exit at
Bradley Park Dr. Go east one mile. Turn right on
Whitesville Rd., go to Veterans Pkwy. It's on the left.

The name of this long-established place was changed from Hamilton Road Bar-B-Q in 1997. Mike and Ed cook hams, Boston butts, and pork shoulders in an open pit with hickory. Their mustard-based sauce is a bit hot. Also on the menu are Brunswick stew, beans, cole slaw, fries, potato salad, non-BBQ meats, and desserts. Dine in, 100 seats.

Date visited _____*Remarks* _____

Miller Brothers Rib Shack (280)

606 E Morris St.
Dalton, Ga. 30721
706/278-7365
County: Whitfield

Tue & Wed 11 a.m. - 7 p.m., Thu - Sat 11 a.m. - 9 p.m.
From I-75, take exit 136, go east. Turn left on Glenwood
Ave. Turn right on E. Morris. Pass two lights.
It's over the hill, on the right.

Miller Brothers uses only top quality meats and pit-cooks and hickory-smokes them daily. You can buy the fruits of their labor by the dinner, sandwich, or pound. The meats are cooked in a closed pit and served sliced, with a mustard-based sauce. Brunswick stew, beans, cole slaw, potato wedges, potato salad, and corn on the cob are on the side. Also catfish, Buffalo wings, wieners. Sweet potato pie is sometimes the dessert of the day. Dine in, 25 seats. Opened 1982. (No beer at this location.)

Date visited _____Remarks _____

Miller Brothers Rib Shack (281)

2103 Chattanooga Rd.
Dalton, Ga. 30720
706/278-8510
County: Whitfield

Tue & Wed 11 a.m. - 9 p.m., Thu - Sat 11 a.m. - 10:30 p.m.
From I-75, take exit 137, go east/south toward Dalton.
It's not far from the exit, on the left.

The menu at Miller Brothers' Chattanooga Road location is pretty much the same as described above. Beer is served here, but not at the Morris Street location. Dine in, table service, seats 80. Opened 1984.

Date visited _____Remarks _____

Miss Mary's Kitchen (282)

U.S. 221 S
Mount Vernon, Ga. 30445
912/583-4306
County: Montgomery

Mon - Sat 6:30 a.m. - 9 p.m., Sun 8 a.m. - 2 p.m.
From Soperton, go south 14 miles on Hwy. 221 to Mount
Vernon. It's at the courthouse square.

Miss Mary Woods' place has been open a couple of years. A smoker outside always seems to be operating. Boston butts and beef rumps are cooked with pecan wood in a smoker. The sauce is homemade, thick, and smoky, and described best as a Texas-style red sauce. Homemade cakes and pies are for dessert. Farm implements given to Miss Mary decorate the walls. She says if her customers bring it in, she'll hang it up. Breakfast anytime. Dine in.

Date visited _____Remarks _____

Bar-B-Fact

Richardson's Pit Bar-B-Que in Iron City opened in 1968, the year the Allman Brothers Band was formed in Macon, Georgia.

Moldin Tillman's (283)

Hwy. 11
Hillsboro, Ga. 31038
706/468-6536
County: Jasper

Fri & Sat 9 a.m. - 9 p.m. Open April - December only.
From Monticello, take Hwy. 11 south 10 miles to
Hillsboro. It's behind a white house on the left.

This out-of-the-way establishment was selected as one of middle Georgia's favorite BBQ places in a recent *Macon Telegraph* poll. Railroad crews rate it highly too; engineers used to stop their trains to get Tillman's barbecue. On the tables are saltines and loaves of white bread. Slim Jims and pickled sausages are on the counter. Tillman's barbecue smokers, fired with pecan, hickory, and oak, are made out of old dairy equipment. Eat here or take-out (whether or not you come by train).

Date visited _____*Remarks* _____

Bar-B-Fact

The Pig, in Waycross, opened in 1947, the year Jackie Robinson,
a young man from Cairo, Georgia, broke the color barrier to
become the first African-American to play major league baseball.

Mountain Man Barbeque (284)

5506 Atlanta Hwy.
Flowery Branch, Ga. 30542
770/967-2424
County: Hall

Mon - Sun 7 a.m. - 7 p.m.
On east side of the tracks in downtown, across from the
Amoco convenience store. From I-985, take Spout Springs
Rd. (exit 3) one mile west to Flowery Branch.

The core of this rambling, ramshackle place is an old school bus. Eat at picnic tables under a wide front porch cluttered with antiques, curios, signs, and junk. The pork, cooked in a closed brick pit, is available by the sandwich, plate, or by the pound. For dessert, there's banana pudding. Mountain Man also sells fresh produce, hot boiled peanuts, and bait.

Date visited _____*Remarks* _____

Mountain Man Barbeque (285)

U.S. 441
Dillard, Ga. 30537
706/746-5646
County: Rabun

Mon 11 a.m. - 7 p.m., Wed & Thu 11 a.m. - 7 p.m.,
Fri & Sat 11 a.m. - 8 p.m.
From Gainesville, take Hwy. 23/365 to Hwy. 441. Continue
north on 441 to Dillard. It's just past town on the left.

This little place is usually overlooked by the crowds headed to the far better-known Dillard House restaurant, but it's definitely worth a visit. The pork is properly smoked and there's a good selection of sides. Although seating several hundred fewer patrons than the more famous place down the road, MMB can accommodate 20 or so.

Date visited _____*Remarks* _____

Mr. B's Hickory House Restaurant (286)

4318 Waters Ave.
Savannah, Ga. 31404
912/354-2122
County: Chatham

Mon - Sat 6 a.m. - 8:30 p.m., Sun 7:30 a.m. - 3 p.m.
From I-16, take exit 34. Go south on I-516, continue
straight on DeRenne Ave. Turn left on Waters Ave.
It's on the right.

Mr. B's barbecue is made "the old way," from Boston butts cooked with hickory in an open pit. Besides pork, beef, and chicken, barbecued turkey is available, too. Mr. B. offers a mild red sauce and a mild tomato/mustard sauce. Daily specials. Also soups, salads, sandwiches, seafood. Dine in. Banquet room. "Since 1968."

Date visited_____Remarks_____

Mr. J's Steak, Potato, and Barbecue (287)

187 N Macon St.
Jesup, Ga. 31545
912/530-9228
County: Wayne

Mon - Sat 10 a.m. - 8 p.m.
From the Welcome Center caboose in downtown Jesup, go
west across the tracks, go to the first traffic light, turn
right. It's at the second corner on the left.

Two of life's greatest pleasures, riding trains and eating barbecue, are available in downtown Jesup. Amtrak has a station here, and Mr. J's sells barbecue a couple of blocks away. It's a walk-up and drive-thru-only place, but there are two picnic tables outside. Hams, butts, and shoulders are cooked in a smoker with oak. The sauce is tomato-based Cattleman's, but Ollie's mustard-based sauce is available by request. (Be careful; Ollie's has a "bite.")

Date visited_____Remarks_____

Mr. Soul Real Pit Bar-B-Q (288)

2292 Fairburn Rd. SW
Atlanta, Ga. 30331
404/629-0656
County: Fulton

Thu - Sat 10 a.m. - 9 p.m.
From I-285 at Hwy. 166 in southwest Atlanta, go west on
166 to Fairburn Rd. Turn left; it's on the right.

Mr. Soul's take-out shack sells closed-pit-cooked, hickory-smoked meats complemented by an excellent, made-from-scratch barbecue sauce. Brunswick stew is available occasionally. Besides barbecue, Mr. Soul has pork chops, wings, steaks, fish, hot dogs, fresh yams, collards, mac-and-cheese, and cole slaw. Take-out only.

Date visited_____Remarks_____

Mt. View BBQ Restaurant & Trout Pond (289)

15520 Hwy. 19 N
Cleveland, Ga. 30528
706/865-3877
County: White

Fri 5 a.m. - 8:30 p.m., Sat 8 a.m. - 8:30 p.m.,
Sun 8 a.m. - 4 p.m.
On U.S. 129 12 miles north of Cleveland.

Voted North Georgia's Best BBQ in an area newspaper survey, Mt. View serves New Orleans-style ribs, trout smoked with apple wood, and pork tenderloin. Locally grown vegetables are available in season. Dine in, table service, seats 60, both indoors and outside.

Date visited_____Remarks_____

Nancy Hart Bar-B-Q

Name/Map ID	Hours/Directions

Nancy Hart Bar-B-Q. (290)

Hwy. 77 S
Hartwell, Ga. 30643
706/376-2523
County: Hart

Thu - Sat 11 a.m. - 9 p.m.
Located in the fork of Hwy. 77 S and Nancy Hart Rd.,
4 miles south of Hartwell.

Open-pit-cooked, hickory-smoked pork and grilled chicken are the main attractions at Nancy Hart Bar-B-Q. The tomato/vinegar–based sauce is served on the side. Brunswick stew, beans, and slaw on the side. Dine in or carry out. Opened 1993.

Date visited _____ *Remarks* _____

Nankipooh Bar-B-Que (291)

7519 Fortson Rd.
Columbus, Ga. 31909
706/327-0499
County: Muscogee

Tue - Sat 11 a.m. - 6 p.m.
From Columbus, take U.S. 27 north. Just past J.R. Allen
Pkwy., turn left at Burger King, cross the tracks, take an
immediate right. It's on the left.

Nankipooh used to be a little town, but it was swallowed up by Columbus. The name survives, however, at Larry Bell's barbecue house. Opened in 1994, it serves prime pig meat slow-cooked on an open pit with love and care by Larry himself. Larry has a special mild tomato-based sauce and a hot mustard-based sauce. Ribs by the full slab or half-slab. Desserts: cakes, pies, and peanut brittle. Dine in, order at counter, 60 seats.

Date visited _____ *Remarks* _____

Neal's Bar-B-Q (292)

U.S. Hwy. 278
Thomson, Ga. 30824
706/595-2594
County: McDuffie

Thu 10 a.m. - 8 p.m., Fri 7 a.m. - 11 p.m., Sat 7 a.m. - 6 p.m.
From I-20, take exit 59. Go south about three miles through
downtown Thomson. Turn left onto U.S. 278. It's about a mile
on the left. Look for a trailer with log siding.

Whole hogs cooked over oak coals in an open pit, hash, and barbecue rice—that's Neal's. The sauce recipe is not only patented, it's also not for sale. A competitor once won a barbecue cook-off while surreptitiously using Neal's sauce, attracting the attention of a food company that sought to buy his winning formula. He was "left with sauce on his face" when he had to admit that it wasn't really his own. As for the Neals, they refused to sell at any price. Dine in, 50 seats.

Date visited _____ *Remarks* _____

Newby-Q (293)

Magnolia St.
Jeffersonville, Ga. 31044
912/945-6470
County: Twiggs

Mon - Thu 7 a.m. - 8 p.m., Fri & Sat 7 a.m. - 9 p.m.
Behind the courthouse in downtown Jeffersonville.

Mayor W. Bradley Newby, who has been smoking meat for thirty years, recently opened this little restaurant. His thin tangy red sauce is made with a bit of mustard, Worcestershire sauce, and red and black pepper. Ribs available on weekends. Newby-Q stew is made with pork roast, a little sweet corn, and a few peas, according to an old family recipe. Dine in, table service, 45 seats.

Date visited _____ *Remarks* _____

O.B.'s Real Pit Out-N-Back BBQ (294)

725 Industrial Blvd.
McDonough, Ga. 30253
770/954-1234
County: Henry

Mon - Sat 11 a.m. - 9 p.m.
From I-75, take exit 70, go east one block, turn right. It's
past McDonald's, on the right.

At O.B.'s the meat is cooked in a closed pit over hickory wood. "No liquid smoke, no pellets, no par-boiling, no pressure cooking," says O.B. He encourages guests to visit the real pits out back. The rustic, roomy building has seating for 164 at tables and booths with table service and a nonsmokers' area.

Date visited _____ *Remarks* _____

Old Brick Pit

O.K.'s Bar-B-Que & Family Restaurant (295)

581 N Main St.
Hiawassee, Ga. 30546
706/896-2238
County: Towns

Tue - Thu 7 a.m. - 11 p.m., Fri & Sat 7 a.m. - midnight,
Sun 11 a.m. - 4 p.m.
On Hwy. 76 on the west side of Hiawassee.

Becky and Donald Woodard have owned this place since 1988, but it has been in the family since 1965. The select pork ribs are a good choice here. The sauce is a sweet ketchup and mustard mix; it's a little tangy. Also: Brunswick stew, homemade cole slaw, fries, potato salad, homemade onion rings, vegetables, hamburgers, hot dogs, chicken strips, sandwiches. Desserts: homemade pies and cobblers, cheesecake. Dine in, table service and order at counter, 100 seats, nonsmokers' area. Drive-thru.

Date visited _____*Remarks* _____

Oga's Hickory Barbecue (296)

1527 Northside Dr. NW
Atlanta, Ga. 30318
404/351-3064
County: Fulton

Mon - Fri 10:30 a.m. - 9 p.m.,
Sat 10:30 a.m. - 2:30 p.m.
From I-75, exit at Northside Drive. Go south a half-mile.
Oga's is on the left.

Oga cooks Boston butts and shoulders in a smoker using hickory and oak and adds a thick, sweet ketchup-based sauce. She serves a tangy Brunswick stew, a wide selection of fresh Southern-style vegetables, barbecue salads, and other sides. The desserts — banana pudding, pecan pie, and fruit cobblers — finish off a meal at Oga's quite nicely. Dine in, table service, 80 seats.

Date visited _____*Remarks* _____

O'Kelley's Barbeque (297)

1501 N. Cherokee Rd.
Social Circle, Ga. 30279
770/464-2424
County: Walton

Tue - Thu 8 a.m. - 3 p.m.,
Fri & Sat 8 a.m. - 3 p.m. & 5 p.m. - 9 p.m.
From I-20, take exit 47. Go north on Hwy. 11 about
7 miles. It's on the left.

Social Circle was named when an early traveler found a group of other frontiersmen gathered around a campfire. Form your own social circle at this place and enjoy some of the best barbecue and fixings around, as well as burgers, seafood, and fresh vegetables. Dine in, table service or order at counter, 60 seats.

Date visited _____*Remarks* _____

Bar-B-Fact

Salt pork was a primary food served to both the
Confederate and Union troops during the
War Between the States.

Old Brick Pit Barbeque (298)

4805 Peachtree Rd.
Chamblee, Ga. 30341
770/457-6083
County: DeKalb

Mon - Sat 11 a.m. - 8 p.m.
From I-285, exit at Peachtree Industrial Blvd., go south 3
miles. It's on the left, past the Frito-Lay plant.

Old-fashioned closed-pit hickory-smoked BBQ is sold out of this one-time Dairy Queen with its brick pits right behind the counter. This is the place for strong tangy, hickory-smoky flavors. The stew is thin, brown, and meat-challenged, but is delicious, nonetheless. Ribs are served dry along with a cup of the thin, zesty sauce. (It's better than the table sauce.) Like the pork, they have the fine taste of smoke, vinegar, and pepper. Whole smoked hogs available at $80. Dine in, order at counter, seats 40. All nonsmoking. Since 1976.

Date visited _____Remarks _____

Old Clinton

Old Clinton Bar-B-Q (299)

Route 6, Box 155
Gray, Ga. 31032
912/986-3225
County: Jones

Sun - Thu 10 a.m. - 7 p.m., Fri - Sat 10 a.m. - 8 p.m.
From I-16 in Macon, take exit 2, go 11 miles north on
U.S. 129. It's on the right, 2 miles south of Gray.

Owners Wayne and Betty Coulter claim that their BBQ is the best in Georgia and they just might be right. The tender and smoky chopped pork is excellent. The barbecue plate comes with chopped pork, stew, slaw, and a choice of white or rye bread. The sauce is thin, vinegary, peppery, and delicious. Also ribs, BBQ turkey, beans, fries, chips, pickles, turkey sandwiches. Smoked chicken on Fri. & Sat. The place seats about 50 inside and there's room for more at picnic tables under the front porch. Opened 1958.

Date visited _____Remarks _____

Old Hickory Barbeque (300)

499 Bankhead Hwy. SW
Mableton, Ga. 30059
770/948-9451
County: Cobb

Mon - Thu 11 a.m. - 9 p.m., Fri & Sat 11 a.m. - 10 p.m.
From I-285, exit at Bankhead Hwy. Go west
about 5 miles. It's on the left.

With over three decades in business at this location, Old Hickory is a local institution of the highest order. Shoulders are cooked with hickory in a closed pit. The sauce is a vinegar and mustard mix. Baby back ribs are served wet or dry. Also steaks, marinated grilled chicken, sandwiches, salads. Apple or pecan pie. Also lemon meringue pie. Dine in, table service, 80 seats.

Date visited _____ *Remarks* _____

Old Hickory House (301)

5490 Chamblee-Dunwoody Rd.
Dunwoody, Ga. 30338
770/671-8185
County: DeKalb

Mon - Sat 7 a.m. - 9 p.m., Sun 8 a.m. - 9 p.m.
On Chamblee-Dunwoody Rd. 2 miles outside I-285 and a
block north of Mt. Vernon Rd. Across the street
from Dunwoody Village.

Old Hickory House is a long-time Atlanta-area favorite. The numbers and locations of OHH have changed over the years, but not the food. The smoky, tangy pork sandwiches are still some of the best in the city. Baby back ribs, Brunswick stew, corn on the cob, and spicy hickory-pit baked beans are also winners. Try the dressed dog smothered in Brunswick stew or chili. Also vegetables, salads, sandwiches, and desserts.

Date visited _____ *Remarks* _____

Old Hickory House (302)

2202 Northlake Pkwy.
Tucker, Ga. 30084
770/939-8621
County: DeKalb

Mon - Thu 7 a.m. - 9 p.m.
Fri & Sat 7 a.m. - 10 p.m., Sun 8 a.m. - 9 p.m.
From I-285 in the NE metro area, exit at LaVista Rd. Go
east to first traffic light. Turn left. It's on the left

Old Hickory House's Northlake location serves the same tasty barbecue and sides as the others.

Date visited _____ *Remarks* _____

Old Hickory House/Jilly's (303)

5750 Roswell Rd. NW
Atlanta, Ga. 30342
404/252-5770
County: Fulton

OHH: Mon - Sun 11 a.m. - 10 p.m.
Jilly's: Mon - Sun 5 p.m. - 10 p.m.
On Roswell Rd. (U.S. 19), just inside I-285 at exit 17
In the Days Inn Motel

Two of Atlanta's favorite smoked-meat places have combined into one. Jilly's, a well-known rib house, is now allied with the Old Hickory Houses at Roswell Road and Cobb Parkway. Items from the Jilly's menu are served after 5:00 each day. Items from the OHH menu continue to be served all day long. Also steaks, chicken, and seafood. Dine in, table service, 75 seats.

Date visited _____ *Remarks* _____

Bar-B-Quote

"Pork, sausage, spareribs, backbone, bacon, and ham are among the most highly esteemed articles of diet in the lowly huts of the poor and the lordly mansions of the rich."
—Georgia Department of Agriculture, 1901

Name/Map ID   **Hours/Directions**

Old Hickory House/Jilly's (304)

2655 Cobb Pkwy. NW
Smyrna, Ga. 30080
770/952-7437 or 770/952-2231
County: Cobb

Mon - Fri 6:30 a.m. - 9:30 p.m.,
Sat & Sun 7 a.m. - 9:30 p.m.
From Cumberland Mall, go north on Cobb Pkwy.
(U.S. 41). It's just past I-285, on the right.

The Old Hickory House on Cobb Parkway serves the same menu items found at all other OHH locations, as well as Jilly's food after 5:00.

Date visited_____Remarks _____

Old McDonald's Real Pit Bar-B-Que (305)

5774 Holiday Rd.
Buford, Ga. 30518
770/945-8608
County: Hall

Tue 11 a.m. - 3 p.m., Wed - Fri 11 a.m. - 9 p.m.,
Sat & Sun 8 a.m. - 9 p.m.
From Buford, take Peachtree Industrial/McEver Rd. north toward
Gainesville. Turn left at Holiday Rd. (Hwy. 347). It's a half mile on the right.

"Good Friends, Great Food" is the motto at Old McDonald's. In business twenty-five years, this place is a long-time stop for folks headed to and from Lake Lanier Islands marina and resort. A variety of smoked meats, including turkey, are served in a good-sized red wood-frame building that seats 40 or so. The sauce is spicy red. Cole slaw, beans, and potato salad are the principal sides. Also hot dogs and hamburgers for the kids.

Date visited_____Remarks _____

Old Smoke House (306)

14th St. SW
Cairo, Ga. 31728
912/377-6655
County: Grady

Fri & Sat 11 a.m. - 8 p.m.
From U.S. 84, take Hwy. 111 south. It's in a converted
gas station on the right, just before the nursery.

Old Smoke House, a take-out place that has been open about three years, sells no Brunswick stew or food other than barbecue and the basic sides, but then, that's a sign that what is available is likely to be good. The sauce is mild and red, and the meat is tender and moist.

Date visited_____Remarks _____

Old South Bar-B-Q (307)

601 Burbank Circle SE
Smyrna, Ga. 30080
770/435-4215
County: Cobb

Tue - Sun 11 a.m. - 9:30 p.m.
At corner of Windy Hill Rd. and Burbank Cir.,
just east of South Cobb Drive.

Helen Llewallyn's award-winning place has been serving peerless pork straight from the open pit since 1968. Her thick, dark, sweet and smoky tomato-based sauce and sweet no-mayo cole slaw go well with the meat. Brunswick stew, chili, steaks, Bar-B-Q salad, franks and beans, hamburgers, green salads, fries, onion rings, potato salad, beans, and garlic toast round out the menu. Sweet tooths will appreciate the cheesecake, and lemon, pecan, and rocky road dessert treats. Dine in, table service, 70 seats.

Date visited _____*Remarks* _____

Old South Bar-B-Que House (308)

1706 West Hill Ave.
Valdosta, Ga. 31601
912/247-0505
County: Lowndes

Sun - Thu 11 a.m. - 9 p.m., Fri & Sat 11 a.m. - 10 p.m.
From I-75, take exit 4. It's 700 yards east.

"Great down-home cooking" and right off the interstate, too. What more could a weary traveler ask for? Old South offers pit-cooked barbecue chopped or sliced, served with a tomato-based sauce. On the side: Brunswick stew, beans, cole slaw, fries, onion rings, deep-fried corn on the cob, and salads. Sausage too. Dine in, table service, 54 seats. Opened 1976.

Date visited _____*Remarks* _____

At Col. Poole's Georgia Bar-B-Q in East Ellijay,
you can have your name immortalized on a
plywood pig. All you need, the Colonel says, is an
honest face, good intentions, and five dollars.

Ole South Bar-B-Que (309)

4972 Hwy. 42
Ellenwood, Ga. 30049
404/366-8130
County: Clayton

Mon - Fri 6:15 a.m. - 2:15 p.m. Closed Sat & Sun.
On Moreland Ave., just south of the main gate
of Fort Gillem.

This southside establishment used to be barbecue only, but meat-and-vegetable meals have been added. Pit-cooked pork is still the main attraction, though. A tasty sandwich slathered with the rich, red sauce has provided sustenance to busy folks here for twenty-one years. May it always continue. Dine in, table service.

Date visited _____ *Remarks* _____

Only Way Bar-B-Que (310)

3714 East Point St.
East Point, Ga. 30344
404/766-5483
County: Fulton

Tue - Sat 11 a.m. - 5:30 p.m.
Take I-75/85 to Lakewood Frwy. (Hwy. 166). Take the
third exit and go to East Point via Main St. At the fork,
keep right. It's on the right. Look for red and white awnings.

Closed-pit, hickory-smoked, chopped pork served with the sweet, mustard-based sauce on the side. It's not the only way it can be done, but many folks believe it is the only way it should be done. Also Brunswick stew, beans, cole slaw, collard greens, black-eyed peas, pinto beans, and mac-and-cheese. Opened 1984. Take-out only. Picnic tables outside.

Date visited _____ *Remarks* _____

Our Place Bar-B-Q (311)

8690 Hwy. 52 E
Dahlonega, Ga. 30533
706/864-4276
County: Lumpkin

Mon - Fri 6 a.m. - 2 p.m., Sat 7 a.m. - 4 p.m., Sun 11 a.m. - 4 p.m.
At the end of Hwy. 400, cross over Hwy. 60 and continue
north on Long Branch Rd. about 5 miles.
It's on the right at the intersection with Hwy. 52.

Order at the window of Bud and Jean's small pre-fab building. Their place is mostly for take-out, but there's a shed with tables next door seating 16 to 20. The meat is cooked in a smoker out front and there's a variety of other food, including stew, hot dogs, burgers, sandwiches, fried pies, and funnel cakes.

Date visited _____ *Remarks* _____

Owens Bar-B-Que (312)

1207 South Main St.
Cedartown, Ga. 30125
770/748-1130
County: Polk

Mon - Sat 5:30 a.m. - 7 p.m.
From Atlanta, take U.S. 278 west to Cedartown, then
U.S. 27 south. It's a half mile on the left.

Outside wood-burning pits about ten feet off the highway make effective ads for Craig Owens' place. People stop and eat at this rustic, antique-filled building because they notice the aroma as they drive by. The 'cue is made from hams cooked with hickory. The sauce is homemade red, thick, and spicy, and served on the meat or on the side. Dine in, order at counter, 30 seats. Drive-thru.

Date visited _____ *Remarks* _____

Owens, Rome

Name/Map ID	Hours/Directions

Owens Bar-B-Que. (313)

4534 Martha Berry Hwy.
Rome, Ga. 30165
706/235-2099
County: Floyd

Mon - Sat 6 a.m. - 7 p.m.
From Rome, go north on U.S. 27. It's 3 or 4 miles
north of town, on the right.

Owens' Rome restaurant is in an old log cabin. The rustic interior is decorated with antiques and old signs. It has the same menu as the other Owens Bar-B-Que places. Dine in, order at counter, seats 28. Drive-thru.

Date visited _____ *Remarks* _____

Owens Bar-B-Que (314)

6798 Adairsville Rd.
Adairsville, Ga. 30103
770/773-1733
County: Bartow

Mon - Sat 6 a.m. - 7 p.m.
From I-75, take exit 128 and go west on Hwy. 140 about a
half mile. It's on the left.

Prime pork lovingly cooked with hickory in a smoker. It's so good, Owens can rely on word of mouth to bring folks to his Adairsville place. It's served with or without the ketchup-based, mildly tangy sauce. Dine in, order at counter, 15 seats.

Date visited _____ *Remarks* _____

Pa-Bill's BBQ (315)

1271 SW Bowens Mill Rd.
Douglas, Ga. 31533
912/383-0642
County: Coffee

Mon - Sat 11 a.m. - 8 p.m. (closes at 6 on Wed).
From downtown Douglas, take Hwy 206
(Bowens Mill Rd.) to Pa-Bill's.

Bill Morgan's barbecue won second place at the Big Pig Jig in Vienna a few
years ago, and Pa-Bill's is where you can try his award-winning pork. It's a
take-out-only place that's been open about four years. Bill cooks the meat in an
open pit over red oak coals. The sauce recipe is, of course, top secret. (It's of the
red and sweet variety.) For dessert, there are pumpkin, pecan, and coconut pies.

Date visited _____ *Remarks* _____

Pa Pete's (316)

Mount Zion St.
Milan, Ga. 31060
912/362-4845
County: Telfair

Tue & Wed 8 a.m. - 2 p.m.,
Thu - Sat 8 a.m. - 9 p.m., Sun 8 a.m. - 2 p.m.
From U.S. 441 at McRae, go west 9 miles on U.S. 280 to
Milan. It's on the right.

"Pa Pete's; Under the Caution Light in Milan." (It's pronounced "MY-lun," by the
way.) Pa Pete's mild tomato/mustard sauce has a secret ingredient that no one
would likely guess. It goes great with the butts cooked with oak in an open pit.
The homemade old-fashioned Brunswick stew is the kind rural Georgians used
to cook in iron kettles in their backyards. Fresh vegetables, too. Dine in, table
service, 200 seats. Nonsmokers' area. Cafeteria-style buffet at lunch. Drive-thru.

Date visited _____ *Remarks* _____

Papa's Bar-B-Que and Deli (317)

4700 U.S. Hwy. 80 E
Savannah, Ga. 31410
912/897-0236
County: Chatham

Mon - Sat 11 a.m. - 9 p.m.
From central Savannah, take U.S. 80 (Victory Dr.) east
to Whitemarsh Island. It's in Whitemarsh Plaza,
across from Publix.

Closed-pit, chopped 'que is topped with a mustard/tomato–blend sauce that
merges the mustard-base-sauce customs of South Carolina with the tomato traditions of Georgia. Similar blends are found elsewhere in Savannah and eastern
Georgia. Dine in, table service. 30 seats. Nonsmokers' area.

Date visited _____ *Remarks* _____

Papa's Bar-B-Que at Malone's (318)

27 Barnard St.
Savannah, Ga. 31401
912/234-3059
County: Chatham

Sun - Sat 11 a.m. - 9 p.m.
At City Market in downtown Savannah.

This restaurant/bar is named Malone's, but the delectable barbecue here is definitely Papa's. The tender chopped pork is mixed with a tomato and mustard
sauce. Dine in, table service, 150 seats. Nonsmokers' area.

Date visited _____ *Remarks* _____

Pappy Red's B-B-Que (319)

867 Buford Rd.
Cumming, Ga. 30131
770/844-9446 770/667-8792
County: Forsyth

Mon - Sun 11 a.m. - 9 p.m.
From Hwy. 400, take exit 14. Go east (toward Lake
Lanier) on Hwy. 20 about 300 yards. It's on the right.

The place is easy to find. It is the only building in town with a wrecked plane on
the roof, an attention-getting stunt intended to attract visitors to this new restaurant. (At night look for the red neon signs.) Inside is a comfortable dining room,
with walls decorated with "Road-kill BBQ" tee-shirts and a mounted deer head
with a bib. The meat is "cooked over hickory wood the old southern way." The
usual sides plus jalapeño bread. Pecan and lemon pies. Dine in or take-out.
Cafeteria-style serving line.

Date visited _____*Remarks* _____

Pappy Red's

Paradise Bar-B-Q Co (320)

1346 Washington Hwy.
Lincolnton, Ga. 30817
706/359-7097
County: Lincoln

Fri & Sat 10 a.m. - "until all the barbecue is gone."
From Augusta, take Hwy. 104 to Pollard's Corner, then
Hwy. 47 to Lincolnton. Turn left on Hwy. 378. It's the
second building on the left.

Owner William B. Paradise Sr. says of his restaurant, "It's not a big place, but we
are Paradise." Unhealthy habits are not supported here: "No beer, no wine, no
smoking; that's Paradise too," says Mr. Paradise. It's at the northern extension
of Georgia hash and rice country, so expect hash, rather than Brunswick stew.
Paradise does a lot of take-out, but there's seating for 24 inside.

Date visited _____*Remarks* _____

Confederate general Joseph L. Hogg (1806-1862) was born in Morgan County. The county is now better known for cows than Hoggs; it's Georgia's leading cattle producer.

Name/Map ID	Hours/Directions

Parker's Barbecue (321)

602 W Franklin St.
Sylvester, Ga. 31791
912/776-9206
County: Worth

Mon - Sat 11:30 a.m. - 8 p.m.
From I-75 in Tifton, take exit 18. Go west 20 miles to Sylvester. It's just past downtown, on the right.

Perry Parker's place opened in 1995, and serves meats cooked in an oak-fired open pit. The sauce is sweet and mustardy. All kinds of vegetables and soul food are available too. Non-barbecue meats include fried chicken, stew beef, and chitterlings. Dine in, cafeteria-line service, 30 seats.

Date visited_____Remarks _____

Pate's Grocery & Bar-B-Q (322)

U.S. 27 S
Louvale, Ga. 31814
912/838-6218
County: Stewart

Mon - Sun 7 a.m. - 7 p.m.
From Columbus, take U.S. 27 south 25 miles to Louvale. It's on the left .

Pate's place used to be a gas station, grocery store, and BBQ outlet. The gas is gone (no intestinal jokes, please), but the groceries and 'que remain. Hams cooked in a closed pit with oak produce the barbecue. Ribs are available by special request. The sauce is tomato-based and mild-to-medium. Dine in, chairs and tables in back.

Date visited_____Remarks _____

Peachtree BBQ (323)

1875 Peachtree Industrial Blvd.
Buford, Ga. 30518
770/932-8090
County: Gwinnett

Tue - Thu 10 a.m. - 2 p.m., Fri & Sat 9 a.m. - 5 p.m.
or 6 p.m., Sun 9 a.m. - 4 p.m.
On Peachtree Industrial Blvd. at Little Mill Rd. in Buford.

If you notice the taste of honey at this place, don't be surprised. Owner Mike McCallister says he uses it on nearly everything. He cooks Boston butts and eye of round in a smoker, using apple wood. He has a mild red sauce and a hot sauce of ketchup, mustard, and spices. The stew is made with pork and beef tenderloin. All sides are homemade. Freshly squeezed lemonade. Peach and apple fried pies. Eight years in a row voted best BBQ in a Lake Lanier–area survey. Praised in Cumming and Lawrenceville newspapers. Take-out only. Tables outside.

Date visited_____Remarks _____

Peanut's

Name/Map ID	Hours/Directions

Peanut's Redneck Barbecue (324)

5170 Atlanta Hwy.
Bogart, Ga. 30622
770/725-7947
County: Clarke

Mon - Fri 6 a.m. - 8 p.m., Sat 11 a.m. - 8 p.m.
From Georgia Square mall in Athens, go west on U.S. 78
Bus. It's on the right a half mile past the U.S. 78 turn-off.

James T. "Peanut" Vincent's place began as a roadside store; he converted it into a restaurant in the early 1980s. He recently sold the business and retired, but still comes in to help out. Inside it's a real down-home place. You might be a redneck if you eat here, but at least you'll be a well-fed one. The pork plate comes with plenty of chopped pork, a goodly portion of all-meat hash, cole slaw, and two slices of white bread. The hash is a thick oniony mixture of Boston butt, ground chuck, and chicken, served straight on the plate (not atop rice). The hot BBQ sauce is brown and peppery; there's a mild sauce, too. Peanut's also serves catfish, shrimp, chicken, vegetables, and cracklin' cornbread. Vegetables change daily. Dine in, table service, 50 seats.

Date visited _____ *Remarks* _____

Peck's Place (325)

101 S Irwin Ave.
Ocilla, Ga. 31774
912/468-4051
County: Irwin

Mon - Sat 4 p.m. - 8 p.m.
In the center of town in Ocilla.

We were told by several people that Peck's has excellent BBQ, and we found one of the reasons why when Peck's owner David Shuman told us that he's a pecan man. He cooks hams, Boston butts, and pork shoulders in a closed pit over pecan coals. Although he makes his own sauce (a thick, nonsweet, tomato-based, moderately spicy blend), he knows it's the meat, not the sauce, that makes great barbecue. Customers have tried to persuade him to enter the rib contest at the Big Pig Jig. Even the winners have praised his bones. Dine in, table service in the evenings (order at counter at lunch). Seats about 40. Opened 1993.

Date visited _____ *Remarks* _____

Perry's Pig (326)

1957 Old Savannah Rd.
Augusta, Ga. 30901
706/724-2387
County: Richmond

Tue - Wed 10 a.m. - 8 p.m., Thu - Sat 10 a.m. - 9 p.m.
From downtown Augusta, go south on U.S. 1 2 or 3 miles
and turn right on Old Savannah Rd.

Leroy Perry has been cooking a long time, and his place has been open more than twenty years. He cooks hams over charcoal in an open pit and adds a homemade ketchup-based sauce (hot or mild). Hash and rice, soul-food-style vegetables, and sweet potato pie are sold, too. George Bush take note: Perry's has home-cooked wash-pot fried pork skins. Take-out only.

Date visited _____*Remarks* _____

Phila's Kitchen (327)

2344 Hwy. 25 S
Waynesboro, Ga. 30830
706/554-5195
County: Burke

Mon - Thu 6:30 a.m. - 8 p.m.,
Fri & Sat 6:30 a.m. - 9 p.m.
On U.S. 25, about 5 miles south
of downtown Waynesboro.

Phila's Kitchen is located at the former "Sam's Stop Shop," and now there are more reasons to stop than ever before. The delicious barbecue is pit-cooked with wood, the way it's supposed to be. Phila also has "sandwiches, beer, cookies, etc." Dine in, order at counter, 30 seats.

Date visited _____*Remarks* _____

The Pig (328)

768 State St.
Waycross, Ga. 31501
912/283-4875
County: Ware

Mon - Sat 9:30 a.m. - midnight.
From Plant Ave. (U.S. 84) in downtown Waycross, go
north toward Alma on Hwy. 4 Bus.
It's a half mile on the right.

A tiny establishment that opened for business in 1947. The open-pit-cooked barbecue is available chopped or sliced. It's usually served with The Pig's Special Sauce, a thin mustard/vinegar mix, already mixed in. There's no stew and few sides, and the only beverages are soft drinks and water, but if you wanted a big, fat menu you would have gone to Shoney's, right? Dine in, table service, about 30 seats.

Date visited _____*Remarks* _____

Pig Out Barbeque (329)

118 Railroad St.
Hazlehurst, Ga. 31539
912/375-0388
County: Jeff Davis

Mon - Thu 10 a.m. - 8 p.m., Fri - Sat 10 a.m. - 9 p.m.
Next to the railroad tracks in downtown Hazlehurst.
Look for the flashing sign.

The meat at Pig Out is cooked with oak and pecan wood and is served with or without the sweet tomato/vinegar–based sauce. There's also Brunswick stew, baked beans, cole slaw, green beans, potato salad, and stuffed potatoes. Non-BBQ items, too. Take-out only. Picnic tables outside. Opened 1992.

Date visited _____*Remarks* _____

Piget BarBQ (330)

202 College St.
Cuthbert, Ga. 31740
912/732-2670
County: Randolph

Tue & Thu 10:30 a.m. - 2 p.m.,
Wed 10:30 a.m. - 2 p.m. & 5 p.m. - 8 p.m.,
Fri & Sat 10:30 a.m. - 2 p.m. & 5 p.m. - 9 p.m.
On U.S. 82 West between the city square and Andrew College.

You might spot the fried chicken place before you see Piget, but hold out for the really good stuff. Open-pit-cooked pork pleasure beats poultry any day. Ketchup-based sauce. Dine in or take out. While in Cuthbert, take a look at the historic old courthouse; it's a beauty.

Date visited _____ *Remarks* _____

Piggie Park (331)

U.S. 19 North
Thomaston, Ga. 30286
706/648-3330
County: Upson

Sun, Tue & Wed 10 a.m. - 10 p.m.,
Thu, Fri & Sat 10 a.m. - 11 p.m.
From downtown Thomaston, take U.S. 19 about 2 miles
north. It's on the right.

One of the South's best-known barbecue places is Maurice's Piggie Park in Columbia, S.C. This Georgia version opened in 1950 on the south side of town. Its owners, the Pasley family, moved it to the present location in 1965. It's a drive-in-only place, but it can accommodate dozens of cars. PP's hams and ribs are smoked with oak and hickory in a huge gas-fired indoor smoker. The ketchup-based sauce is semi-hot. Brunswick stew, cole slaw, and fries are the chief sides. All barbecue and sides are cooked from scratch.

Date visited _____ *Remarks* _____

Piggie Park, Thomaston

Piggyback's Bar-B-Que (332)

6012 Ga. Hwy. 42
Rex, Ga. 30273
770/961-4706
County: Clayton

Mon - Sat 11 a.m. - 8 p.m.
From I-285, take the Moreland Ave. exit. Go south 6 or 7
miles. It's on the left in the community of Rex.

Hams cooked with oak and hickory (and sometimes pecan) are cut up and served with your choice of two homemade sauces or a couple of commercial sauces. Brave souls will want to try Piggyback's "Hot O' Mighty" hot pepper sauce. The ribs get rave reviews, and other people-pleasing items are the stew and the "pig puffs." Homemade fried pies. Dine in, order at counter, 40 seats.

Date visited_____Remarks _____

Piggy's Rib Shack (333)

7080 North Hwy. 53 NE
Rome, Ga. 30161
706/295-1736
County: Floyd

Mon - Sat 10 a.m. - 9 p.m.
On New Calhoun Highway (Hwy. 53), north of Rome.

Real pit-cooked, hickory-smoked, pulled pork. Douse it with the vinegar-based sauce and dig in. Or try the baby back rib dinner; it's the shack specialty. Not in a BBQ mood? Piggy's serves catfish, wings, several non-BBQ meats, pintos and cornbread, and a variety of vegetables. Desserts include apple turnovers, sundaes, and banana splits. Dine in, table service, 60 seats. Opened 1992.

Date visited_____Remarks _____

The Pink Pig (334)

P.O. Box 100
Cherry Log, Ga. 30522
706/276-3311
County: Gilmer

Thu - Sun 11 a.m. - 9 p.m.
From Ellijay, take GA Hwy. 515 (Zell Miller Pkwy.) about
8 miles north to Cherry Log.

Inside this long, low rustic building by the old highway is a comfortable dining area seating a hundred or so. Cutesy pig stuff and antiques decorate the walls. Quality 'que is hickory-smoked in a closed pit, then chopped. A tomato and vinegar sauce is served on the meat or on the side. Try the thick and tomato-rich stew, garlic salad, and cornbread. Dine in, table service. Opened 1967.

Date visited_____Remarks _____

The Pink Pig B-B-Q (335)

310 Redfern Village
St. Simons Island, Ga. 31522
912/638-1003
County: Glynn

Mon - Sat 11 a.m. - 10 p.m.
From Torras Causeway/Demere Rd. turn left onto
Frederica Rd., go one block, turn left on Landing Field Rd.
into Redfern Village shopping center.

This pleasant nook among the live oaks serves barbecue made from Boston butts cooked over oak in an open pit. Choose a sweet tomato-based or a spicy mustard-based sauce to go with it. Also corn on the cob, wings, burgers, hot dogs, and chicken breast sandwiches. Dine in, 20 seats inside and 20 outside.

Date visited_____Remarks _____

Pippin's Bar-B-Q #1 (336)

40 Sims St.
McDonough, Ga. 30253
770/957-2539
County: Henry

Tue - Sat 10 a.m. - 8 p.m.
From I-75 southbound, take exit 71 and go left. Go
straight into McDonough, around the square, toward
Covington; turn right on Sims.

You know it's good because Pippin's has made the Top Ten in the Stone Mountain BBQ Cook-Off four times. Pippin's offers both sandwiches and plates, Brunswick stew, and the usual sides. The pork is hand-chopped as it is ordered. Dine in, order at counter, 30 seats. Opened 1986.

Date visited _____*Remarks* _____

Pippin's Bar-B-Q (337)

10115 Alcovy Rd.
Covington, Ga. 30209
770/784-1966
County: Newton

Mon - Sat 11 a.m. - 9 p.m.
From Atlanta, take I-20 east to exit 45A. Go left on
Alcovy Rd. It's a quarter mile on the left.

High standards of quality and consistency are a source of pride at Pippin's. Hickory-smoked hams are converted into people-pleasing sandwiches and pork plates. Baby back ribs are served sweet and tender. The tomato-based sauce, hot or mild, is smooth and rich. Dine in, order at counter, 50 seats. Drive-thru. Opened 1988.

Date visited _____*Remarks* _____

Pippin's Bar-B-Q (338)

4580 Hwy. 20 SE
Conyers, Ga. 30208
770/922-9730
County: Rockdale

Mon - Thu 11 a.m. - 8 p.m., Fri & Sat 11 a.m. - 9 p.m.
From I-20, take exit 42. Go south 6 miles on Hwy. 20.
Look for the sign.

Same menu. This Pippin's opened in 1990. Its dining area will accommodate about 50 pork lovers. Place your order at the counter.

Date visited _____*Remarks* _____

Pistol Pete's Bar-B-Que (339)

1425 Sam Nunn Blvd.
Perry, Ga. 31069
912/988-4373
County: Houston

Mon - Sat 11 a.m. - 9:30 p.m., Sun 11 a.m. - 8:30 p.m.
From I-75, take exit 43. Go east toward Perry.
It's on the right.

Pistol Pete's was voted one of middle Georgia's favorite BBQ places in a *Macon Telegraph* poll. Hams, butts, and beef brisket are cooked in a smoker with oak and hickory. The homemade sauce — a mix of ketchup, mustard, vinegar, and spices, and available in hot or mild — pleasingly complements the meat. Sides include baked beans and corn on the cob, and onion sticks instead of onion rings. Dine in, table service, 76 seats. Drive-thru.

Date visited _____*Remarks* _____

The Pit Bar-B-Q (340)

3802 Hwy. 193
Flintstone, Ga. 30725
706/820-2692
County: Walker

Tue - Sat 10 a.m. - 7 p.m.
From LaFayette, take Hwy. 193 about 25 miles north. It's
next to the feed store in Flintstone,
on the way to Rock City.

In the shadow of Lookout Mountain is a little community named not for Fred and Wilma, but for the rock found hereabouts. Dinosaur meat is not an option, but pit-cooked, hickory-smoked, hand-chopped pork, served with a sweet sauce, certainly is. (Wilma would be as big as Fred if she ate here.) Sides include beans, cole slaw, fries, potato salad, onion rings, and chips. Dine in, order at counter, 35 seats, nonsmokers' area.

Date visited_____Remarks _____

Bar-B-Quote

"PIG, n.   An animal (Porcus omnivorus) *closely allied to the human race by the splendor and vivacity of its appetite. . . ."*
—*Ambrose Bierce,* The Devil's Dictionary

Pit Stop (341)

442 W Howell St.
Hartwell, Ga. 30643
706/376-7867
County: Hart

Mon 5 a.m. - 2 p.m., Tue - Thu 5 a.m. - 8 p.m.,
Fri & Sat 5 a.m. - 9 p.m.
On Hwy. 77, on the south side of town.

Barbecued pork, cooked on an open pit out back, is available every day at Pit Stop, but barbecued chicken and riblets are served only on Friday and Saturday. A vinegar-based sauce is served mixed in with the smoked meat, or can be had on the side. It's also available by the bottle. Brunswick stew and the standard sides are served, along with several non-BBQ dinners and sandwiches. Opened 1990.

Date visited_____Remarks _____

Pit Stop BBQ (342)

409 W College St.
Bowdon, Ga. 30108
770/258-7415
County: Carroll

Mon - Wed 11 a.m. - 8 p.m.,
Thu 11 a.m. - 9 p.m., Fri & Sat 11 a.m. - 9:30 p.m.
On Hwy. 166 just west of downtown Bowdon.

Pit Stop's barbecued pork is made from hams and Boston butts cooked in a smoker with hickory wood. The sauce is a tangy red mixture of secret ingredients. Thirteen vegetables are served daily. Spare ribs are available by the rack (or by the truckload if that is your desire). Also steak, catfish, liver, shrimp (liver?!!). Dine in, 64 seats. Drive-thru too. Open 1986.

Date visited_____Remarks _____

Pit Stop BBQ (343)

P.O. Box 1644
Tifton, Ga. 31794
912/387-0888
County: Tift

Tue - Thu 11 a.m. - 8 p.m., Fri & Sat 11 a.m. - 9 p.m.
From I-75, take exit 18 and go east on U.S. 82 about a
mile. It's on the right at Seventh St., in downtown Tifton.

Pit Stop is a favorite of Tiftonians and tourists alike. Customers from as far away as Canada praise Pit Stop's barbecue and ribs as the best anywhere. Hams, Boston butts, and shoulders are cooked 15 hours with oak and hickory in a closed pit out back. A thin, mild, red sauce is served on the meat or on the side. Ribs are available as sandwiches, dinners, or slabs. Sides include Brunswick stew, beans, cole slaw, fries, potato salad, and hot dogs. Pound cake for dessert. Take-out only. Drive-thru.

Date visited _____ *Remarks* _____

Pitts Barbeque Diner (344)

1715 W Savannah Ave.
Valdosta, Ga. 31601
912/247-6224
County: Lowndes

Wed 11 a.m. - 2 p.m., Thu 11 a.m. - 6 p.m.,
Fri & Sat 11 a.m. - 11 p.m..
From downtown Valdosta, take W. Savannah Ave. west.
(W. Savannah Ave. runs beside the railroad.)

Mary Pitts invites you to come inside and sit down at her Valdosta establishment and enjoy some fine home cooking. The chipped pork is tender, the red sauce is wonderful, the Brunswick stew is tasty, the sides are fine, and, for dessert, there's sweet potato pie. It's the Pitts, and it's good!

Date visited _____ *Remarks* _____

Po Boys Bar-B-Que (345)

Hwy. 221 E
Douglas, Ga. 31533
912/384-1704
County: Coffee

Wed - Sat 9 a.m. - 8:30 p.m.
From downtown Douglas, go north on U.S. 221.
It's on the left.

The po boys cook hams and shoulders with oak in a closed pit. To go with the delectable results, there's a thick and tasty homemade red sauce, along with all of the usual barbecue-related sides. A big buffet is an option, and steaks and seafood are served, too. Open since 1983, it's a big, roomy place that is often packed on weekends. There's a busy drive-thru too.

Date visited _____ *Remarks* _____

Po' Freddie's Bar-B-Q (346)

2661 Campbellton Rd. SW
Atlanta, Ga. 30311
404/349-9000
County: Fulton

Tue - Sat 11 a.m. - 12 p.m.
Exit Hwy. 166 at Greenbriar Pkwy. Go north one block,
turn right on Campbellton Rd. It's about a mile on the left
at the corner of Dodson Dr.

Both pork and beef ribs are served at Po' Freddie's. The pork barbecue is carefully made from Boston butts cooked in a smoker with hickory wood. A special thick and sweet sauce is served on the meat or on the side. Brunswick stew, beans, cole slaw, and vegetables too. Dine in, table service, 50 seats.

Date visited _____ *Remarks* _____

Pomo's House of Barbecue (347)

2766 Watson Blvd.
Centerville, Ga. 31028
912/953-2060
County: Houston

Mon - Sat 11 a.m. - 9 p.m.
On GA Hwy. 247C between I-75 and Warner Robins.

Voted one of middle Georgia's favorite BBQ places in a *Macon Telegraph* poll, Pomo's is famous for its open-pit barbecue and tasty sides including smoked beans, creamed corn, fried corn, cornbread, fried okra, baked potato (evenings only), chef salad, pickles, and gravy. Also smoked sausage, fried chicken, burgers, and vegetable plates. Homemade desserts include peanut butter pie, apple crisp, chocolate squares, and lemon squares. Country-style lunches on weekdays. Dine in, table service, 200 seats, all nonsmoking. Opened 1981.

Date visited_____Remarks_____

Pop's Place (348)

5614 Holiday Rd.
Buford, Ga. 30518
770/945-8736
County: Hall

Mon - Sun 10 a.m. - 10 p.m.
From Buford, take Peachtree Industrial Blvd./McEver Rd.
north toward Gainesville. It's on the left
at Holiday Road (Hwy. 347).

Pop's is one of the dozen or so BBQ places surrounding Lake Lanier, and one of three clustered near this busy intersection. (Old McDonald's and Mary's Flying Pig are the other two.) Order from a window at Pop's little blue barbecue building. It's at a corner of a convenience store/bait shop parking lot. You can eat at tables and chairs under a large wooden shelter. Try the spicy Brunswick stew, jalapeño poppers, and boiled peanuts.

Date visited_____Remarks_____

Purvis Barbecue (349)

514 Hwy. 1 Bypass S
Louisville, Ga. 30434
912/625-8148
County: Jefferson

Thu - Sat 9 a.m. - 6 p.m.
From Augusta, take U.S. 1 to Louisville and beyond
(about 55 miles total). It's on the right.

It's strictly 'que, stew, and fixings at this place which has been here forever (or at least since 1964). Jeanne and Lonnie Purvis try their best to keep their food consistently good, and they consistently do a good job of it. They cook hams and Boston butts over an open pit with charcoal and add a homemade moderately hot vinegar-based sauce. Brunswick stew, cole slaw, and potato salad accompany the barbecue nicely. Coconut and pecan pies are the desserts. Dine in, 60 or so seats.

Date visited_____Remarks_____

Bar-B-Fact

Title 4, Section 4, Paragraph 22 of The Official Code of Georgia
prohibits the feeding of garbage to swine.

Quinnie's Barbecue Restaurant (350)

2856 LaVista Rd.
Decatur, Ga. 30033
404/728-8763
County: DeKalb

Mon - Fri 11 a.m. - 8 p.m., Sat 11:30 a.m. - 6 p.m.
From downtown Decatur, take Clairmont Rd. (U.S. 23)
north about 3 miles to LaVista Rd., turn right. Quinnie's
is about a mile on the left in a small shopping center.

Three or four meat entrees and 10–12 veggies daily are served at Quinnie's little storefront place. Veggies are cooked without grease or fat, but somehow still taste good. (It's a miracle!) Brunswick stew is available sometimes. Fried fish and a few non-BBQ meats look tasty enough that they could almost substitute for barbecue. Desserts: banana pudding, peach cobbler, cakes, and pies. Seats 20. Cafeteria line. All nonsmoking.

Date visited _____*Remarks* _____

R.W.'s Bar-B-Que (351)

201 E Atlanta Rd.
Stockbridge, Ga. 30281
770/474-7675
County: Henry

Tue - Thu 11 a.m. - 2 p.m. and 5 p.m. - 8 p.m., Fri & Sat 11 a.m. - 8 p.m.
From I-75, take exit 75 and go east about 2 miles
on Hwy. 138 to Stockbridge. After crossing an overpass,
take the first street on the left. It's a half mile on the right.

R.W.'s claims to offer no specials because all of their food is special. Plenty of people agree, apparently. The food is praised by serious barbecue eaters from all over. Pork shoulders are cooked in an old pit with indirect heat. Baby back ribs are served "dry" or with the mild red sauce. The cole slaw and potato salad are perfect complements to the meat. Dine in, table service, 50 seats. Opened 1989.

Date visited _____*Remarks* _____

Rawl's Country Mall (352)

U.S. 17 N
Woodbine, Ga. 31569
912/576-5630
County: Camden

Mon - Sat 6 a.m. - 9 p.m., Sun 8 a.m. - 6 p.m.
From I-95, take exit 4, then Hwy. 25 Spur to U.S. 17.
Turn right. Rawl's is on the right at the
Fina station in downtown Woodbine.

Rawl's is a good stop for hunting and fishing supplies, gas, and, surprisingly, a barbecue sandwich. The sliced pork sandwich is the only barbecue item available, but it is a fine sandwich, with pieces of outside meat, doused with a thin, mild, smoke-flavored, tomato-based sauce, as good as any in the area. A smoke ring indicates the meat was slowly cooked with wood coals. The meat is cooked every day using water oak in a smoker. Sweet tomato-based sauce. Hot sauce available. For dessert, there are sweets in the store and an ice cream stand next door. Order at counter. 12 seats between the grocery aisles.

Date visited _____*Remarks* _____

Bar-B-Fact

Johnny Harris Restaurant, Georgia's oldest barbecue place, was established in 1924. Rock City, high atop Lookout Mountain in the opposite corner of Georgia, was begun the same year.

The Red Pig

Name/Map ID	Hours/Directions

The Red Pig Bar B Que (353)

3763 Peach Orchard Rd.
Augusta, Ga. 30906
706/796-9694
County: Richmond

Mon, Thu - Sun 11 a.m. - 8 p.m.
From I-520 (Bobby Jones Expressway), exit at Peach
Orchard Rd. and go right. It's down a bit on the right.

It was closed when we visited. We were able to contact the owners, and they told us they plan to reopen it after several months of remodeling. When it's back in business, expect the pork to be cooked on an open pit with hickory, the sauce to be mustard/ketchup/vinegar-based, hash and rice to be served instead of Brunswick stew, and the other menu items to be home-cooked. Lunch and dinner specials are planned, too.

Date visited _____ *Remarks* _____

Rib Hut Bar-B-Que & Seafood Restaurant (354)

1629 W. Bay St.
Savannah, Ga. 31401
912/233-2195
County: Chatham

Mon - Sat 11:30 a.m. - 3 a.m.,
Sun 12:30 p.m. - 2 a.m.
From downtown Savannah, go upriver on West Bay
Street, across the viaduct. It's on the left.

Open-pit, chopped pork, or fresh seafood? Decisions, decisions. Just eat some barbecue first, and then order the fishy stuff afterwards. With your 'que, have some fries, potato salad, fried vegetables, or lettuce and tomato salad. And a beer or cooler. Then some cake or pie. By the time you finish, seafood won't be appealing at all. Dine in, order at counter, 150 seats, nonsmokers' area. Opened 1976.

Date visited _____ *Remarks* _____

The Rib Rack (355)

500 Tripp St.
Americus, Ga. 31709
912/931-0606
County: Sumter

Mon - Wed 10:30 a.m. - 9 p.m., Thu 10 a.m. - 11 p.m., Fri &
Sat 10 a.m. - 12 p.m.
From U.S. 19, turn east onto Lamar St., go through downtown,
turn right on Tripp St. It's on the left next to the Chevy dealer.

In 1923, Charles Lindbergh made his first solo flight here in Americus and went on to cross the Atlantic alone. If the Rib Rack had been here then, he probably would have just hung around town to enjoy the smoky pork, chicken, and ribs, the flavorful homemade red sauce, both mild and sweet and spicy hot, the potato salad, beans, and collards, and other delicious food found herein. Dine in, order at counter, 24 seats.

Date visited _____*Remarks* _____

The Rib Ranch (356)

25 Irby Ave. NW
Atlanta, Ga. 30305
404/233-7644
County: Fulton

Mon - Sat 11 a.m. - 11 p.m., Sun 12 p.m. - 10 p.m.
In the heart of the Buckhead area of northside Atlanta.
From the Peachtree Rd./Roswell Rd. fork, take Roswell Rd.
one block north and turn left on Irby.

Texas-theme decor, beef ribs, sausage sandwiches, and Mexican cornbread mark the Rib Ranch as more a foreign restaurant than a Georgia barbecue place. But the tomato-based sauce is sweet and smoky, and pork and pork ribs are on the menu, along with Brunswick stew and other standard sides, so we'll include them. Beef brisket is a specialty, and the big beef ribs (the owner calls them Fred Flintstone ribs) are popular, too. For dessert: blackberry cobbler and brownies. They serve beer at the Ranch and have a full bar as well. Dine in, table service, 150 seats, nonsmokers' area.

Date visited _____*Remarks* _____

The Rib Ranch (357)

2063 Canton Hwy.
Marietta, Ga. 30066
770/422-5755
County: Cobb

Sun - Thu 11 a.m. - 10 p.m., Fri - Sat 11 a.m. - 11 p.m.
From I-75 northbound take exit 114-A (Hwy. 5 Spur). Go
toward Canton. It's about 1.5 miles on the left.

This Lone Star State outpost is convenient to I-75. It serves the same big ole ribs and other sweet smoky stuff as the Atlanta ranch.

Date visited _____*Remarks* _____

The Rib Ranch (358)

1150 Powder Springs Rd., SW
Marietta, Ga. 30064
770/422-7001
County: Cobb

Sun - Thu 11 a.m. - 10 p.m., Fri - Sat 11 a.m. - 11 p.m.
From I-75 north, take exit 112. Go west to Marietta and
turn left onto Powder Springs Rd. Look for the big sign a
half mile on the right.

Rib Ranch's other Cobb County place is farther from I-75, but not so far that you wouldn't want to go there.

Date visited _____*Remarks* _____

Rib Shack Blues Cafe (359)

4848 Memorial Dr.
Stone Mountain, Ga. 30083
404/292-0056
County: DeKalb

Mon - Thu 11 a.m. - 10 p.m.,
Fri & Sat 11 a.m. - 2 a.m., Sun 12 p.m. - 7 p.m.
At the corner of Memorial Dr. and Rockbridge Rd.,
next to Wachovia Bank.

"The place where BBQ meets LIVE Blues. Excellent BBQ, great music and a good time! Featuring a live blues band on Friday and Saturday nights." How could anyone resist an ad like that? Closed-pit, hickory-smoked, chopped pork, beef, and chicken are among the favorites here. Smoked turkey is available, too. Sweet tomato-based sauce. Also, Brunswick stew, beans, cole slaw, fries, country vegetables, fried chicken, fried fish, and sandwiches. Desserts include peach cobbler, sweet potato pie, and chocolate cake. Rib Shack Blues Cafe was the winner of the 1993 Great Atlanta Smoke-Out.

Date visited _____*Remarks* _____

Rib Shack Blues Cafe

Ribs Etc. (360)

4233 Roswell Rd. NE
Atlanta, Ga. 30342
404/843-8200
County: Fulton

Mon - Thu 11 a.m. - 10 p.m.,
Fri & Sat 11 a.m. - 10 p.m., Sun 11 a.m. - 10 p.m.
From Peachtree Rd. in Buckhead, take Roswell Rd.
(Hwy. 9/19) about 2 miles north. It's on the right.

The pork ribs served here are wonderful, and the "et cetera" isn't bad either. Open-pit-cooked with oak and hickory, the pork is served chopped and the beef is sliced. The sauce is red, hickory-flavored, mildly tangy, and a little sweet. On the side: Brunswick stew, beans, cole slaw, barbecue fries, sweet potato fries, and potato salad. Try the "barbecue sundae" appetizer. Desserts include Key lime pie and cheesecake. Full bar. Dine in, seats about 70. Opened 1986.

Date visited _____*Remarks* _____

> *Holcomb's Barbecue in White Plains opened in 1971, the year Macon's Allman Brothers Band released their album "Eat a Peach."*

Name/Map ID	**Hours/Directions**

Richardson's Pit Bar-B-Que (361)

171 Durham St.
Iron City, Ga. 31759
912/774-2469
County: Seminole

Mon - Sat 9 a.m. - 9 p.m.
On old Hwy. 84 East. From the post office on the new Hwy. 84, go north a couple of blocks to the old highway. It's on the right.

One of the oldest and best-known barbecue places in southwest Georgia is Richardson's. Although no longer on the main highway, it's still in business and the barbecue is still among the best. The meats are cooked in an open pit and in a smoker using oak and pecan. The red sauce is sweet and tangy. Sides include cole slaw, beans, and potato salad. Dine in, table service, 80 seats. Drive-thru. Opened in 1968.

Date visited _____ *Remarks* _____

Ricks' Bar-B-Que (362)

2303 Hwy. 80 W
Dublin, Ga. 31021
912/272-7903
County: Laurens

Tue - Wed 10 a.m. - 7 p.m.,
Thu - Fri 10 a.m. - 8 p.m., Sat 10 a.m. - 7 p.m.
From the courthouse in downtown Dublin, take Hwy. 80 east about 3 miles. It's on the right about 8/10 mile past Dublin Mall.

We heard more praise for Ricks' than for any other barbecue place in the area. Even some of the local competition says the barbecue here is superb. The secret is in the sauce, they say at Ricks'. The business is mostly take-out, but there's seating for 24 in a little building next door. Try Mom's Own Brunswick Stew. Vanilla pudding pound cake is only 60 cents a slice.

Date visited _____ *Remarks* _____

River BBQ & Breakfast (363)

U.S. Hwy. 84
Atkinson, Ga. 31553
912/778-5390
County: Brantley

Mon - Sun 6 a.m. - 10 p.m.
From I-95 exit 6, take U.S. 82 west 18 miles to Atkinson. It's on the right just before the three river bridges.

At the Satilla River about halfway between Waycross and Brunswick is River BBQ and Breakfast. A favorite of truckers, it's a roomy place with 75 seats and table service. The barbecue is cooked with oak in a smoker, and the sauce comes in hot, spicy, or mild. Lima beans, green beans, cole slaw, and corn on the cob are among the sides.

Date visited _____ *Remarks* _____

River Road Barbecue (364)

4222 River Rd.
Columbus, Ga. 31904
706/571-0807
County: Muscogee

Mon - Wed 6:30 a.m. - 8 p.m., Thu & Fri 6:30 a.m. - 9 p.m.,
Sat 6:30 a.m. - 8 p.m., Sun 6:30 a.m. - 6 p.m.
From Manchester Expressway headed south, take the River
Road exit. Go left. It's two blocks down on the left.

Columbus and Phenix City, the Alabama town across the river, are blessed with an abundance of fine barbecue outlets. River Road Barbecue is no exception. The red sauce comes in mild and hot, as well as extra hot for those who like to live on the edge.

Date visited_____Remarks _____

Riverside Restaurant at Pappy's Marketplace (365)

Hwy. 19/129 S
Blairsville, Ga. 30512
706/745-9885
County: Union

Wed - Fri 11 a.m. - 9 p.m., Sat & Sun 7 a.m. - 9 p.m.
(Open May 1st - Oct 31st).
Five miles south of Blairsville on Hwy. 19/129
at the Nottely River.

On the picturesque Nottely River in the Georgia mountains. Feed the fish and ducks from Pappy's porch on the river, and then go inside and feed yourself on hickory-smoked barbecued pork or beef (sliced or chopped), chicken, pork ribs, and homemade stew. The many sides include fried okra, fried squash, and hush-puppies. Trout, catfish, shrimp, and hamburger steaks are served, too.

Date visited_____Remarks _____

Roberson Barbecue (366)

1115 Telfair St.
Dublin, Ga. 31021
912/272-6709
County: Laurens

Mon 10 a.m. - 2:30 p.m., Tue - Sat 10 a.m. - 5 p.m.
From the county courthouse in downtown Dublin, go
south on Hwy. 441. It's about a mile
on the right, near Telfair St.

Roberson's is a small cinderblock shack with a Coke machine in front and a large stack of oak on the side. It's take-out only, but there are a couple of picnic tables out front. Open-pit-cooked Boston butts and a mild red sauce join to create some of the best barbecue in town. To go with it, get some homestyle vegetables and, of course, some of Roberson's sweet potato pie for dessert.

Date visited_____Remarks _____

Robison's Barbecue (367)

132 W. Spring St.
Monroe, Ga. 30655
770/207-7675
County: Walton

Wed - Sat 11 a.m. - 8 p.m. or 9 p.m.
From Atlanta, take U.S. 78 east. Take the Monroe exit.
Go east on W Spring St. (Hwy. 10 Bus.). It's on the left.

Truman Robison cooks hams in a closed pit with hickory and charcoal. Sometimes he cooks a whole hog (with the head on) by special order. His sauce is vinegar-based. Everything in the Brunswick stew is ground, creating a thick, smooth and somewhat spicy dish. Winner of 6th-place award at 1995 Stone Mountain Smoke-Off in BBQ pro category. Table service, seats 100.

Date visited_____Remarks _____

The Rock House Grill (368)

360 S Piedmont St.
Calhoun, Ga. 30701
706/625-8000
County: Gordon

Mon - Thu 11 a.m. - 9 p.m.,
Fri 11 a.m. - 10 p.m., Sat 4 p.m. - 10 p.m.
From the courthouse go south on U.S. 41 and turn left
onto Piedmont; the Rock House is on the right.

Housed in (of course) an old rock house at the south edge of downtown
Calhoun, this place serves closed-pit, hickory-smoked, pulled and chopped pork.
Ribs and barbecued turkey are available, too. The sauce is tomato/vinegar-
based. Seats 78, table service, nonsmokers area.

Date visited _____*Remarks* _____

Roger's Pit Cooked Bar-B-Que (369)

210 E 10th St.
West Point, Ga. 31833
706/645-2383
County: Troup

Mon - Thu 11 a.m. - 9 p.m., Fri & Sat 11 a.m. - 10 p.m.
From I-85 southbound, take GA exit 1, turn right.
It's 1.5 miles on the left.

A West Point tradition since 1945, Roger's is known for its Brunswick stew. Still
prepared fresh daily in a big black cast-iron kettle the old-fashioned way, it's
made with hams, not leftovers, and is hand-stirred. The pork is pit-cooked with
hickory, and there are two different red sauces (not sweet), one for the pork and
one for the ribs and chicken. Dine in, table service, 120 seats, drive thru.

Date visited _____*Remarks* _____

Roger's Pit Cooked Bar-B-Que (370)

117 New Franklin Rd.
LaGrange, Ga. 30240
706/812-0041
County: Troup

Mon - Thu 11 a.m. - 9 p.m., Fri & Sat 11 a.m. - 10 p.m.
From I-85, take exit 4 and go west. Go past three traffic
lights and turn right on New Franklin Rd. Go past one
more light. It's on the left.

The original Roger's began in West Point in 1945 and expanded to LaGrange in
the early 1990s. Interestingly, the name of the place was supposed to be
Rodgers', but the sign maker spelled it incorrectly. The error was left
unchanged. Although under different ownership, the menu here is the same.

Date visited _____*Remarks* _____

Rowan's BBQ House (371)

Hwy. 82 E
Enigma, Ga. 31749
912/533-1055
County: Berrien

Fri & Sat 10 a.m.- 8 p.m.
From Tifton, take U.S. 82 about 9 miles to Enigma. It's
on the left as you're leaving town.

Nobody knows how Enigma got its name (really!), but there's no mystery about
why Enigmans and others come to Rowan's BBQ House. It's to get The Special,
a cup of Brunswick stew and a side order of cracklin' cornbread. Bobby Rowan,
a sometime gubernatorial candidate, designed his own cooker. For dessert, try
the thin-layer chocolate cake. Outside seating only.

Date visited _____*Remarks* _____

Sam's Bar-B-Que (372)

Hwy. 82
Georgetown, Ga. 31754
912/334-5912
County: Quitman

Mon - Sun 10 a.m. - 10 p.m.
On U.S. 82 in Georgetown, Ga., across the lake from
Eufaula, Ala.

Sam Nickerson's place serves closed-pit, hickory-smoked, chopped barbecue with a sauce made of ketchup, mustard, and vinegar. It's available in hot or mild. He's justifiably proud of the sauce; the recipe has been in the Nickerson family for over fifty years. His Bar-B-Q Potato is a large baked potato stuffed with a quarter pound of meat, covered with Sam's special sauce and melted cheese, and served with sour cream and Texas toast on the side. Dine in, table service. 80 seats. Opened 1993.

Date visited _____*Remarks* _____

Bar-B-Fact

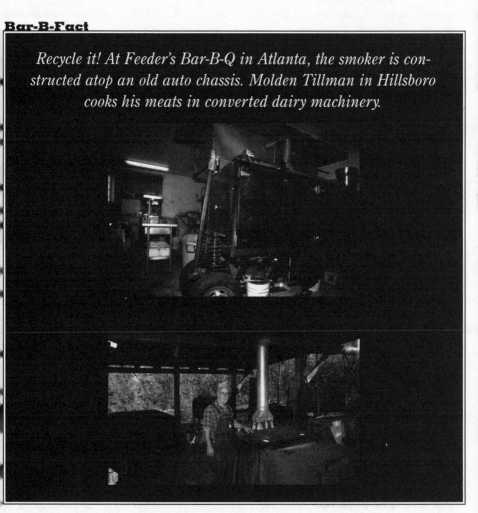

Recycle it! At Feeder's Bar-B-Q in Atlanta, the smoker is constructed atop an old auto chassis. Molden Tillman in Hillsboro cooks his meats in converted dairy machinery.

Satterfield's (373)

120 New St.
Macon, Ga. 31201
912/742-0352
County: Bibb

Mon - Sat 10:30 a.m. - 9 p.m.
From I-16, exit at Spring St., cross the river, and take the
first left onto Riverside. Turn right at New St.
It's on the left.

"Porker portions at piggy prices." Pick up some pork by the plate, platter, pound, or sandwich at Satterfield's. Sliced Angus beef, smoked chicken, smoked turkey, smoked pork chops, and pork spare ribs are also on the menu. Sides, salads, sandwiches, and vegetable plates are other options. Premium and domestic beers and boiled peanuts provide even more reasons to visit Satterfield's. Dine in, table service, 135 seats, nonsmokers' area.

Date visited _____ *Remarks* _____

Sconyers Bar-B-Que (374)

2250 Sconyers Way
Augusta, Ga. 30906
706/790-5411
County: Richmond

Thu - Sat 10 a.m. - 10 p.m.
From Bobby Jones Expressway (Hwy. 415), exit at
Windsor Spring Rd. It's behind Wal-Mart.

Seating is on two levels in a large two-story glass-roofed log building. The short menu includes Heineken beer and pork skins. The "small bar-b-que pork plate" is a stupendous, gravity-defying mound of wonderful chipped pork, hash and rice, and cole slaw. A loaf of white bread is already on the table. This unusual Georgia barbecue place, owned by Augusta mayor Larry Sconyers, has been ranked as one of the nation's top ten barbecue restaurants by *People* magazine. Opened 1956. Drive-thru.

Date visited _____ *Remarks* _____

Sconyers Bar-B-Que, Augusta

Bar-B-Fact

> *The heaviest pig on record was named Big Bill. He weighed in at 2,552 pounds, was five feet tall and nine feet long. Bill's belly was so large it dragged the ground. After suffering a broken leg, Bill was mounted and put on display in Weekly County, TN, until he was sold to a traveling carnival in 1946.*

Scott's Barbecue (375)

P.O. Box 560, Macon Hwy.
Cochran, Ga. 31014
912/934-6069
County: Bleckley

Mon - Thu 10 a.m. - 8 p.m., Fri & Sat 10 a.m. - 9 p.m.
From downtown Cochran, take Old U.S. 129 (the old Macon Hwy.) about a mile and a half north.
It's on the left.

Open since 1952, this is one of the oldest barbecue places in central Georgia. Scott's cooks the meat in an open pit and offers a mild vinegar-based sauce. Brunswick stew and the standard sides are also served, along with salads and hamburgers and pecan pie for dessert. Dine in, table service, 50 seats.

Date visited_____Remarks_____

Shelia's BBQ (376)

21970 Providence Rd.
Alpharetta, Ga. 30201
770/442-9878
County: Fulton

Mon - Sat 8 a.m. - 7 p.m.
From Alpharetta, take Mayfield Rd. west, bear right at the third stop sign onto Providence Rd.
It's 3 or 4 miles on the right.

In business for several years as Hester's, but now operated by Shelia Foote, this little country store/barbecue place is popular with local construction workers, housewives, and golfers. Mostly a take-out operation, it sells tender pulled pork barbecue and wonderful Brunswick stew. Shelia's mild tomato-based sauce is applied sparingly to preserve the smoky flavor of the meat. Sides include baked beans, cole slaw, garlic bread, potato salad, and corn on the cob.

Date visited_____Remarks_____

The Sheppard House (377)

1610 Vienna Hwy.
Americus, Ga. 31709
912/924-8756
County: Sumter

Sun - Fri 11 - 2:30, Wed, Thu & Fri 6 p.m. - 8:30 p.m.
Closed Sat.
On U.S. 280 on the east side of Americus in the Americus Village shopping center.

Although the Sheppard House serves a wide variety of food, barbecue is their specialty. Hungry hordes can be fed quickly and well; there are 100 or so seats and a lunchtime cafeteria line helps folks get back to work without delay. Opened 1977.

Date visited_____Remarks_____

> *Of all domestic animals, a pig's diet is closest to that of human beings.*

Name/Map ID	**Hours/Directions**

Shirley's Real Pit BBQ (378)

1794 Industrial Blvd. NW
Conyers, Ga. 30207
770/860-0020
County: Rockdale

Mon - Sat 10:30 a.m. - 5 p.m.
From I-20 eastbound, take exit 40. Turn left on Sigman Rd., then right on Covington Hwy./Industrial Blvd. Go to third light. It's behind Bio-Lab.

One of Georgia's newest barbecue places is Shirley's. It wasn't yet open when this was written, but it will be by the time you read it. Shirley Wilson will be offering barbecued pork, beef, chicken, and ribs, as well as stew, sides, and a variety of fresh vegetables daily. Her sauce is a sweet and tangy red. Hot dogs, fish, burgers, fried chicken, and other non-barbecue items will be on the menu. Dine in, order at counter, about 80 seats, all nonsmoking.

Date visited _____ *Remarks* _____

Shorty's Wood-Cooked Barbecue (379)

1330 Boone Rd. E
Kingsland, Ga. 31548
912/729-6005
County: Camden

Mon - Sat 10 a.m. - 8 p.m., Sun 10 a.m. - 4 p.m.
From I-95, take exit 2 (Hwy. 40) It's on the east side of the exit, next to the Chevron station.

The enticing aroma and drifting smoke will help you find this tiny take-out operation. Shorty's sells chopped pork and sliced beef sandwiches and plates. The sauce is sweet and tomato-rich, and the Brunswick stew is a spicy concoction of meat, corn, butter beans, and tomatoes. Also available are ribs, chicken, hot dogs, slaw, beans, potato salad, and corn on the cob. There's outdoor seating at five picnic tables.

Date visited _____ *Remarks* _____

Simmons' Smokehouse (380)

2719 Hwy. 16 W
Jackson, Ga. 30233
770/227-9444
County: Butts

Mon - Sat 9 a.m. - 9 p.m.
From I-75 southbound take exit 67 (Hwy. 16), turn left, cross the bridge. It's on the right.

You can get your pork sliced instead of chopped here, if you like. Simmons sells barbecue sandwiches and plates, grilled chicken, chicken tenders, country-fried steak, hot dogs, and hamburgers out of this converted gas station right off of I-75 between Atlanta and Macon. Dine in, order at counter, plenty of seats.

Date visited _____ *Remarks* _____

Slope's BBQ of Roswell (381)

10360 Alpharetta St.
Roswell, Ga. 30075
770/518-7000
County: Fulton

Mon - Thu 11 a.m. - 9 p.m., Fri & Sat
11 a.m. - 9:30 p.m., Sun 11 a.m. - 2:30 p.m.
From downtown Roswell, go north on Alpharetta St.

The hickory-smoked meats at Slope's are delicious when eaten alone, but they're even better with the sweet and tangy brown sauce, a splendid mix of tomatoes, mustard, vinegar, and spices. A big selection of sides (beans, cole slaw, fries, potato salad, corn on the cob, green beans, black-eyed peas, collard greens, lima beans) accompanies the main dishes. Desserts include cobblers and banana pudding. All-you-can-eat specials Monday, Tuesday, and Wednesday. Dine in, nonsmoking only, 85 seats. Opened 1991.

Date visited _____ *Remarks* _____

Slope's BBQ of Woodstock (382)

10020 Hwy. 92
Woodstock, Ga. 30188
770/516-6789
County: Cherokee

Mon - Thu 11 a.m. - 9 p.m.,
Fri & Sat 11 a.m. - 9:30 p.m., Sun 11 a.m. - 2:30 p.m.
From I-575 northbound take the Hwy. 92/Woodstock exit.
Turn right. It's a half mile on the right, next to Ingles.

Slope's other place also serves real hickory-smoked and hand-pulled barbecue, a variety of appealing sides, and tasty desserts.

Date visited _____ *Remarks* _____

The Smokehouse (383)

Hwy. 32 W
Alma, Ga. 31510
912/632-4787
County: Bacon

Tue - Sat 11 a.m. - 9 p.m. (hours vary, call ahead).
From Waycross, go 25 miles north on U.S. 1.
Turn left onto Hwy. 32.

Owner Morris Chaffin Jr. learned to cook from his mother, and he loved it so much as a hobby that he decided to open a restaurant. He makes his barbecue from Boston butts cooked with oak and pecan (and other hardwoods sometimes) in a closed pit/smoker. For his sauce, he uses Cattleman's, to which he adds "a little something extra." Ribs are available by the full rack. Dine in, table service.

Date visited _____ *Remarks* _____

Bar-B-Fact

Pigs wallow in the mud not because they like to be dirty, but because they want to cool off on hot days. Having no perspiration systems, they must rely on evaporation and conduction to move heat away from their bodies.

Smoke House,
Gainesville

Name/Map ID	Hours/Directions

Smoke House Bar-B-Q (384)

3205 Atlanta Hwy.
Gainesville, Ga. 30507
770/536-7971
County: Hall

Fri & Sat 11 a.m. - 8 p.m.
From I-985, take exit 4, go south on Hwy. 53 a half mile,
turn left at the light onto Hwy. 13. It's straight ahead on
the right at junction with Hwy. 332.

Wayne Vaughn started out as a caterer. He decided to go into the restaurant business after so many of his customers asked where they could buy his barbecue on a regular basis. He's the only two-time first-place winner of the Stone Mountain BBQ Cook-off. Vaughn makes his sauce and Brunswick stew according to old family recipes. Sides include Brunswick stew, beans, cole slaw, potato salad, and chips. Order at a window and eat at picnic tables in the 80-seat "Woodshed Dining Room," a tin-roofed wooden shed next door. Opened 1980.

Date visited _____*Remarks* _____

Smoke House BBQ (385)

101 Recreation Rd.
Eatonton, Ga. 31024
706/485-0800
County: Putnam

Mon - Thu 10:30 a.m. - 9 p.m.,
Fri & Sat 10:30 a.m. - 10 p.m., Sun 11 a.m. - 5 p.m.
From the courthouse in Eatonton go south on old U.S.
441. It's near the ambulance service and the sheriff's dept.

Eatonton's Smoke House opened in late 1995 to rave reviews. They cook with hickory in a smoker, and offer a tangy mustard-based sauce. Smoked turkey is available, and on the side are potato salad, cole slaw, and beans. Steaks, fries, baked potatoes, and desserts are available on Thursday, Friday, and Saturday. Dine in, table service, 65 seats, nonsmokers' section.

Date visited _____*Remarks* _____

Smokehouse Ribs (386)

1873 Piedmont Rd. NE
Atlanta, Ga. 30324
404/607-0474
County: Fulton

Mon - Thu 11 a.m. - 10 p.m., Fri & Sat 11a.m. - 11 p.m.,
Sun 11 a.m. - 9 p.m.
In Rock Springs Plaza shopping center on Piedmont Rd.,
just south of Cheshire Bridge Road.

"Take your bones home" is the motto at Smokehouse Ribs. Get baby back pork ribs or beef ribs to go, or dine in at this little storefront place. Sweet 'n' tangy tomato-based sauce. Also grilled corn, veggies, cornbread, and desserts. If you like Brunswick stew thick and meaty and easy on the tomatoes, you'll find Smokehouse's version to be among the tastiest in town. Opened 1994.

Date visited _____ *Remarks* _____

Smokey Jim's BBQ (387)

401 N Main St.
Pearson, Ga. 31642
912/422-7881
County: Atkinson

Fri & Sat 11 a.m. - 10 p.m..
On North Main St. (U.S. 441) about two blocks
north of Hardee's.

Smokey Jim's is a take-out-only place serving pork, beef, chicken, ribs, Brunswick stew, and the usual sides. The meats are cooked in a smoker over oak coals. The red barbecue sauce isn't sweet, and comes in a choice of hot or mild. Opened 1992.

Date visited _____ *Remarks* _____

Smokey Joe's Bar BQ (388)

1174 Calhoun Falls Hwy.
Elberton, Ga. 30635
706/283-4653
County: Elbert

Fri & Sat 9:30 a.m. - 8 p.m.
From Athens, take Hwy. 72 east to Elberton.
It's on the left.

During the week, Joe runs the hunting and fishing store next door. On weekends he cooks hams in a smoker/grill with hickory and sells 'que until it runs out. Ribs are available by the full rack (baby back and short end), and a hot or mild vinegar-based red sauce is served. Dine in, table service, 30 seats.

Date visited _____ *Remarks* _____

Smokey Pig Barbecue (389)

1617 Eleventh Ave.
Columbus, Ga. 31901
706/327-9253
County: Muscogee

Mon - Fri 10 a.m. - 7 p.m., Sat 10 a.m. - 5 p.m.
From downtown, take Sixth Ave north, turn right on
Linwood Blvd. It's behind Electronic Tune
and Linwood Lunch.

Open-pit barbecue is served with a red sauce at this old intown place, established in 1953. On the side are Brunswick stew, beans, potato salad, fruit salad, and BBQ slaw. Dine in, order at counter, 75 seats. (This is Smokey Pig No. 1. Across the river in Phenix City, Alabama, at 1502 Opelika Rd. is No. 2.)

Date visited _____ *Remarks* _____

Smokin' Branch Barbecue (390)

4389 Victory Dr.
Columbus, Ga. 31903
706/685-0222
County: Muscogee

Mon - Sat 11 a.m. - 9 p.m.
From I-185, take exit 1, go a half mile west on Victory Dr.
(U.S. 27). It's on the right.

"We do it all good," they say at Smokin' Branch. Apparently, Columbians agree. The place attracts blue-collar and white-collar workers alike, as well as a lot of military personnel. Smokin' Branch cooks Boston butts in an open pit with oak and hickory. Pork ribs are served "dry." A homemade ketchup-based BBQ sauce, in a choice of hot or mild, is available to go on them. For dessert, there's homemade lemon, pecan, sweet potato, and chocolate meringue pies. Dine in, table service, 60 seats. Opened 1990.

Date visited _____*Remarks* _____

Sonny's Real Pit Bar-B-Q (391)

11170 Alpharetta Hwy.
Roswell, Ga. 30076
770/664-8930
County: Fulton

Sun - Thu 11 a.m. - 9 p.m., Fri & Sat 11 a.m. - 10 p.m.
On Hwy. 9 on the north side of Roswell, near Pep Boys.

With seventeen locations throughout Georgia, Sonny's surely sells more barbecue than any other restaurant chain in the state. The tender sliced pork served here is pink on the inside, as properly smoked meats should be. Sweet 'n' smoky pork ribs are served daily, and they're available as an all-you-can-eat item on a regular basis. The mild and medium sauces are tomato-based, and there's a mustardy hot sauce. Thick, dark, and sweet beans are flavored with shreds of smoked meat. Dine in, table service, about 200 seats, nonsmokers' area.

Date visited _____*Remarks* _____

Sonny's Real Pit Bar-B-Q (392)

1235 Indian Trail-Lilburn Rd.
Norcross, Ga. 30093
770/381-7357
County: Gwinnett

Sun - Thu 11 a.m. - 9 p.m., Fri & Sat 11 a.m. - 10 p.m.
From I-85 North, take exit 38 (Indian Trail-Lilburn Rd).
Go east/south 1.5 miles. It's on the right.

Date visited _____*Remarks* _____

Bar-B-Fact

A few of Georgia's many porky place names:
Hog Bay, Hog Bed Branch, Hog Creek, Hog Fork, Hog Gallus Island, Hog Hammock, Hog Heaven Branch, Hog Marsh Island, Hog Mountain, Hog Wallow Creek, Hogback Mountain, Hogcrawl Creek, Hogjawl Valley, Hognose Point, and Hogpen Branch.

Sonny's Real Pit Bar-B-Q (393)

1380 Boone Rd. E
Kingsland, Ga. 31548
912/673-7262
County: Camden

Sun - Thu 10:30 a.m. - 9 p.m.,
Fri & Sat 10:30 a.m. - 9:30 p.m.
From I-95, take exit 2. Go east on Hwy. 40 a half mile.
It's on the right.

Date visited _____ Remarks _____

Sonny's Real Pit Bar-B-Q (394)

160 Cobb Pkwy. SE
Marietta, Ga. 30062
770/428-1534
County: Cobb

Sun - Thu 11 a.m. - 9 p.m., Fri & Sat 11 a.m. - 10 p.m.
From I-75, take exit 112 and go west toward Marietta.
Turn right at third light onto Cobb Pkwy. (U.S. 41).
It's on the left in front of Sam's Club.

Date visited _____ Remarks _____

Sonny's Real Pit Bar-B-Q (395)

1870 Hwy. 20 SE
Conyers, Ga. 30208
770/860-0099
County: Rockdale

Sun - Thu 11 a.m. - 9 p.m., Fri & Sat 11 a.m. - 10 p.m.
From I-20, take exit 42. Go south on Hwy 138 one or
two miles. It's on the left.

Date visited _____ Remarks _____

Sonny's Real Pit Bar-B-Q (396)

1900 N. Slappey Blvd.
Albany, Ga. 31701
912/883-7427
County: Dougherty

Sun - Thu 11 a.m. - 9:30 p.m., Fri & Sat 11 a.m. - 10:30 p.m.
From the junction of U.S. 19 north and U.S. 82, go south on N.
Slappey Blvd. (U.S. 19 Bus.). It's about a mile on the left.

Date visited _____ Remarks _____

Sonny's Real Pit Bar-B-Q (397)

2037 Bemiss Rd.
Valdosta, Ga. 31602
912/242-8257
County: Lowndes

Sun - Thu 11 a.m. - 9 p.m., Fri & Sat 11 a.m. - 9:30 p.m.
From downtown Valdosta, go north on Ashley St. to
Bemiss Rd. (Hwy. 125). It's at the intersection.

Date visited _____ Remarks _____

Sonny's Real Pit Bar-B-Q (398)

2717 New Spring Rd. SE
Smyrna, Ga. 30080
770/955-1597
County: Cobb

Sun - Thu 11 a.m.- 9 p.m., Fri & Sat 11 a.m. - 10 p.m.
From Cumberland Mall, go north on Cobb Pkwy.
(U.S. 41). Turn left at the first light past I-285.
It's just ahead on the right.

Date visited _____ Remarks _____

Sonny's Real Pit Bar-B-Q (399)

3755 Atlanta Hwy.
Athens, Ga. 30622
706/546-0385
County: Clarke

Sun - Thu 11 a.m. - 9 p.m., Fri & Sat 11 a.m. - 10 p.m.
On Atlanta Hwy. (U.S. 78 Bus.) across from Georgia
Square mall, about 6 miles west of downtown Athens.

Date visited _____ *Remarks* _____

Sonny's Real Pit Bar-B-Q (400)

5328 New Jesup Hwy.
Brunswick, Ga. 31525
912/264-9184 or 9185
County: Glynn

Mon - Sun 11 a.m. - 9 p.m.
From I-95, take exit 7 (U.S. 341). It's about
a quarter mile toward Jesup, on the right.

Date visited _____ *Remarks* _____

Sonny's Real Pit Bar-B-Q (401)

625 Morrow Industrial Blvd.
Jonesboro, Ga. 30236
770/968-0052
County: Clayton

Fri & Sat 11 a.m. - 10 p.m., Sun - Thu 11 a.m. - 9 p.m.
From I-75, take exit 77 (U.S. 19/41, Tara Blvd.). Go
south one mile to Morrow Ind. Blvd. Turn left.
It's on the right.

Date visited _____ *Remarks* _____

Sonny's Real Pit Bar-B-Q (402)

6869 Peachtree Industrial Blvd.
Doraville, Ga. 30360
770/447-6616
County: DeKalb

Sun - Thu 11 a.m. - 9 p.m., Fri & Sat 11 a.m. - 10 p.m.
From Peachtree Industrial Blvd. exit at Winters Chapel
Rd., a little over a mile north of I-285. It's on
the east side of the intersection.

Date visited _____ *Remarks* _____

Sonny's Real Pit Bar-B-Q (403)

811 Russell Pkwy.
Warner Robins, Ga. 31088
912/929-3333
County: Houston

Sun - Thu 11 a.m. - 9 p.m., Fri & Sat 11 a.m. - 9:30 p.m.
From I-75, take exit 45, go east to third traffic light. Turn
right onto Houston Rd. At second light, turn left onto
Russell Pkwy. It's on the right, past Lowe's.

Date visited _____ *Remarks* _____

Sonny's Real Pit Bar-B-Q (404)

2103 Shorter Ave. SW
Rome, Ga. 30165
706/234-1441
County: Floyd

Sun - Thu 11 a.m. - 9 p.m, Fri & Sat 11 a.m. - 10 p.m.
From the Floyd Medical Center at Turner McCall and
Martha Berry, go west on Hwy. 20 (Shorter Ave.)
a little over a mile

Date visited _____ *Remarks* _____

Sonny's Real Pit Bar-B-Q (405)

30975 U.S. Hwy. 441 S
Commerce, Ga. 30529
706/335-4741
County: Banks

Sun - Thu 11 a.m. - 9 p.m., Fri & Sat 11 a.m. - 10 p.m.
From I-85, take exit 53. Go toward Commerce on U.S.
441. It's just past the Tanger Factory Outlet.

Date visited _____ *Remarks* _____

Sonny's Real Pit Bar-B-Q (406)

7830 Hwy. 92
Woodstock, Ga. 30188
770/926-7848
County: Cherokee

Sun - Thu 11 a.m. - 9 p.m., Fri & Sat 11 a.m. - 10 p.m.
From I-575 northbound take the Hwy. 92/Woodstock exit.
Turn left at the top of the ramp. It's 1.5 miles on the left.

Date visited _____ *Remarks* _____

Sonny's Real Pit Bar-B-Q (407)

1510 Hwy. 82 W
Tifton, Ga. 31793
912/386-0606
County: Tift

Mon - Sun 11 a.m. - 9 p.m.
From I-75, take exit 18. Go west on Hwy. 82.
It's on the left.

Date visited _____ *Remarks* _____

Old Brick Pit Barbeque,
Chamblee (see p.115)

Southern Bar-B-Q (408)

906 Hwy. 301 S
Glennville, Ga. 30427
912/654-3884
County: Tattnall

Tue - Thu 10:30 a.m. - 8 p.m.,
Fri & Sat 10:30 a.m. - 9 p.m.
From downtown Glennville, go south on U.S. 301/25. It's
on the right at the outskirts of town.

This take-out and drive-thru establishment offers barbecue basics and a tangy mustardy sauce. The usual sides are available, with baked potatoes as a plus. Besides barbecue, Southern sells burgers, chicken sandwiches, fish sandwiches, and other seafood items. It has outside seating at picnic tables for 6 to 10.

Date visited _____*Remarks* _____

Southern Boys Barbecue (409)

2811 N Columbia St.
Milledgeville, Ga. 31061
912/453-9444
County: Baldwin

Tue - Sat 11 a.m. - 9 p.m.
On Hwy. 441 North about 2 miles north of Holiday Inn.

The standard meal during the week at Southern Boys' is their barbecue plate, a flavorful repast of smoked pork, Brunswick stew, slaw, pickles, and bread. Barbecue sandwiches and sides (baked beans, cole slaw, and potato salad) are available, too. Chicken is served Thursday, Friday, and Saturday, and ribs on Friday and Saturday. Old-fashioned Brunswick stew is served all the time, as are homemade desserts.

Date visited _____*Remarks* _____

Signs at Spring House
Bar-B-Q on Jefferson
Road near Athens

outhpork Barbecue (410)

01 S Church St.
homaston, Ga. 30286
06/647-4288
ounty: Upson

Mon - Wed 11 a.m. - 8 p.m., Thu - Sat 11 a.m. - 9 p.m.
From the courthouse square, take S. Church St. (U.S. 19)
south. It's on the left.

ravelers on U.S. 19 have two opportunities in Thomaston to pick up some bar-
ecue for the road, and they don't even have to get out of their cars. On the
orth side of town, Piggie Park offers drive-in 'que. A drive-thru is available
ere. Southpork has a thin, mild tomato/vinegar sauce on its pork, and a sweet
d sauce on the ribs and chicken. The barbecue chef salad here is a favorite.
ine in, order at counter, about 40 seats inside, picnic tables out front.

te visited _____*Remarks* _____

peedi Pig 1 Barbecue (411)

146 Hwy. 85
nesboro, Ga. 30236
70/471-4111
ounty: Clayton

Mon - Thu 11 a.m. - 8:30 p.m., Fri & Sat 11 a.m. - 9 p.m.
On Hwy. 85 between Riverdale and Fayetteville, at Flint
River Rd. and Helmer Rd.

eedi Pig 1 is housed in a small building with a take-out window. In a separate
ructure next door is the dining room. Besides barbecued meats, SP 1 offers
ew, smoked buffalo wings, slaw, garlic bread, fries, chips, and barbecue beans.
omemade apple, peach, and sweet potato fried pies are available for dessert.

te visited _____*Remarks* _____

peedi Pig Barbecue (412)

15 S Glynn St.
ayetteville, Ga. 30214
70/719-2720
ounty: Fayette

Mon - Thu 11 a.m. - 8:30 p.m., Fri & Sat 11 a.m. - 9 p.m.
From the old courthouse in downtown Fayetteville, go
south on GA 85. It's not far past Melear's, on the right.

his is Speedi Pig no. 2; the original is in Jonesboro. It serves the same fine
ods as the other place.

te visited _____*Remarks* _____

piced Right Bar-B-Que (413)

364 Lawrenceville Hwy. NW
lburn, Ga. 30247
70/564-0355
ounty: Gwinnett

Mon - Sat 11 a.m. - 9 p.m.
From I-85 northbound, exit at Indian Trail-Lilburn Rd.
Turn right, go about 3 miles to U.S. 29. Turn right.
It's a short distance ahead on the left.

iced Right's all-you-care-to-eat buffet features old-fashioned real barbecue and
l the fixings. The superb pulled pork here is championship quality, and the buf-
t features items such as turnip greens, rice, cornbread, and white bread. A red
uce comes in mild, hot, "Lilburner," and "Killer," while a South Carolina-style
ustard sauce is available in hot or mild. A mild North Carolina vinegar sauce is
so available. Dine in, table service, seats 120. Nonsmokers' area. Opened 1988.

te visited _____*Remarks* _____

*Sprayberry's,
Jackson Street*

Name/Map ID	**Hours/Directions**

Sprayberry's Barbecue (414)

229 Jackson St.
Newnan, Ga. 30263
770/253-4421
County: Coweta

*Mon - Sat 10:30 a.m. - 9 p.m.
U.S. 29 North at Sprayberry Rd.
on the north side of town.*

A historic marker should be put up in front of this place. Family owned and operated since 1926, Sprayberry's has been a favorite of several generations of Georgians. Fresh hams are barbecued daily in outside pits. Try the Houston Special sandwich, a succulent pile of chopped outside pork piled on a bun and topped off with a big glop of Brunswick stew. Tangy tomato/vinegar sauce. Vinegary cole slaw. Fried apple and peach pies are among the desserts. Basic, clean dining rooms. Curb service, too.

Date visited _____*Remarks* _____

Sprayberry's Barbecue (415)

1060 East Hwy. 34
Newnan, Ga. 30265
770/253-5080
County: Coweta

*Mon - Sat 7 a.m. - 9 p.m.
Hwy. 34 at I-85 (exit 9). On the east side of interchange.*

The menu and the quality are the same as at the original location, so that means good eating right next to an interstate highway. It doesn't happen often, so enjoy

Date visited _____*Remarks* _____

Bar-B-Quote

"Health food makes me sick."
—*Calvin Trillin*

*Spring House Bar-B-Q,
Broad Street, Athens*

Name/Map ID	**Hours/Directions**

Spring House Bar-B-Q (416)

1078 Baxter St.
Athens, Ga. 30606
706/613-1979
County: Clarke

*Sun - Thu 11 a.m. - 10 p.m., Fri - Sat 11 a.m. - 11 p.m.
On Baxter Street between Milledge Ave. and Alps Rd.,
on the west side of Athens.*

Spring House's smoky, tender pork is complemented perfectly by the black-peppery-hot red sauce (mild sauce available, too). Choose baby back, regular, or Texas-style ribs. Also served are a variety of salads, fried chicken, grilled chicken, wings, grilled tuna, cheesesteaks, vegetable plates, burgers, and a good selection of beer. Sweet potato pie and cheesecake for dessert. Dine in, table service.

Date visited _____ *Remarks* _____

Spring House Bar-B-Q (417)

12240 Jefferson Rd.
Athens, Ga. 30607
706/548-5880
County: Clarke

*Mon - Wed 11 a.m. - 2:30 p.m., Thu - Sat 11 a.m. - 8:30 p.m.
From the north Athens Bypass, take the Prince Ave. exit, go
north on Hwy. 129 about 5 miles. It's on the left.*

No beer at this location. Otherwise, the menu is pretty much the same. Dine in, table service.

Date visited _____ *Remarks* _____

Spring House Bar-B-Q (418)

111 E May St.
Winder, Ga. 30680
770/867-8550
County: Barrow

*Sun-Thu 11 a.m. - 9:15 p.m., Fri & Sat 11 a.m. - 10:15 p.m.
From downtown Winder, go east on East May St.
(Old U.S. 29). It's on the right.*

Same menu as the Spring House on Baxter St. in Athens. Dine in, table service, plenty of seats.

Date visited _____ *Remarks* _____

Spruce's Bar-B-Q (419)

1201 Meriwether St.
Griffin, Ga. 30223
770/412-1007
County: Spalding

Tue 5 p.m. - 7 p.m., Mon - Thu 10 a.m. - 7 p.m.,
Fri & Sat 10 a.m. - 8 p.m.
In a brown cinderblock building on Meriwether St. at College
Extension, southwest of downtown Griffin at the railroad.

An old roadside place on an old highway, it looks just like a barbecue joint should look. Owner Terry Belvin is carrying on the tradition begun by founder Emerson Spruce in 1938. Advertised as the "place where Presidents have eaten," it also has fed train crews who would sometimes pull their engines onto the nearby spur track just to get some barbecue.   All-you-can-eat rib special every Tuesday.

Date visited _____*Remarks* _____

Stew & Que (420)

Willingham Ave./Hwy. 23 S
Baldwin, Ga. 30511
706/778-6419
County: Habersham

Tue - Sat 10:30 a.m. - 9 p.m.
Take I-85 North to I-985 North to Hwy. 365 north to Hwy.
441 Bypass South to Hwy. 23 South. It's on the right,
across the street from the Baldwin post office.

Pit-cooked 'que and awesome stew and country decor. They smoke hams in an open pit with hickory wood and add a bit of their homemade, just-a-little-tangy red sauce. They have both pork and beef ribs, a wide selection of sides, and a big choice of desserts. Try the Oh Yeah! Buffet. Dine in, order at counter.

Date visited _____*Remarks* _____

Stinson's Old Fashioned Bar-B-Q (421)

Hwy 341
Lumber City, Ga. 31549
912/363-4788
County: Telfair

Mon - Sat 10:30 a.m. - 9 p.m.
At U.S. 23/341 and Hwy. 19, next to the Huddle House.

Stinson's, voted one of middle Georgia's favorite barbecue places in a 1996 *Macon Telegraph* poll, serves up some fine smoked meat and delicious stew in a little blue house near the Ocmulgee River. Cole slaw, potato salad, fries, and onion rings are the only sides. Dine in, order at counter, 80 seats, nonsmokers' area. Drive-thru window.

Date visited _____*Remarks* _____

Sweetwater Inn Barbeque (422)

2471 Bankhead Hwy.
Austell, Ga. 30001
770/948-4200
County: Cobb

Mon - Thu 11 a.m. - 9 p.m., Fri 11 a.m. - 1 a.m.,
Sat 11 a.m. - 12 a.m., Sun 12 p.m. - 12 a.m..
From I-285, exit at Bankhead Hwy. go west through Mableton.
It's in an octagonal cedar building on the left.

This restaurant/bar on the old highway to Alabama opened in 1946. It serves barbecued pork, burgers, wings, fresh vegetables, and other items daily. Hours vary, depending on how good business is. The kitchen sometimes stays open 'til 10 p.m. on weeknights. Dine in, table service, 100 seats.

Date visited _____*Remarks* _____

Tasty Chick/Country Bar-B-Q (423)

Hwy. 91 S
Newton, Ga. 31770
912/734-7362
County: Baker

Mon - Thu 8 a.m. - 8 p.m., Fri & Sat 8 a.m. - 9 p.m..
From Albany, take Hwy. 91 South about 20 miles. It's at
the junction with Hwy. 37 in Newton.

In the summer of 1994, the waters of the nearby Flint River rose almost to the first-floor ceiling of the county courthouse here in tiny Newton. The town suffered extensive damage, but fortunately this little place remained in business to keep Baker County on the barbecue map. The barbecue part of the menu is fairly limited, but the pork, cooked in a big steel smoker outside, is tasty. Dine in, seats 23.

Date visited _____ *Remarks* _____

Taylor's Barbecue (424)

1213 Liberty St.
Waynesboro, Ga. 30830
706/554-4478
County: Burke

Mon - Thu 4 a.m. - 11 p.m., Fri & Sat 4 a.m. - midnight,
Sun 4 a.m. - 9 p.m.
From Augusta, take U.S. 25 south 30 miles to
Waynesboro. It's on the right, across from the Holiday Inn.

Taylor's has served up pit-cooked, hickory smoked ham meat for thirty years. To go on it is a homemade orange/red sauce made according to a patented recipe. It's bottled and available for sale in the restaurant. It's just a bit spicy and is great on fries. A big buffet is a twice-daily feature. Desserts are homemade and are different every day. Taylor's serves breakfast, lunch, and dinner. It opens early. During hunting season, it's open by the time the deer get up.

Date visited _____ *Remarks* _____

Terry's Hickory House Bar-B-Que (425)

U. S. 19
Camilla, Ga. 31730
912/336-7406
County: Mitchell

Tue - Sat 11 a.m. - 9 p.m.
From Camilla, take U.S. 19 two miles north.
It's on the right.

Terry's barbecue sandwiches feature huge flavorful smoky chunks of pork direct from the pit. The hickory-smoked meats are accented by hot or mild red sauces or a thin, sweet "special" sauce. Brunswick stew, beans, cole slaw, curly fries, corn on the cob, potato salad, and fried okra are available on the side. Dine in, seats 130. Opened 1991.

Date visited _____ *Remarks* _____

Bar-B-Quote

> *"To eat is human; to digest, divine."*
> — *Mark Twain*

Texas Bar-B-Q (426)

2555 Delk Rd.
Marietta, Ga. 30067
770/955-2767
County: Cobb

Mon - Fri 11 a.m. - 8:30 p.m., Sat 11 a.m. - 5 p.m.
From I-75 north, exit at Delk Rd., go east a quarter mile
and turn left into Delk Village shopping center.
Look for the sign.

While Texas-style barbecue places are extremely rare in Georgia, Cobb County has three of them (see Rib Ranch). This one serves beef ribs, beef sausage, jalapeño cornbread, and other western favorites of the Lone Star County. Pork ribs and BBQ turkey are available, too. Desserts are carrot cake and pecan pie. Dine in, table service, about 80 seats.

Date visited _____*Remarks* _____

Thelma's Rib Shack (427)

302 Auburn Ave. NE
Atlanta, Ga. 30303
404/523-0081
County: Fulton

Mon - Thu 11 a.m. - 4 p.m., Fri & Sat 11 a.m. - 7 p.m.
On historic Auburn Avenue downtown, just east of the
I-75/85 Downtown Connector.

For years this small storefront place was well known as the Auburn Avenue Rib Shack. It closed some time ago, but now it has been recently reincarnated under the name Thelma's. Pork ribs are the specialty, of course, but don't overlook the open-pit-cooked barbecue. A dark red sauce, available hot or mild, combines with the meat quite nicely. Brunswick stew, green peas, sweet potatoes, okra, cabbage, and other home-style vegetables are served, too. Dine in, 55 seats.

Date visited _____*Remarks* _____

Thigpen Bar B Que (428)

2679 Mesena Rd.
Thomson, Ga. 30824
706/595-8513
County: McDuffie

Saturday mornings only.
From the First Methodist Church on Main St. in
Thomson, take Lumpkin St./Mesena Rd. west. At fork, go
left. Thigpen's is 4 miles on the right.

The only things on the menu at this backyard shack are barbecued pork and hash (not hash-on-rice). Take-out only. Picnic tables outside.

Date visited _____*Remarks* _____

Third Street Bar-B-Q (429)

Third St.
Vienna, Ga. 31092
912/268-4000
County: Dooly

Thu - Sat 11 a.m. - 7 p.m.
From the Dooly County Courthouse square in Vienna, go
north on U.S. 41 and look for the sign.

Vienna is the home of the Big Pig Jig, Georgia's official championship barbecue-cooking contest. People who've participated in it now can't drive through here without getting a powerful desire for smoked pig meat. If it happens to you (on a Thursday, Friday, or Saturday), just stop in at Third Street Bar-B-Q. You will be satisfied. Take-out only. No inside or outside seating.

Date visited _____*Remarks* _____

The Big Pig Jig in Vienna, Georgia's official barbecue cook-off, began in 1982 as a result of a bet on who could cook the tastiest pig. Colorfully named cooking teams (for example, Ham Hock Jocks and Swine Lake Ballet) now compete in cooking whole hogs, ribs, shoulders, and stew. The contests, which also include non-food events like hog calling and showmanship, are preceded by parades, pageants, concerts, crafts shows, livestock shows, and a variety of other events. The 1996 schedule featured a Lighting of the Flame ceremony and other "Olym-pig" activities. The Atlanta Journal and Constitution Barbecue Fest is not a competition; it's an "eating event." Vendors, cooking demonstrations, food samples, and live music attract ten thousand or more. It's held in a different location each year.

This & That Bar-Be-Que (430)

87 Main St.
Luthersville, Ga. 30251
770/927-0804
County: Meriwether

Tue - Sat 11:30 a.m. - 10 p.m.
From I-85, take exit 8. Go 8 miles south on U.S. 27 Alt.
It's on the left, a half-mile north of Luthersville.

Look for a little red wooden take-out shack next to a liquor store. This & That serves meat cooked over an open pit stoked with charcoal, oak, and hickory. Chipped pork and rib sandwiches are the specialties. Brunswick stew and the usual sides are available also. Take-out only. Opened 1996.

Date visited _____*Remarks* _____

This Is It Bar-B-Q & Seafood (431)

2056 Campbellton Rd. SW
Atlanta, Ga 30311
404/758-7294
County: Fulton

Mon - Wed 11 a.m. - 11 p.m., Thu 11 a.m. - 12 p.m.,
Fri & Sat 11 a.m. - 1 a.m., Sun 1 p.m. - 10 p.m.
From Lakewood Frwy. (Hwy. 166), exit at DeLowe Dr. Go
north to Campbellton Plaza shopping center.

What it is is Boston butts cooked in a closed pit with hickory, red sauce in a choice of hot or mild, beans, cole slaw, fries, potato salad, onion rings, vegetables, hot dogs, cheesesteaks, and homemade cakes. Dine in, order at counter, 40 seats, nonsmokers' area. Opened 1983.

Date visited _____*Remarks* _____

This Is It Bar-B-Q & Seafood (432)

2776 Hargrove Rd. SE
Smyrna, Ga. 30080
770/435-3159
County: Cobb

Mon - Thu 10:30 a.m. - 10 p.m.,
Fri & Sat 10:30 a.m. - 10:30 p.m., Sun 12 p.m. - 8 p.m.
From I-285, go north on Cobb Pkwy. (U.S. 41). Turn left
at first light. Turn right at Hargrove Rd.

Jumbo Buffalo wings, shrimp, rib tips, fish, hushpuppies, sandwiches, thick Brunswick stew, fried okra, red velvet cake, potato pie, banana pudding, and peach cobbler. And more. All-you-can-eat buffet. Dine in, order at counter, about 30 seats.

Date visited _____*Remarks* _____

Bar-B-Quote

"Corn bread is not supposed to be sweet. That's in the Bible, too. The Book of Martha White, 7:11. If you want something sweet, order the pound cake. Anybody who puts sugar in the corn bread is a heathen who doesn't love the Lord, not to mention Southeastern Conference football."

— Lewis Grizzard

This Is It Bar-B-Q & Seafood (433)

Greenbriar Mall, SW
Atlanta, Ga. 30331
404/344-1009
County: Fulton

Mon - Sat 8:30 a.m. - 9 p.m , Sun 12 p.m. - 6 p.m.
From I-285 in southwest Atlanta, exit at Hwy. 166 and
head east. The mall is at the first exit, on the right.

Also rib tips, beans, cole slaw, potato salad, mac-and-cheese, collard greens, rice souffle, and more. (This This Is It is in the food court at Greenbriar Mall.)

Date visited _____ Remarks _____

This Is It Bar-B-Q & Seafood (434)

4065 Memorial Dr.
Decatur, Ga. 30032
404/292-5616
County: DeKalb

Sun - Wed 10:30 a.m. - 11 p.m.,
Thu - Sat 10:30 a.m. - 2 a.m.
From I-285, exit at Memorial Dr. and go west, toward Atlanta,
about 1.5 miles. It's on the left in a small shopping center.

It's another one of those This Is It places with the same extensive menu. Dine in, order at counter, 40 seats, all nonsmoking. Opened 1987.

Date visited _____ Remarks _____

This Is It Bar-B-Q (435)

4514 Washington Rd.
College Park, Ga. 30349
404/669-9517
County: Fulton

Sun - Wed 11 a.m. - 10 p.m., Thu 11 a.m. - 11 p.m.,
Fri & Sat 11 a.m. - 12 p.m.
From I-285, take exit 2 to Washington Rd. and go a half block
west "outside" of I-285. It's in Washington Village shopping center.

This This Is It sells barbecue (and plenty of other foods), but not seafood. This Is It Seafood is in a separate building nearby. Dine in, order at counter, 25 seats.

Date visited _____ Remarks _____

This Is It Express (436)

447 Ponce de Leon Ave. NE
Atlanta, Ga. 30308
404/875-1113
County: Fulton

Mon - Thu 10 a.m. - 11 p.m., Fri & Sat 10 a.m. - 12 a.m.
From the Fox Theater on Peachtree St. in midtown
Atlanta, go east on Ponce de Leon Ave. It's on the right.

Smoked meats, baby back ribs, rib tips, short ends, full racks of ribs, Brunswick stew, beans, cole slaw, fries, potato salad, fish, shrimp, collard greens, other tasty vegetables, and homemade desserts such as sweet potato pie and carrot cake. Take-out only (except for eight or so seats at picnic tables). Opened 1996.

Date visited _____ Remarks _____

This Little Piggy Bar-B-Q (437)

63 E Johnston St.
Forsyth, Ga. 31029
912/994-0618
County: Monroe

Tue - Fri 10:30 a.m. - 7 p.m., Sat 10:30 a.m. - 2 p.m.
From the courthouse in downtown Forsyth, take East
Johnston Street to This Little Piggy.

This Little Piggy went to the market, bought some prime meat, smoked it, served it with an old-fashioned mustard-based sauce, added a few delicious sides, and made a lot of people live happily ever after (or at least until the next mealtime).

Date visited _____ Remarks _____

Thomas Bar-B-Q (438)

Hwy. 32
Leesburg, Ga. 31763
912/759-2921
County: Lee

Fri & Sat 1 p.m. - 9 p.m.
From Albany, take U.S. 19 north about 10 miles to
Leesburg. Turn left onto Hwy. 32.
"Drive on down. You'll see the sign."

Strictly barbecue and fixings. The meat is open-pit-cooked over charcoal. The
sauce is a regular red sauce. The combination of the two makes for some
mighty good eating.

Date visited _____*Remarks* _____

Thompson & Thompson Barbeque (439)

342 W Jackson St.
Thomasville, Ga. 31792
912/228-5999
County: Thomas

Wed - Sun 10:30 a.m. - 9 p.m.
From Broad St. in the center of Thomasville, turn onto
Hwy. 319 Bus. (W. Jackson St.). It's a short distance
ahead at the edge of downtown.

Thompson & Thompson is a small place that does a lot of take-out business.
The meat is open-pit-cooked with oak and pecan. The sauce is a modified commercial sauce. It's a little sweet. Vegetables include collards, turnips, butter
beans, and peas, all cooked fresh. Roast beef and oxtails are among the other
items. Dine in, order at counter, 20 seats.

Date visited _____*Remarks* _____

Tracy's Bar-B-Que (440)

4934 Cleveland Hwy.
Gainesville, Ga. 30506
770/983-3592
County: Hall

Wed - Sat 10:30 a.m. - 9 p.m., Sun 11 a.m. - 9 p.m.
On U.S. 129, about 9 miles north of Gainesville, on the
right. It's 7/10 mile south of Hwy. 52.

Tracy learned how to cook barbecue in the early 1970s. She cooks fresh hams in
a closed pit with hickory wood. Her homemade red sauce is not too sweet and
not too spicy. That's all that Tracy will reveal about it. The Brunswick stew is
excellent, and the homemade pies are worth every pound that they put on your
body. Also, burgers, fish, chicken tenders. Dine in, 50 seats. In business twenty-
two years.

Date visited _____*Remarks* _____

Treybon (441)

520 Reynolds St.
Augusta, Ga. 30901
706/724-0632
County: Richmond

Mon - Wed 11 a.m. - 3 p.m., Thu 11 a.m. - 8 p.m.,
Fri & Sat 11 a.m. - 9 p.m.
On Reynolds St. between 5th and 6th Sts. in downtown
Augusta, a block from the river.

Treybon features Memphis-style Bar-B-Que "with a Cajun twist" and a "sauce bar"
with twelve very different homemade sauces (and more being added all the time).
One sauce includes bourbon in the recipe, and one, called "High Plains Drifter," is
very, very hot. Also served are barbecued turkey, St. Louis-style ribs, and Cajun
shrimp and sausage dishes. No fried foods. Fifty kinds of beer. Opened 1997.

Date visited _____*Remarks* _____

Troy's Bar-B-Que (442)

4 Calhoun Ave.
Rome, Ga. 30161
706/291-7188
County: Floyd

Mon - Thu 6 a.m. - 3 p.m., Fri & Sat 6 a.m. - 9 p.m.
From U.S. 27 (Turner McCall Blvd.) go north (away
from town) on Broad St. It's at the corner of
Broad St. and Calhoun Ave.

When in Rome, do as the Romans do and head to Troy's for barbecue. It's made from hams cooked with hickory over an open pit. Troy's red sauce is mild, but bottles of hot sauce are available to spice it up. Baked beans, potato salad, cole slaw, vegetables, fries, and other sides are offered. Desserts: homemade cobblers, banana pudding. Homemade food makes the difference. Dine in, table service, 100 seats. Seating at tables and at the counter.

Date visited _____ Remarks _____

Tucker's Bar-BQ Drive-In (443)

4591 Broadway
Macon, Ga. 31206
912/788-9940
County: Bibb

Mon - Sat 10 a.m. - midnight, Sun 2 p.m. - 10 p.m.
From I-75, take exit 49 and go south on Pio Nono Ave. At
1st light, turn left on Guy Paine Rd. Turn right onto
Broadway. It's on the right.

A drive-in specializing in barbecue on a street named Broadway? Sounds like retro fun to us. Tucker's offers old-fashioned curb service until midnight. The half-century-old place serves pulled and chopped barbecue with a tomato/mustard/vinegar sauce. Brunswick stew, beans, cole slaw, and fries are the chief BBQ sides. Also burgers, hamburger steaks, BLTs, egg sandwiches, and hot dogs. Beer and skins, too. Drive-in, dine in, table service, 45 seats.

Date visited _____ Remarks _____

Twelve Oaks Bar-B-Que (444)

2948 Cleveland Hwy.
Dalton, Ga. 30721
706/259-7675
County: Whitfield

Thu - Sat 11 a.m. - 8 p.m.
From I-75, take exit 137 (Rocky Face). Go east toward
Dalton on the bypass. Turn left onto Cleveland Rd.
(Hwy. 71). It's on the right at the end of the 4-lane road.

This take-out operation serves pork barbecue made from hams and beef barbecue made from brisket cooked in a smoker using hickory. The homemade barbecue sauce is sweet and spicy. Ribs by the full rack.

Date visited _____ Remarks _____

Bar-B-Fact

"Never order barbecue in a place that also serves quiche."

— Lewis Grizzard

Twin Oaks

Twin Oaks Drive In (445)

2618 Norwich St.
Brunswick, Ga. 31520
912/265-3131
County: Glynn

Mon - Thu 10:30 a.m. - 8 p.m.,
Fri & Sat 10:30 a.m. - 9 p.m.
From Gloucester St. in downtown Brunswick, go north
one mile on Norwich St. It's on the right.

"Brunswick's Best Bar-B-Q for Over 50 Years." This classic place, with its old neon sign out front, has been serving fine smoked meat "Hot from the Pit" since 1943. Besides barbecue, it has catfish, fried chicken, liver, sandwiches, and salads. Brunswick stew, beans, cole slaw, potato salad, onion rings, blooming onions, and deep-fried corn on the cob too. Dine in, take-out, or curb service under the big oaks.

Date visited _____ *Remarks* _____

Two Brothers Bar-B-Que (446)

1695 Old Canton Rd.
Ball Ground, Ga. 30107
770/735-2900
County: Cherokee

Wed & Thu 10:30 a.m. - 9 p.m.,
Fri - Sun 10:30 a.m. - 10 p.m.
From Marietta, take I-575 north to Ball Ground (Howell
Bridge Rd.) exit. Turn right, then left at the first stop sign.

In business about twenty-five years, Two Brothers Bar-B-Que is a sawdust-floor, antique-decorated, country-cooking place serving closed-pit, hickory-smoked, chopped pork with a red sauce on the side or on the meat. Brunswick stew, beans, cole slaw, and fries are on the side. Homemade pies and ice cream are the desserts. Dine in, table service, seats 90.

Date visited _____ *Remarks* _____

Uncle Sargeant's Barbeque (447)

885 Bouldercrest Dr. SE
Atlanta, Ga. 30316
404/241-7050
County: DeKalb

Mon - Thu 11:30 a.m. - 10 p.m., Fri & Sat 11:30 a.m.- 11 p.m.
From I-285 southeast of the city,
take Bouldercrest Rd. north about 2 miles.
It's on the left in Meadows Plaza shopping center.

Sgt. Henry Wyatt opened this place a couple of years ago. His open-pit-cooked barbecue, pork ribs, and beef ribs are the main attractions, but he also serves up some excellent freshly made sides and vegetables such as potato salad, collards, macaroni-and-cheese, and black-eyed peas. Rib tips, pig ears, and oxtails are also available. Desserts include pound cake, peach cobbler, and banana pudding. Dine in, order at counter, 12 seats, all nonsmoking.

Date visited_____Remarks _____

Vandy's Barbeque (448)

22 W Vine St.
Statesboro, Ga. 30458
912/764-2444
County: Bulloch

Mon - Sat 6 a.m. - 6 p.m.
From I-16, take U.S. 25 to downtown Statesboro. Turn left
at the post office. It's a couple of blocks down on the left.

Housed in a small plain building in downtown Statesboro, Vandy's is a step-back-in-time local institution that serves one of the best barbecue sandwiches in the state. Fresh-off-the-pit juicy pork is plopped onto white bread and then united with Vandy's delicious mustardy sauce to create a masterpiece. From Rabun Gap to Tybee Light, there's nothing better.

Date visited_____Remarks _____

Vandy's,
Vine Street

163

Vandy's Barbeque (449)

Hwy. 80 E
Statesboro, Ga. 30458
912/764-3033
County: Bulloch

Mon - Sat 9 a.m. - 9 p.m.
At Statesboro Mall on Northside Drive (U.S. 80 East) at Veterans Memorial Pkwy.

It offers white-bread pork sandwiches and the same mustardy sauce, but this Vandy's is a full-service restaurant with fried chicken, catfish, shrimp, a variety of vegetables, and other items. Daily specials. Dine in, table service, 100 seats, nonsmokers' section.

Date visited _____*Remarks* _____

Varsity Bar-B-Q (450)

314 Forrester Dr.
Dawson, Ga. 31742
912/995-4888
County: Terrell

Mon - Sun 9 a.m. - 9 p.m.
On Hwy. 82/520 about a mile south of downtown Dawson. It's 23 miles northwest of Albany.

The tasty Brunswick stew here is so thick and meaty, you can eat it with a fork. In fact, it's so thick that the Varsity serves it as a sandwich, too. Superb cornbread. Other sides include slaw, baked beans, fries, mashed potatoes, turnip greens, and tossed salad. Also meat-and-two-vegetable meals, ribeye steaks, hamburger steaks, sandwiches, and a small salad bar. Two dessert choices: pecan pie and peanut butter chiffon pie. Table service, 130 seats. Opened 1984.

Date visited _____*Remarks* _____

Village Bar B Que Restaurant (451)

2098 Blue Ridge Dr.
McCaysville, Ga. 30555
706/492-4592
County: Fannin

Sun - Thu 8 a.m. - 8 p.m., Fri & Sat 8 a.m. - 8:30 p.m.
From Hwy. 515 (Zell Miller Pkwy.) in Blue Ridge, go north 8 miles on Hwy. 5. It's on the left just south of McCaysville.

"Fresh makes the difference" is the slogan at Village Bar B Que. Boston butts and shoulders are cooked on an open pit with hickory. The red sauce is available hot or mild. A hot food bar and a salad bar are options. Non-barbecue items vary, but fried chicken and pork chops are usually available. Homemade cakes and pies. Dine in, table service, seats 72. Drive-thru.

Date visited _____*Remarks* _____

Bar-B-Quote

"To people with an allegiance to barbecue, the pig is a sacred cow."
— Jane and Michael Stern, Real American Food

Bar-B-Quote

> *"It is a social event, whether a family's Sunday dinner or a town's Saturday night celebration. Barbecue signifies home, or hometown, or home state; to eat it again is to taste where you came from."* — Jane and Michael Stern, Real American Food

Name/Map ID	Hours/Directions

Wagner's Bar-B-Que (452)

2406 Sylvester Rd.
Albany, Ga. 31705
912/436-7177
County: Dougherty

Mon - Thu 11 a.m. - 9 p.m., Fri & Sat 11 a.m. - 10 p.m.
On Sylvester Rd. (U.S. 82 Bus.) at Cordele Rd. next to
Georgia 7 Theatres, on the east side of Albany.

"Everything is special" at this family-run place on the east side of Albany. Meats smoked with oak coals are complemented with a choice of sauces, including a mustard-based mix. corn on the cob and onion rings are tasty sides. Smoked turkey, grilled chicken breasts, seafood, hot dogs, hamburgers, and chicken fingers, are served, too. Pecan and lemon pies. Dine in, table service, plenty of seats.

Date visited _____ *Remarks* _____

Walker's Bar-B-Que Pit (453)

71 E Willis St.
Sycamore, Ga. 31790
912/567-2333
County: Turner

Mon - Fri 8 a.m. - 6 p.m., Sat 8 a.m. - 12 p.m.
Sycamore is three miles south of Ashburn on U.S. 41.
(From I-75, take exit 27, and go west one mile.)

Originally opened in 1976, this long-established take-out place sells barbecue only by the pound, and similarly sells its other items in quantity rather than individual servings. It's a great place to pick up the main courses for a picnic.

Date visited _____ *Remarks* _____

Walker's Bar-B-Que (454)

U.S. 80
Roberta, Ga. 31078
912/836-4970
County: Crawford

Tue - Sat 11 a.m. - 9 p.m.
On U.S. 80 at the eastern edge of Roberta.

Known for friendly service, Walker's in Roberta is a great place to be on Friday nights. That's when they have an all-you-can-eat rib special. A combination hot bar and salad bar is featured during lunch on weekdays. Walker's barbecue is made with hams that have been slow-cooked with oak and hickory in a closed pit. A non-sweet ketchup-based sauce is available in hot or mild to put on it. Brunswick stew, beans, cole slaw, fries, potato salad, and other sides are served, too. Dine in, table service, seats 75. Drive in. Opened 1988.

Date visited _____ *Remarks* _____

Wall's

Name/Map ID	Hours/Directions

Wall's Bar B Que Restaurant (455)

515 East York Lane
Savannah, Ga. 31401
912/232-9754
County: Chatham

Wed 11 a.m. - 5 p.m., Thu 11 a.m. - 10 p.m.,
Fri & Sat 11 a.m. - 10:30 p.m.
Off Oglethorpe Ave., between E. Houston St. and W. Price
St. in the downtown historic district.

Wall's specialties are chicken and ribs, but be sure to try the pork sandwich; it's one of the biggest you'll ever see. The meat is open-pit-cooked and chopped, and a creamy mustard-based sauce goes nicely with it. Also on the menu are small ends, fried chicken, deviled crab, fried fish, fresh vegetables, cole slaw, and fries. All dinners are served with red rice, potato salad, and one vegetable. Canned drinks. Assorted cake slices and sweet potato pie for dessert. Dine in, order at counter, seats 12 in three booths. Opened 1968.

Date visited _____ Remarks _____

Wallace Barbecue (456)

3035 Bankhead Hwy.
Austell, Ga. 30001
770/739-1686
County: Cobb

Tue - Thu 10:30 a.m. - 9 p.m.,
Fri & Sat 10:30 a.m. - 10 p.m.
From I-20 west of Atlanta, take exit 12 (Hwy 6), go north
to U.S. 78/278, turn right. It's just ahead on the right.

Mustard-sauce lovers definitely need to visit this place. Wallace's superb barbecue sauce is a thin pungent mixture of vinegar, mustard, and black pepper that works exceptionally well with pit-cooked pork. A long-time favorite in the south Cobb area, the restaurant has been in Austell since 1966 and in the present building since 1988. Ice-box pies and fried pies for dessert. Dine in, table service, 175 seats.

Date visited _____ Remarks _____

Ware's Bar-B-Q (457)

303 N Main St.
Swainsboro, Ga. 30401
912/237-6942
County: Emanuel

Thu - Sat 11 a.m. - 9 p.m.
From the courthouse in Swainsboro, go north on U.S. 1.
It's a couple of blocks on the right.

The courthouse in Swainsboro has been destroyed by fire five times, and recently the century-old Durden Hotel next door burned down in a spectacular blaze. Fire is put to productive use, though, just up the street. Ware's uses it to turn Boston butts into delectable barbecue. Ware's tangy red sauce provides the finishing touch. Take-out only. One picnic table outside. Opened 1995.

Date visited _____ Remarks _____

Washington Food Market (458)

1010 E Robert Toombs Ave.
Washington, Ga. 30673
706/678-2233
County: Wilkes

Mon - Sun 8:30 a.m. - 7 p.m. (BBQ after 11)
From the city square in Washington, go east on
U.S. 78 Bus. to the edge of town. It's on the right,
across from Hardee's.

Washington Food Market sells barbecue as a sideline from about 11 a.m. until closing (unless they run out before then). It's available with other food on a steam table. (Barbecue chicken and ribs available only on Saturday.)

Date visited _____ Remarks _____

Wayne's Bar-B-Que (459)

617 Hwy. 80
Jeffersonville, Ga. 31044
912/945-6838
County: Twiggs

Tue - Thu 9 a.m. - 5 p.m., Fri & Sat 9 a.m.- 8 p.m.
On U.S. 80, a quarter-mile east of the courthouse.

Wayne and Lelia Huston started barbecuing for church events. Lelia's secret-recipe spicy-sweet yellow sauce was so good it put the Hustons in the restaurant business in 1993. It's positively sublime when added to the chopped pork that Wayne makes from charcoal-cooked hams. On the side are Brunswick stew, baked beans, cole slaw, fries, potato salad, and home-style vegetables. Cakes and potato pie for dessert. Dine in, order at counter. 16 - 20 seats. All nonsmoking. Drive-thru.

Date visited _____ Remarks _____

Westside Barbeque (460)

89 Temple Ave.
Newnan, Ga. 30263
770/253-6900
County: Coweta

Mon - Sat 6 a.m. - 9 p.m.
From I-85, take exit 9, and go west. At cemetery get in
center lane, go straight onto Temple Ave. It's on the right,
before the traffic light.

Hams cooked with oak and hickory, the usual barbecue-related sides, a good selection of vegetables, and a comfortable place to enjoy it all, that's Westside. Dine in, order at counter, plenty of tables, nonsmokers' area. Opened 1991.

Date visited _____ Remarks _____

White Diamond Grill & Barbecue (461)

497 S Hwy. 247
Bonaire, Ga. 31005
912/922-8686
County: Houston

Mon - Sat 9 a.m. - 6 p.m.
From Warner Robins, take Hwy 247 south 5 miles.
It's on the right at Hwy. 96, next to the Exxon station.

It's a tradition in the area to eat at White Diamond. People come from a hundred-mile radius for the hams and shoulders cooked with oak and hickory in an open pit the old way. The sauce is homemade, a mustard/vinegar–based mix that is very popular in the area. It's been in business fifty years and looks much the same as it did when it opened. The name, by the way, comes from the white, diamond-shaped stonework on the exterior.

Date visited _____*Remarks* _____

White House Bar-B-Q (462)

1778 Hwy. 42 N
McDonough, Ga. 30253
770/957-2440
County: Henry

Tue - Thu 11 a.m. - 6 p.m., Fri & Sat 11 a.m. - 8 p.m.
From McDonough, take Hwy 42 toward Stockbridge about
3 miles. It's on the right, near
Eagle's Landing Baptist Church.

This 20-seat establishment opened in the mid-1980s and has fed Henry County folks some pretty good barbecue since then. Pork shoulders cooked with hickory wood in an open pit is how they start it. A homemade red sauce that's not too sweet and not too spicy is how they finish it. Dine in, order at counter, 20 seats.

Date visited _____*Remarks* _____

Williams Bar-B-Que (463)

Hwy. 29 N
Danielsville, Ga. 30633
706/795-5394
County: Madison

Mon - Sat 11 a.m. - 6 p.m.
From Athens, take U.S. 129 north about 16 miles to Hwy.
98 on the north side of Danielsville. It's on the right.

Good luck and a roll of the dice eleven or so years ago got owner Ricky Williams into the take-out barbecue business. He's been doing okay ever since, he says. His hickory-smoked ham meat is certainly okay. The homemade red sauce goes well with it. He sells hash, too; it's a mix of beef, pork, chicken, onions, and tomatoes served with rice, found in the Athens and Augusta regions. Also burgers, sandwiches, and chips.

Date visited _____*Remarks* _____

Bar-B-Quote

"To ask a barbecue man to tell you his sauce recipe is
like asking to borrow his wife."
— Ed Powers of the Georgia Pig in Brunswick

Williams Barbecue (464)

Hwy. 49 S
Oglethorpe, Ga. 31068
912/472-8687
County: Macon

Tue - Sat 10 a.m. - 6 p.m. (later in summer).
Two miles south of Oglethorpe on Hwy. 49 and just north
of Hwy. 26 ("the Bypass").

This family place, a favorite in a *Macon Telegraph* poll, serves lean hams cooked over oak and hickory coals in an open pit. The chicken and ribs are dipped in the mild red sauce as they come off the pit. Everything is made from scratch. Great fried pies. Dine in, order at counter, 32 seats. (When this was written, Williams was closed due to illness. They hope to reopen by June 1997.)

Date visited _____ *Remarks* _____

Williams Country Barbecue (465)

2500 Martin L. King Jr. Dr. SW
Atlanta, Ga. 30311
404/699-2169
County: Fulton

Mon - Thu 11 a.m. - midnight, Fri & Sat 11 a.m. - 2 am.
From I-20 West exit at Hightower Rd., go south, under the
bridge. At the second light, turn right on MLK, Jr. Dr. It's
on the left, across from the MARTA station.

Is this what they eat in the country? Tender smoky pork fresh off the open pit served with a sweet red sauce, mouth-watering pork and beef ribs, pork chops, fried chicken, collards, fried corn, rutabagas, and peas? We're gonna move to the country! Dine in, one table. Take-out, mostly.

Date visited _____ *Remarks* _____

Williamson Brothers Bar-B-Q (466)

1425 Roswell Rd. NE
Marietta, Ga. 30062
770/971-7748
County: Cobb

Mon - Thu 10:30 a.m. - 9 p.m., Fri 10:30 a.m. - 10 p.m., Sat 10:30 - 9.
From I-75, take exit 112, go west. At Cobb Pkwy. (U.S. 41), turn right.
Turn right at the Big Chicken onto Roswell Road (Hwy. 120).
It's a half mile on the left.

Succulent chopped pork is cooked atop an open pit right in the dining room. A sweet and tangy tomato-based sauce complements it. The thin Brunswick stew has a nice bite to it. Creamy cole slaw. Also beans, corn on the cob, onion rings, fries, and salad. All-you-can-eat platters available. Beer and wine. Homemade pies: chocolate, lemon, coconut, and banana. Dine in, table service, seats 200.

Date visited _____ *Remarks* _____

Will's BBQ (467)

Old U.S. 29
Winder, Ga. 30680
770/867-3757
County: Barrow

Fri & Sat 9 a.m. - 8 p.m.
From downtown Winder, go east on
East May St. about 4 miles to the airport.
It's about a mile farther on a hilltop on the left.

Greg Willoughby's restaurant is a small brown building in the backyard of his parents' house. It seats 25 inside, and there's room for more at picnic tables outside. Greg's concrete block pit holds 40 whole hams at once. He cooks them 24 hours using hickory wood. His red sauce achieves a perfect balance of tomatoes and vinegar, and is offered in mild or hot.

Date visited _____ *Remarks* _____

Wish Bone Bar-B-Que (468)

585 S Harris St.
Athens, Ga. 30601
706/369-8800
County: Clarke

Fri - Sun 12 p.m. - 10 p.m. (Bar hours differ. Call ahead.)
From downtown, take Broad St. west. Turn left on Milledge
Ave., then left on Baxter. Second street on right.

On weekend nights, this big tin-roofed log cabin offers an all-you-can-eat barbecue buffet, frequently with live music (bluegrass, folk rock, soul, jazz). On Friday nights it's "Barbecue, Bluegrass, and Beer." Accompanying the meats are a variety of vegetables, including fried green tomatoes. Catfish too. Ribs sometimes. Full bar. Dine in, table service, 100 seats, nonsmokers' section. Opened 1996.

Date visited _____ *Remarks* _____

Worley's Bar-B-Que (469)

3000 Hwy. 93 S
Cairo, Ga. 31728
912/377-2386
County: Grady

Wed - Sat 10 a.m. - 10 p.m., Sun 11 a.m. - 2 p.m.
From downtown Cairo, take Hwy. 93 5 or 6 miles south.
It's on the right.

"Quality food; expect the best" they say at Worley's. Their Boston butts cooked with oak in an open pit meet expectations. Wide selection of side orders (buttered grits and cheese grits, for example). The sauce is red, sweet, and mild. Apple and pecan pie for dessert. Dine in, table service, 150 seats.

Date visited _____ *Remarks* _____

WW The Boss's Bar-B-Que (470)

3838 Glenwood Rd.
Decatur, Ga. 30032
404/289-4507
County: DeKalb

Tue - Sat 10 a.m. - 11 p.m.
From I-285 east, exit at Glenwood, go west. It's a half-mile
past Columbia Dr. on the right, 3 miles inside I-285.

Look for the smoke rolling across the parking lot. Seven seats are inside, but it's mostly take-out. Try the Boss's ribs, by the slab or sandwich. Also rib tips, turkey wings, jalapeño sausage sandwiches, and collards. The stew is thick, sweet, and abundant with tomatoes. Peach cobbler or sweet potato pie for dessert. Opened 1990. Owner Willie White Jr.

Date visited _____ *Remarks* _____

Wynnton Pitt BBQ & Diner (471)

2500 Buena Vista Rd.
Columbus, Ga. 31906
706/322-5676
County: Muscogee

Mon - Wed 7 a.m. - 7 p.m., Thu 7 a.m. - 8 p.m.,
Fri & Sat 7 a.m. - 9 p.m.
From I-185 take exit 3, go west.
It's on the left in Vista Center.

The proprietor, Rev. Richard Street, also cuts hair and runs the barber shop next door. When we asked who owned the place, the Rev. Street told us, "God owns everything. I just smoke the meat." Well, He chose someone who does it well. Hams, butts, and shoulders are marvelously smoked with red oak. Also down-home meat-and-vegetable cooking and sweet potato pie. Dine in, 60 seats.

Date visited _____ *Remarks* _____

> *"Part of the secret of success in life*
> *is to eat what you like and let the food fight it out inside."*
> — *Mark Twain*

Name/Map ID | **Hours/Directions**

Yancey's Bar-B-Que (472)

U.S. Hwy. 41
Lenox, Ga. 31637
912/546-4655
County: Cook

Mon - Sat 10 a.m. - 8 p.m.
From I-75 take exit 13, go east a quarter-mile to Lenox
and turn left onto U.S. 41. It's on the left.

If traffic is getting your goat, get off the highway and get Yancey's goat (sandwich). Goat is served every day here. Yancey's specializes in hams cooked in a pit fired with mostly oak and a little hickory. Farmer-turned-pitmaster Emmett Yancey, opened the place on Memorial Day 1991. The sauce is thin, mild and brown. The sides are baked beans, potato salad, and chips. For dessert there's 8-layer chocolate or coconut cake. Seats about 50. Order at the counter.

Date visited _____ *Remarks* _____

York's Seafood and BBQ. (473)

128 Paul Murphy Rd.
Moultrie, Ga. 31768
912/985-8522
County: Colquitt

Thu - Sat 11:30 a.m. - 2 p.m. and 4:30 p.m. - 9:30 p.m.
From downtown, take South Main St. and turn right onto
Lower Meigs Rd. It's about 1 1/2 miles on the right, on
Paul Murphy Rd.

The first owner of this place was a fisherman who cooked and sold his catch on weekends. His restaurant was a converted chicken coop/horse barn to which he added periodically. The walls aren't particularly square, but it works. York's serves barbecue from an oak-fired open pit. On the side: beans, slaw, grits, and salads. Also several kinds of fish, steaks, frog legs, quail, fried chicken, etc. Dine in, table service, 100 seats, nonsmokers' area.

Date visited _____ *Remarks* _____

Zeb's Place Bar-B-Que (474)

U.S. 29
Danielsville, Ga. 30633
706/795-2701
County: Madison

Tue - Sat 9 a.m. -9 p.m., Sun 12 p.m. - 4 p.m.
On U.S. 29, 5 miles north of Danielsville.

Family owned and operated since 1947, when it was started up by Zeb Dean. The original structure has been expanded several times. It now has 75 seats, with table service. Hams are cooked over hickory in an open pit. The mild Brunswick stew is unusual in that the only meat in it is beef. The red vinegar–based sauce is spiced with red and black pepper. It's the favorite barbecue of many people in northeast Georgia.

Date visited _____ *Remarks* _____

DIGEST

**Maps
Index
Glossary**

REGION 1

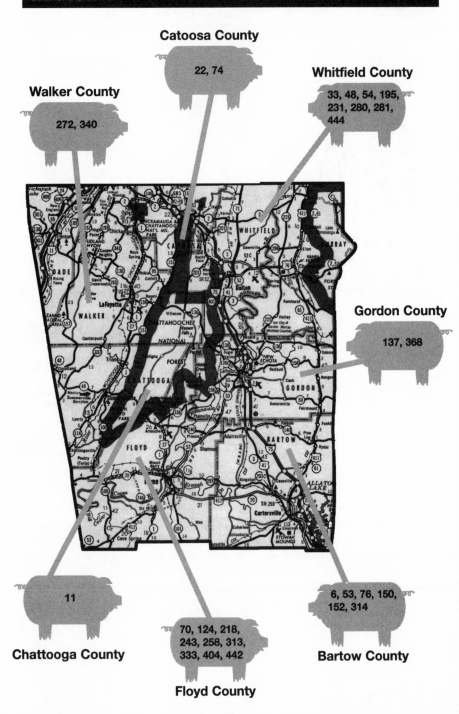

Catoosa County
22, 74

Whitfield County
33, 48, 54, 195, 231, 280, 281, 444

Walker County
272, 340

Gordon County
137, 368

Chattooga County
11

Floyd County
70, 124, 218, 243, 258, 313, 333, 404, 442

Bartow County
6, 53, 76, 150, 152, 314

174

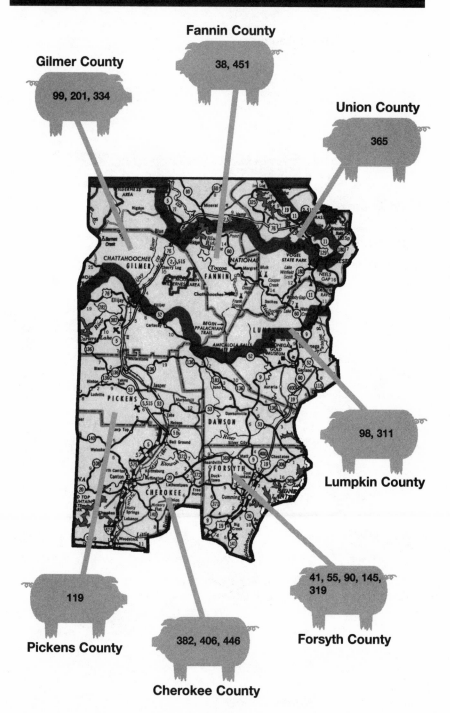

Fannin County

38, 451

Gilmer County

99, 201, 334

Union County

365

Lumpkin County

98, 311

Forsyth County

41, 55, 90, 145, 319

Pickens County

119

Cherokee County

382, 406, 446

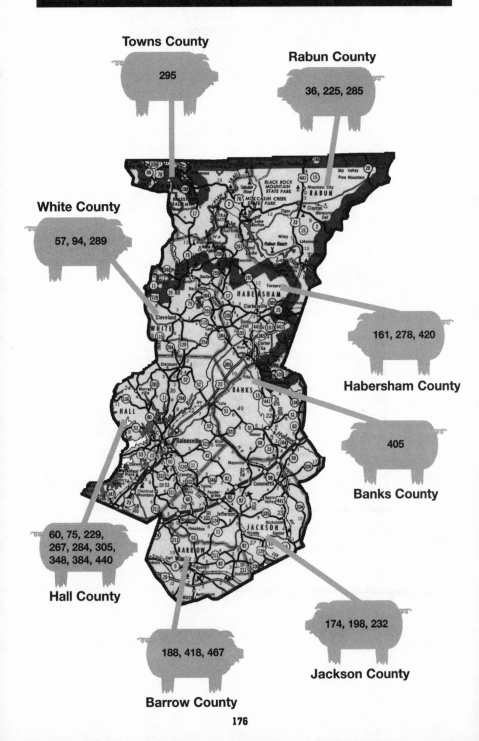

Towns County

295

Rabun County

36, 225, 285

White County

57, 94, 289

161, 278, 420

Habersham County

405

Banks County

60, 75, 229,
267, 284, 305,
348, 384, 440

Hall County

174, 198, 232

Jackson County

188, 418, 467

Barrow County

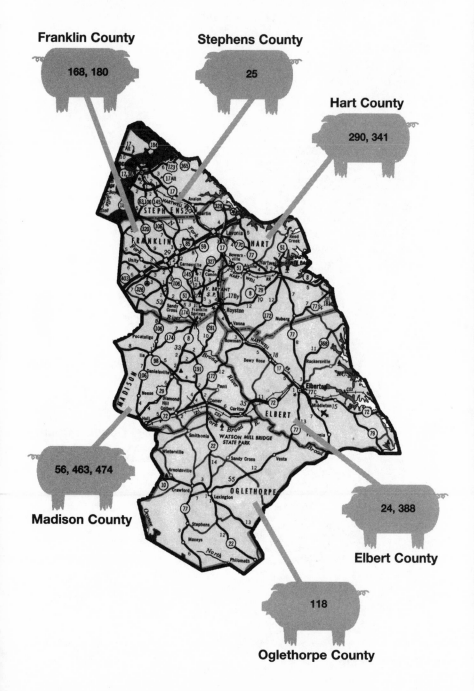

Franklin County
168, 180

Stephens County
25

Hart County
290, 341

56, 463, 474
Madison County

24, 388
Elbert County

118
Oglethorpe County

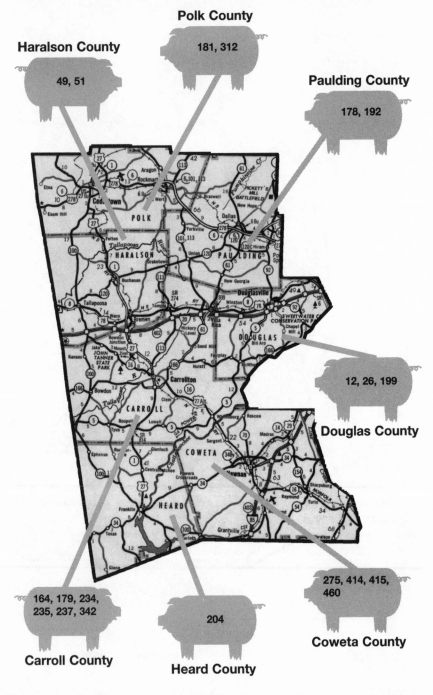

Polk County

181, 312

Haralson County

49, 51

Paulding County

178, 192

12, 26, 199

Douglas County

164, 179, 234, 235, 237, 342

Carroll County

204

Heard County

275, 414, 415, 460

Coweta County

Cobb County

19, 39, 46, 91, 123, 230, 240, 247, 300, 304, 307, 357, 358, 394, 398, 411, 422, 426, 432, 456, 466

Fayette County

128, 274, 412

10, 23, 40, 45, 47, 78, 81, 95, 131, 159, 185, 248, 298, 301, 302, 350, 359, 402, 434, 447, 470

Dekalb County

4, 5, 7, 8, 9, 13, 21, 28, 37, 97, 111, 142, 143, 144, 151, 155, 160, 163, 171, 208, 212, 219, 220, 254, 273, 288, 296, 303, 310, 346, 356, 360, 376, 381, 386, 391, 427, 431, 433, 435, 436, 465

Fulton County

120, 154, 172, 182, 309, 332, 401, 411

Clayton County

REGION 7

Gwinnett County

1, 100, 122, 166, 167, 187, 191, 211, 223, 323, 392, 413

Rockdale County

165, 266, 338, 378, 395

Walton County

106, 121, 202, 242, 297, 367

Henry County

259, 271, 294, 336, 351, 462

257, 337

Newton County

Spalding County

73, 101, 205, 253, 270, 419

Butts County

44, 156, 158, 268, 380

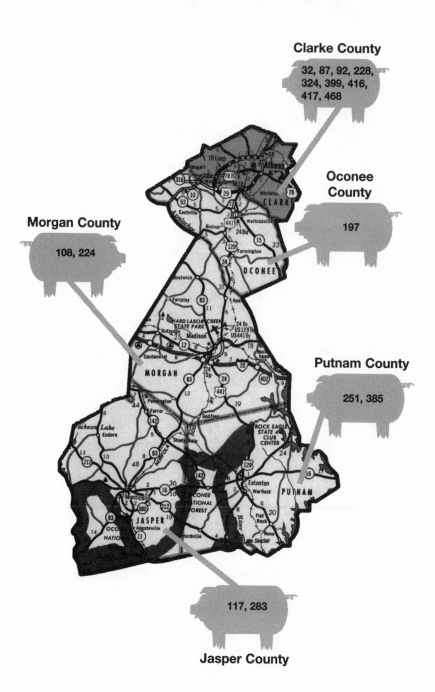

Clarke County

32, 87, 92, 228, 324, 399, 416, 417, 468

Oconee County

197

Morgan County

108, 224

Putnam County

251, 385

Jasper County

117, 283

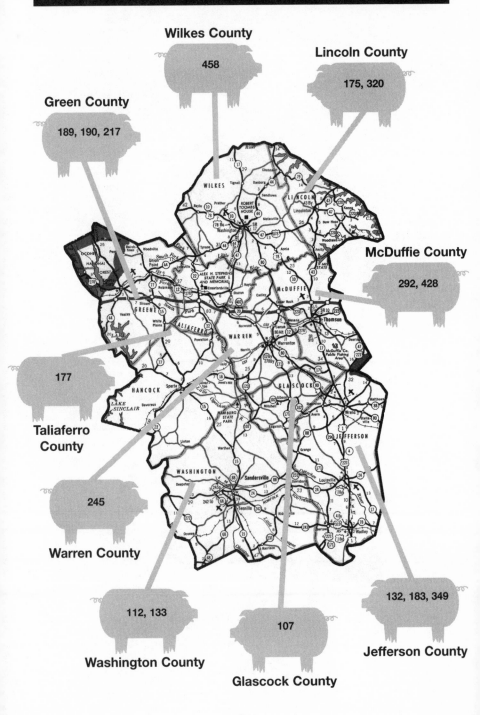

Wilkes County

458

Lincoln County

175, 320

Green County

189, 190, 217

McDuffie County

292, 428

177

Taliaferro County

245

Warren County

112, 133

Washington County

107

Glascock County

132, 183, 349

Jefferson County

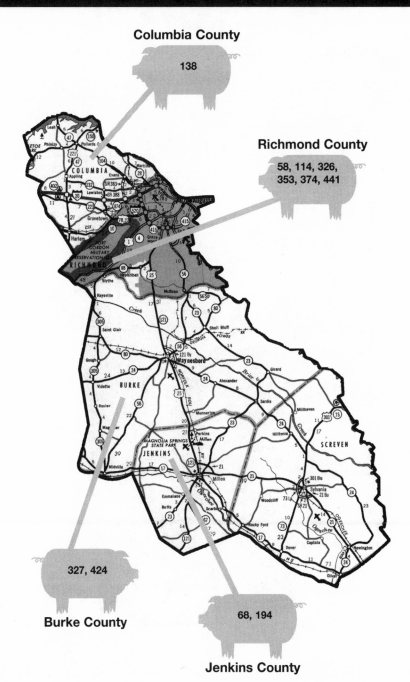

Columbia County

138

Richmond County

58, 114, 326, 353, 374, 441

327, 424

Burke County

68, 194

Jenkins County

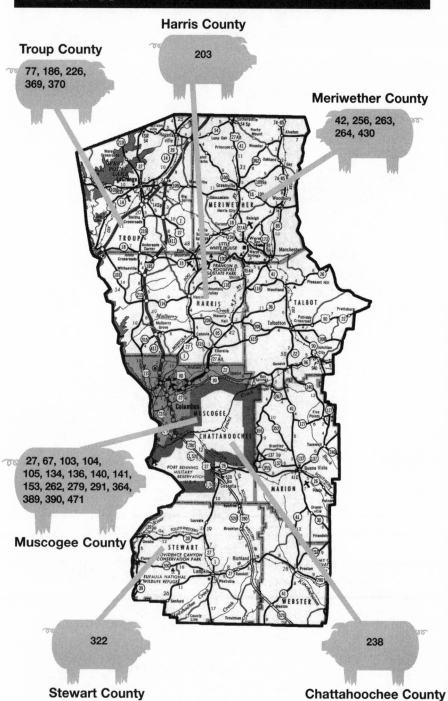

Harris County
203

Troup County
77, 186, 226, 369, 370

Meriwether County
42, 256, 263, 264, 430

27, 67, 103, 104, 105, 134, 136, 140, 141, 153, 262, 279, 291, 364, 389, 390, 471

Muscogee County

322

Stewart County

238

Chattahoochee County

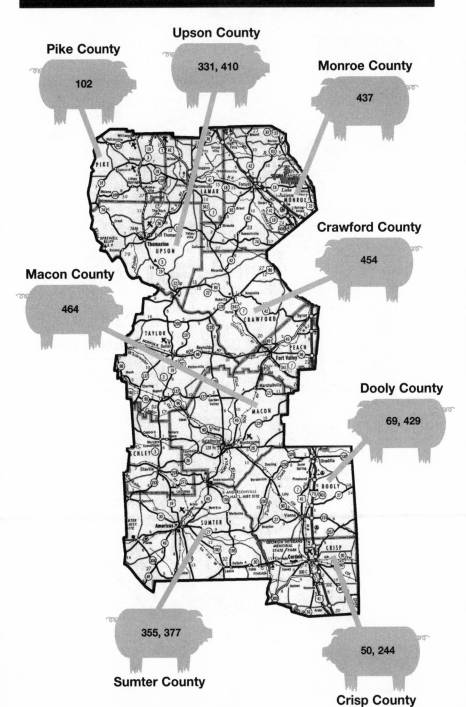

Pike County
102

Upson County
331, 410

Monroe County
437

Crawford County
454

Macon County
464

Dooly County
69, 429

Sumter County
355, 377

Crisp County
50, 244

REGION 13

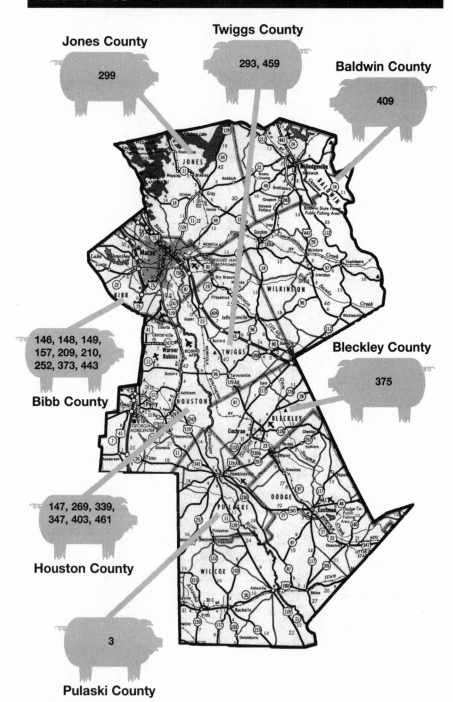

Jones County
299

Twiggs County
293, 459

Baldwin County
409

Bibb County
146, 148, 149,
157, 209, 210,
252, 373, 443

Bleckley County
375

Houston County
147, 269, 339,
347, 403, 461

Pulaski County
3

Laurens County

2, 64, 109, 362, 366

Montgomery County

282

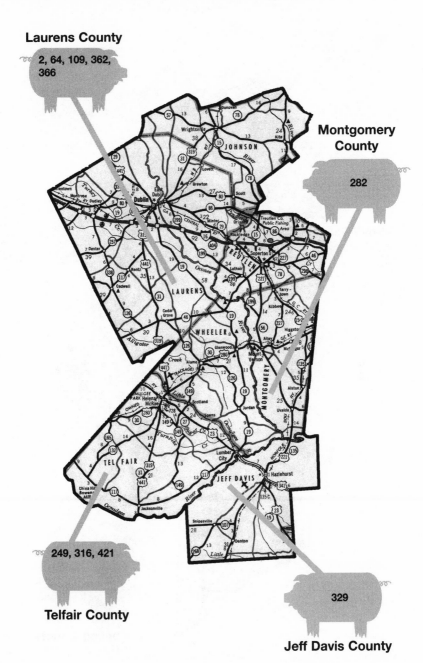

Telfair County

249, 316, 421

Jeff Davis County

329

REGION 15

Emanuel County

260, 457

Candler County

29, 214, 233

Evans County

173

Tattnall County

408

Toombs County

65, 88, 184

Appling County

239, 255

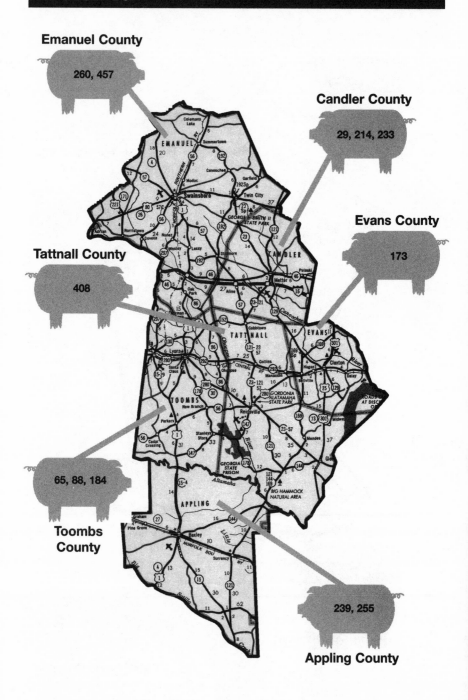

188

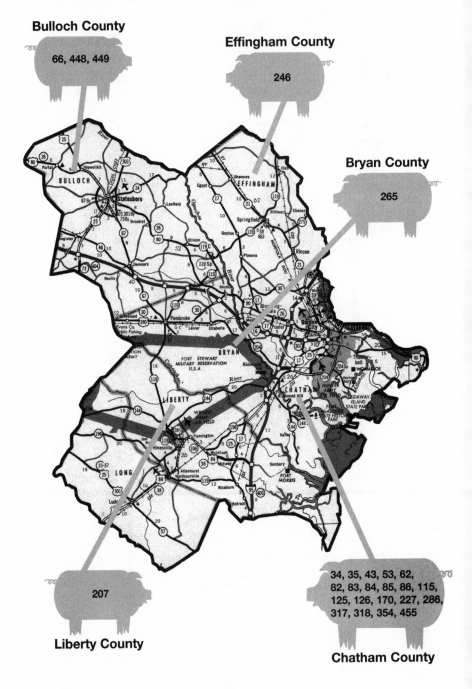

Bulloch County

66, 448, 449

Effingham County

246

Bryan County

265

Liberty County

207

Chatham County

34, 35, 43, 53, 62, 82, 83, 84, 85, 86, 115, 125, 126, 170, 227, 286, 317, 318, 354, 455

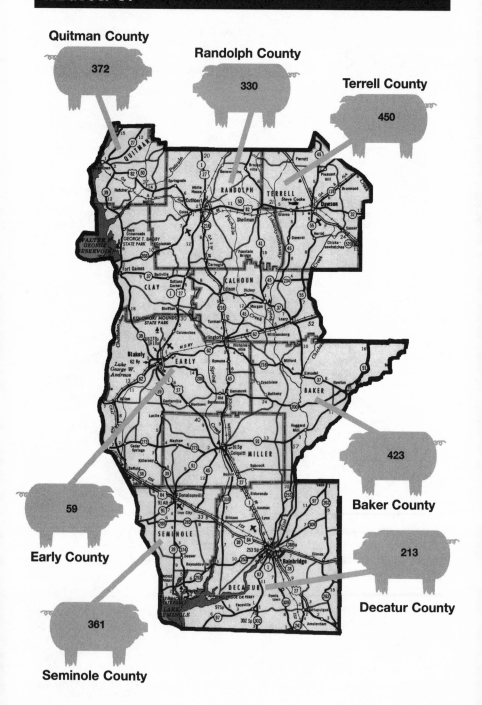

Quitman County
372

Randolph County
330

Terrell County
450

Baker County
423

Early County
59

Decatur County
213

Seminole County
361

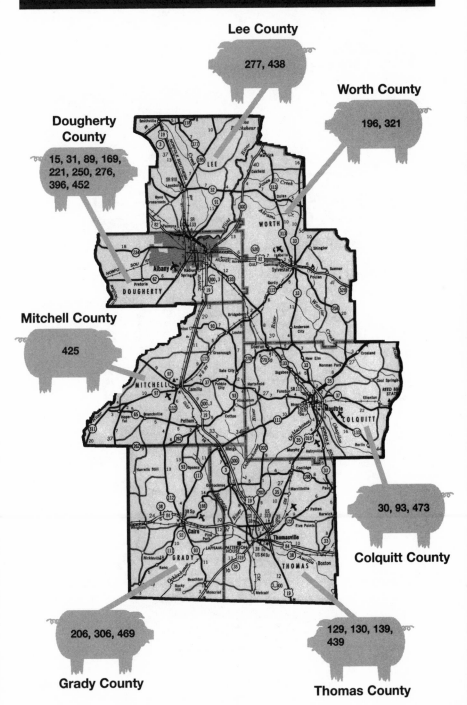

Lee County

277, 438

Worth County

196, 321

Dougherty County

15, 31, 89, 169, 221, 250, 276, 396, 452

Mitchell County

425

Colquitt County

30, 93, 473

Grady County

206, 306, 469

Thomas County

129, 130, 139, 439

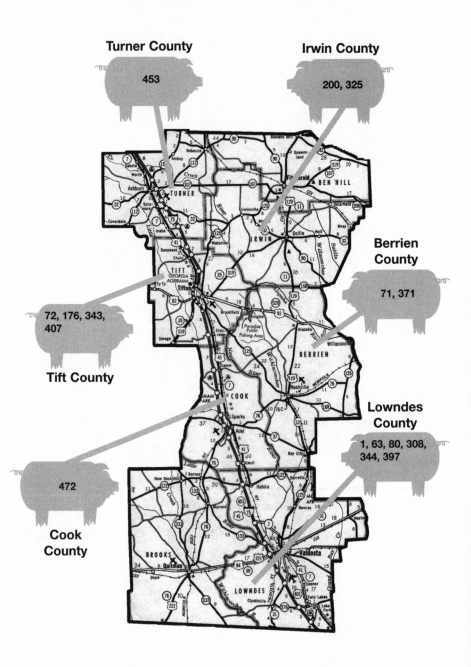

Turner County
453

Irwin County
200, 325

Berrien County
71, 371

Tift County
72, 176, 343, 407

Lowndes County
1, 63, 80, 308, 344, 397

Cook County
472

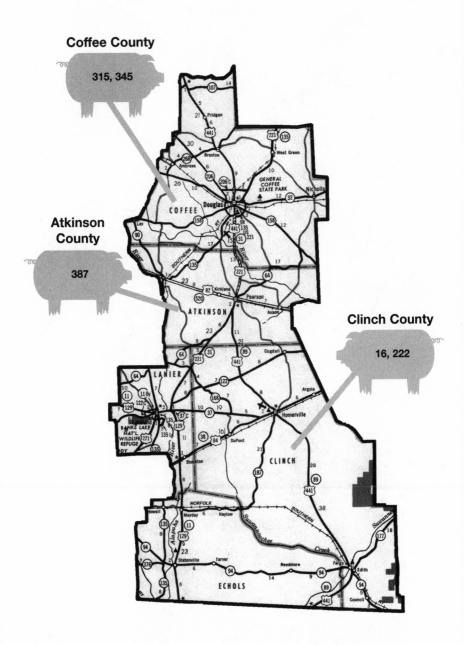

Coffee County
315, 345

Atkinson County
387

Clinch County
16, 222

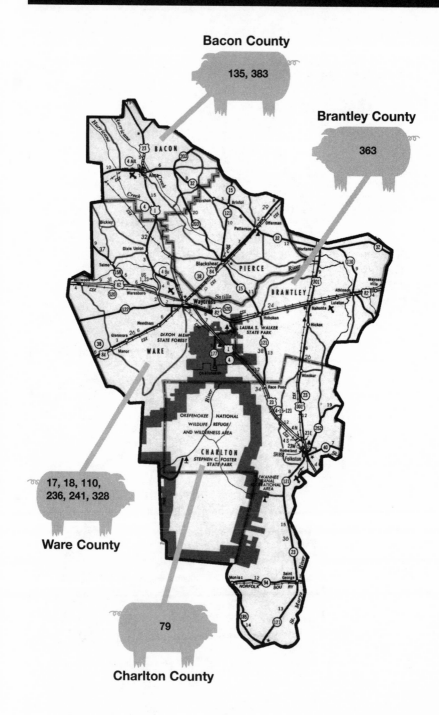

Bacon County

135, 383

Brantley County

363

17, 18, 110, 236, 241, 328

Ware County

79

Charlton County

Wayne County

20, 287

McIntosh County

116

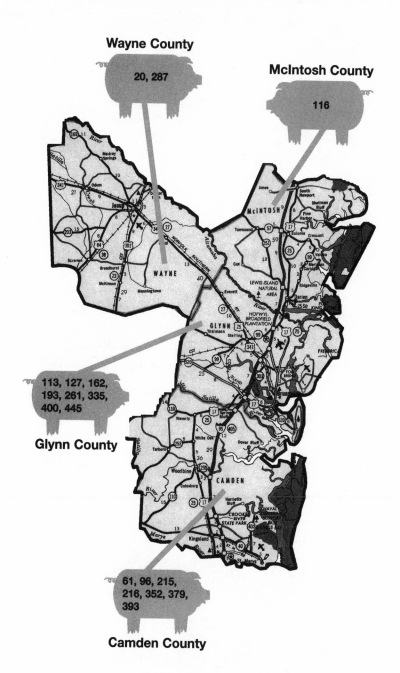

113, 127, 162, 193, 261, 335, 400, 445

Glynn County

61, 96, 215, 216, 352, 379, 393

Camden County

| CITY | RESTAURANT | ID Number |

INDEX

CITY	RESTAURANT	ID Number

REGION 5

INDEX

INDEX

INDEX

INDEX

CITY	RESTAURANT	ID Number

Barbecue (BBQ)(v)(n) — (*v*) The act of preparing meat by the use of one or more cooking methods. These methods include the use of burning **Hardwood** and or **Charcoal**, which imparts a distinctive smoke flavor to the meat. (*n*) The product of the above-noted cooking method. That thing of which we dream at night. *See also* **Indirect Heat, Direct Heat** and **Smoked Meat.**

Barbecue Sauce — The finishing touch to **Barbecue.** A concoction consisting of often unknown ingredients. Swabbed on the finished product prior to presentation or used as a baste. Usually added to a sandwich or plate of meat. *See also* **Red Sauce** and **Vinegar-based Sauce.**

Bark — The dark crusty outer layer of a slow-cooked pork shoulder or ham. The density and texture of bark is influenced by the use of sauce; more sauce = more bark.

Baby Back Ribs — The **Loin (Back) Ribs** of a small hog, usually less than 85 pounds dressed weight.

Beef Brisket — Quintessential **Texas Barbecue.** The front chest portion of meat taken from select beef cattle. Usually smoked using **Indirect Heat** due to the dangers of overcooking, resulting in meat which is tough, similar to a high-grade radial tire.

Boston Butt — The top half of a pork **Shoulder.** North end of a northbound pig. Name bestowed by a Yankee, who didn't know any better.

Brunswick Stew — A thick, rich soup made from pork, beef, chicken, tomatoes, corn, and spices. Might also include onions, okra, peas, potatoes, or other vegetables.

Carolina Barbecue — Barbecue meat as prepared in the Carolinas. Usually **Pit**-cooked, then **Chopped.** Most often served with cole slaw (*see* **Sides**) and a **Vinegar-Based Sauce.**

Charcoal — **Hardwood** that has been burned in the absence of air leaving it less dense and more porous. Advantages to dry wood are slow burning, generally without a flame, but with somewhat less heat emitted. Used in either the **Smoker** or **Pit.**

Chicken — Domestic fowl raised for the purpose of being eaten or laying eggs. Often crosses the road just to show the possum it can be done. One of the primary meats used for **Barbecue**. See Barney Fife.

Chipped — A method of serving pork **Shoulder** or **Ham**. Similar to **Chopped** meat but has a coarser texture. What happens to a glass when you drop it in the sink.

Chopped — Barbecue pork **Shoulder** or **Ham** which has been pulverized by a sharp blade. A common preparation for **Pit-Cooked** meat. Often done when the meat is a bit tough. Also preferred by those lacking their molars.

Direct Heat — A process by which meat is cooked directly above an open flame or smoldering coals of **Hardwood** or **Charcoal**. *See also* **Pit** barbecue. What is applied by spouse after you've stayed out too late.

Dry Rib — Pork ribs cooked without the aid of **Barbecue Sauce**. Usually includes preparation of the meat using a **Dry Rub**.

Dry Rub — A collection of spices and occasionally herbs used to add flavor to **Barbecue**. Rubbing is undertaken prior to cooking, with **Ribs** and **Beef Brisket** being the primary recipient. This is the preferred method of meat preparation for **Texas Barbecue** and **Memphis Barbecue**. This has nothing to do with locker-room pranks.

Ham — The rear quarter of a hog. The south end of a north-bound pig. Most often slow-smoked.

Hardwood — That which is burned to produce smoke and heat. Consists of any variety of natural cellulose products. The most often used woods are hickory, oak, pecan, cherry, and apple. *See also* **Charcoal**.

Hash — A very thick, rich mixture of stewed pork, onions, and potatoes, usually served atop rice. In Georgia, hash is found only in the Athens and Augusta areas.

High on the Hog — Common term for the best or "that which comes at a premium." In literal language, the loin or top portion of the hog, where the most tender cuts are found. This being considered superior to the bottom portion or "pork belly."

Indirect Heat — A process by which meat is cooked away from an open flame or smoldering coals of **Hardwood** or **Charcoal**. Implicit in this definition is the use of a **Smoker**. *See also* **Smoked Meat**.

Inside Meat — The inner portion of barbecue pork **Shoulder** or **Ham** which is tender and juicy. May be **Chopped, Chipped,** or **Sliced**. Referred to when ordering **Pit**-cooked meat. *See also* **Outside Meat** and **Mixed**.

Loin (Back) Ribs — Ribs as found **High on the Hog**. Ribs found attached to the backbone. *See also* **Baby Back Ribs**.

Memphis Barbecue — Likely the preeminent school of barbecue thought and practice. The high art of smoking meat by **Indirect Heat**, with liberal applications of **Dry Rub** (ribs only) and often a sweet **Red Sauce**. Pork is the word.

Mixed — The combination of **Inside Meat** with **Outside Meat**. A veritable mixture. Only for the undecided or well-practiced. Served **Chopped, Chipped** or **Sliced**.

Outside Meat — Outer portion of barbecue pork **Shoulder** or **Ham** which is generally tough and dry. Often indistinguishable from **Charcoal**. May be **Chopped, Chipped,** or **Sliced**. Referred to when ordering **Pit-Cooked** meat. *See also* **Inside Meat** and **Mixed**.

Pig Pickin' — The art of swine selection. Adopting the best hog. Choosing the right mate for your **Pit** or **Smoker**. Also the celebration surrounding such an event. Also the removal (pickin') of meat from a cooked pig.

Pit — An apparatus designed for barbecuing meat by **Direct Heat**. Usually consisting of enclosed masonry walls and a steel grate cooking surface. The portable versions are constructed of steel. *See also* **Smoker**.

BBQ DIGEST

Pulled Pork — Most often referred to when speaking of **Memphis Barbecue**. Barbecue pork **Shoulder** or **Ham** which has been slow smoked. The smoking process breaks down the fibers in the meat and allows it to shred naturally. Sharp instruments are unnecessary with this serving method, so check your knives at the door.

'Q ('Cue) — Slang for *barbecue*.

Red Sauce — **Barbecue Sauce** consisting of a tomato base and other ingredients. Genuine tomato catsup is the number one source for that scarlet hue. Sometimes has a smoky, sweet and/or spicy quality. Mostly served warm, to bring out the flavor. *See* **Texas Barbecue, Memphis Barbecue** and **Vinegar-Based Sauce**.

Rib — The universal **Barbecue** meat. Like Swiss chocolate to the trained palate of a barbecue taster. The midpoint of the hog or an occasional cow. The least common denominator still considered a meal. That from which woman was created. *See also* **Slab, St. Louis Cut Ribs, Baby Back Ribs, Loin (Back) Ribs, Spare Ribs** and **Dry Rub**.

St. Louis Cut Ribs — **Spare Ribs** from which the skirt meat and brisket have been removed. The finished cut consists only of rib meat and large rib bones. *See also* **Rib** and **Spare Ribs**.

Shoulder — The front quarter taken from a mature hog. Usually weighing from 14 to 18 pounds. The cut includes the top blade bone down to the knuckle. The top half is referred to as a **Boston Butt**, while the bottom is called the picnic. A favorite cut for smoking. Served alone, or most commonly in a sandwich.

Sides — Cole slaw, baked beans, potato salad, cornbread, fries, onion rings, and corn on the cob are typical. Steamed vegetables are unlikely.

Slab — One quarter section of a **Whole Hog** rib. Consisting of 12 to 13 interconnected ribs. When ordering out, nothing else need be mentioned. *See also* **Rib**.

Sliced — Barbecue pork **Shoulder** or **Ham** which has been carved using a sharp blade. A common preparation for **Pit-Cooked** meat. Often done when the meat is tender. Also preferred by those having strong molars.

Smoke Ring — The bright red ring found just inside the outer layer (Bark) of **Smoked Meat**. A mark of distinction. The most done part of the meat, next to the **Bark**. Often sent back for being undercooked — an extreme display of ignorance.

Smoked Meat — Meat cooked by the application of heat with benefit of **Hardwood** smoke. Smoke-cured meat differs from smoked **Barbecue** only in the duration and temperature involved in the cooking process. Smoked barbecue is generally cooked at temperatures above 200 degrees with a shorter cooking time. Lower temperatures and longer periods are reserved for the smoke-curing process. *See also* **Smoker, Indirect Heat** and **Smoke Ring**.

Smoker — An apparatus designed for barbecuing meat by **Indirect Heat**. Usually consisting of an enclosed cooking chamber with an attached fire box. Convection pulls heat and smoke from the fire box through the cooking chamber, finally exiting through a smoke stack. Water is often added to the cooking chamber to avoid over-drying. **Hardwood** coals or **Charcoal** are the most common fuels. *See also* **Smoked Meat**.

Spare Ribs — The primary cut of **Ribs** served in most barbecue houses. Taken from the lower or belly portion of the whole rib. Left un-trimmed, contains skirt meat and brisket. *See also* **St. Louis Cut Ribs**.

Sweet Tea — The consummate drink with **Barbecue**. An embellishment without equal. Rumored to be unavailable in parts of the country — against which there should be a law.

DIGEST

Texas Barbecue — A unique dining experience. Possibly the most widely known form of **Barbecue**. The process of slow-smoking over mesquite **Hardwood** adds a distinctive strong flavor. **Beef Brisket** is first rubbed then slow-smoked. Pork ribs get the same treatment. Meat is generally served wet with a spicy **Red Sauce**. *See also* **Dry Rub**.

Vinegar-Based Sauce — Barbecue Sauce consisting of a vinegar base and other ingredients. Often fruit juices and ciders are added for a sweet and sour flavor. Red and black pepper are common ingredients as is sugar. Commonly served at room temperature. *See also* **Carolina Barbecue** and **Red Sauce**.

Wet Rib — Pork ribs cooked with the aid of **Barbecue Sauce**. Usually entails little preparation of the meat other than cooking. Sauce added as a final step in the cooking process. Most common method when cooking over a **Pit**. May also be added to a **Dry Rub** rib.

Whole Hog — The whole thing from snout to tail. Preferred, a pig weighing approximately 100 pounds. Usually split in half and smoked skin side down, but rotated and basted if **Pit-Cooked**. The pinnacle of the barbecue cooker's art. The question for the ages: "How do I cook deep into the **Ham** and not burn the **Rib**?"

Name: _____

Address: _____

Phone Number: (___) _____

Hours: _____

Comments: _____

_____

_____

Name: _____

Address: _____

Phone Number: (___) _____

Hours: _____

Comments: _____

_____

_____

Name: _____

Address: _____

Phone Number: (___) _____

Hours: _____

Comments: _____

_____

_____

Name: _____

Address: _____

Phone Number: (___) _____

Hours: _____

Comments: _____

_____

_____

Name: _____

Address: _____

Phone Number: (___) _____

Hours: _____

Comments: _____

_____

_____

Name: _____

Address: _____

Phone Number: (___) _____

Hours: _____

Comments: _____

_____

_____

Name: _____

Address: _____

Phone Number: (___) _____

Hours: _____

Comments: _____

_____

_____

Name: _____

Address: _____

Phone Number: (___) _____

Hours: _____

Comments: _____

_____

_____

Name: _____

Address: _____

Phone Number: (___) _____

Hours: _____

Comments: _____

_____

_____

Name: _____

Address: _____

Phone Number: (___) _____

Hours: _____

Comments: _____

_____

_____

BARBECUE DIGEST NEWSLETTER

You love barbecue and you're proud of it. You're not alone. Now you have the opportunity to join the ranks of a very special group of people: **The Divine Order of Barbecue Eaters**.

Yes, it's true. There *is* such an organization, and we're here to tell you how you can join. Membership has a lot of benefits above and beyond sheer pride. Most important, as a member, you'll receive a one-year subscription to the bi-monthly newsletter *Barbecue Digest*.

In this newsletter you will receive:

- in-depth interviews and photos of some select barbecue establishments across this great land of ours
- recipes from some master barbecue cooks
- tips on smoking meat from some of the best barbecue cooks in America
- articles on the history and lore of barbecue
- information to help you understand how barbecue varies from region to region
- fun facts about the world of barbecue
- a calendar of events pertaining to the world of barbecue

Plus, you'll receive:

- a suitable-for-framing certificate citing you as an official member of the **Divine Order of Barbecue Eaters** (complete with membership number)
- a wallet-size membership card
- and more

To join, all you need to do is fill out the membership form below. Keep in mind that this might make a great gift for a friend who also loves barbecue. Just let us know if you want us to send an announcement directly to your friend or if you'd rather us send it to you and let *you* present it to your friend with the appropriate ceremony. The newsletters will go to your friend.

For Your Membership:

The cost is $10.00 per annual membership.

Name: _____

Address: _____

Phone number: _____

Gift membership: ☐ Please send the announcement to me   ☐ Please send it to the name below

Name: _____

Address: _____

Phone number: _____

Please send a check or money order payable to:
BBQ Digest, Inc., P.O. Box 531324, Birmingham, Alabama 35253

BBQ DIGEST

Please e-mail comments, questions, or suggestions to bbqdigest@mindspring.com. Or call 205-595-0028.

The map below shows how we divided the state into seven regions. Larger maps of each region with a list of restaurants found in each county begin on page 173. Each region also has its own index, with county-by-county and city-by-city listings. The indexes begin on page 196.

Below you will find the key to the symbols indicating some of the food items and features you can expect to find at a given restaurant.

 Pork Barbecue

 Beef Barbecue

 Chicken Barbecue

 Ribs

 French Fries

 Onion Rings

 Dessert

 Other food

 Alcoholic Beverages

 Brunswick Stew

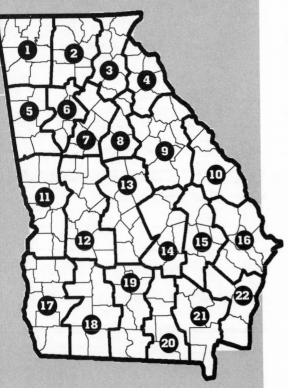